INTERNATIONAL DEVELOPMENT CENTRE LIBRARY

Pathways of Change in Africa

Crops, Livestock & Livelihoods in Mali, Ethiopia & Zimbabwe

Edited by Ian Scoones & William Wolmer
Institute of Development Studies, University of Sussex

JAMES CURREY
OXFORD

HEINEMANN
PORTSMOUTH (N.H.)

James Currey
73 Botley Road
Oxford
OX2 0BS

Heinemann
A division of Reed Elsevier Inc.
361 Hanover Street
Portsmouth NH 03801-3912

1 2 3 4 5 06 05 04 03 02

British Library Cataloguing in Publication Data
Pathways of change in Africa: crops, livestock &
livelihoods in Mali, Ethiopia & Zimbabwe
1. Agricultural productivity – Mali 2. Agricultural
productivity – Ethiopia 3. Agricultural productivity – Zimbabwe
I. Scoones, Ian II. Wolmer, William
338.1'6'096

ISBN 0-85255-422-2 (James Currey paper)
ISBN 0-85255-423-0 (James Currey cloth)

Library of Congress Cataloging-in-Publication Data available on request
ISBN 0-325-07124-1 (Heinemann cloth)

Typeset in 10½/11½ Bembo by Saxon Graphics Ltd, Derby
Printed & bound in the United Kingdom by Woolnough, Irthlingborough

Contents

1

Pathways of Change

Crop-Livestock Integration in Africa

IAN SCOONES & WILLIAM WOLMER

2

Crop-Livestock Integration in Mali

Multiple Pathways of Change

KAREN BROCK, N'GOLO COULIBALY, JOSHUA RAMISCH &
WILLIAM WOLMER

3

Complexity, Change & Continuity in Southern Ethiopia

The Case of Crop-Livestock Integration

GRACE CARSWELL

4

Crops, Livestock & Livelihoods in Zimbabwe

WILLIAM WOLMER, BEVLYNE SITHOLE & BILLY MUKAMURI

5

Crop-Livestock Policy in Africa

What is to be Done?

JOSHUA RAMISCH, JAMES KEELEY, IAN SCOONES &
WILLIAM WOLMER

Figures & Maps

Tables

Boxes

Abbreviations

AV	Associations Villageoises, Mali
BoA	Bureau of Agriculture, Ethiopia
CBPP	Contagious bovine pleuro-pneumonia
CFA	Communauté Financière d'Afrique
CFDT	Compagnie Française de Développement des Textiles, Mali
CMDT	Compagnie Malienne de Développement des Textiles, Mali
DA	Development Agent, Ethiopia
DDF	District Development Fund, Zimbabwe
DfID	Department for International Development, UK
DRAMR	Direction Régional d'Appui au Monde Rural, Mali
DRSS	Department of Research and Specialist Services, Zimbabwe
EARO	Ethiopian Agricultural Research Association
ESAP	Economic Structural Adjustment Programme
FAO	Food and Agriculture Organisation
FSRU	Farming Systems Research Unit, Zimbabwe
IAR	Institute of Agricultural Research, Ethiopia
IDS	Institute of Development Studies, University of Sussex
IER	Institut d'Economie Rurale, Mali
ILCA	International Livestock Centre for Africa
ILRAD	International Laboratory for Research on Animal Diseases
ILRI	International Livestock Research Institute
LGDA	Lower Guruve Development Association, Zimbabwe
MDRE	Ministère du Développement Rural et de l'Eau, Mali
NGO	non-governmental organisation
NLHA	Native Land Husbandry Act, Zimbabwe
OPAM	Office des Produits Agricoles du Mali
PA	Peasant Association, Ethiopia
PRMC	Programme de Restructuration des Marchés Céréalières, Mali
RCR	range to cropland ratio
SAP	Structural Adjustment Programme
SF	State Farm, Mali
SIP	Societés Indigènes de Prévoyance, Mali
SSCF	Small-Scale Commercial Farms, Zimbabwe
WADU	Wollamo Agricultural Development Unit, Ethiopia

Preface & Acknowledgements

Mixed farming, involving the integration of crops and livestock on a single farm, is often seen as an important route to meeting the vital 21st-century challenge of increasing the productivity and sustainability of small-scale African farming systems. Advocates of mixed farming argue that such systems improve on what are claimed to be low productivity and destructive forms of shifting cultivation or transhumant pastoralism, and that mixed farming is more sustainable and appropriate to many African settings than high external input alternatives.

Over many years a huge amount of investment in technology development has occurred in order to support mixed farming – soil fertility management, animal traction and livestock fodder systems are thus all key components of both national and international research efforts. Alongside such technological developments, the individualisation of tenure arrangements, settlement schemes and the planning of land use to encourage integration of crop and livestock production are also regularly promoted through extension efforts and development programmes.

In discussions of mixed farming it is often assumed that such systems represent part of a natural evolutionary progression towards an ideal state. In this book we argue that such evolutionary concepts – either explicitly or implicitly – lie behind much policy debate and often form the underlying rationale for technology choices. But such a deterministic, linear evolutionary view can be questioned on a number of counts. In particular, it fails to recognise the diverse pathways of change that occur in agricultural systems and the wide range of technology options that are pursued by farmers and herders.

Through a series of detailed case studies from Ethiopia, Mali and Zimbabwe, we have explored the range of pathways of change that have occurred over time and the multiple determinants of these. While mixed farming is certainly one possible outcome, it is only one of many. Historical analysis allowed us to highlight the range of processes and events that have resulted in changes in cropping and livestock systems. Setting an understanding of such changes in a broader livelihood context also enabled us to see how choices made about crops or livestock were conditioned by a range of other factors, many unrelated to farming or livestock keeping. An analysis of social differentiation also highlighted how diverse social actors have varying access to resources, facilitated or constrained by a range of institutions, both formal and informal. Unfortunately, many previous studies of crop–livestock integration have ignored these diverse institutional arrangements. Yet these are seen to be critical, and central to any explanation of the observed diversity of pathways of change.

Two important conclusions follow. First, an excessive emphasis on mixed farming as the desired model for the future of small-scale farming in Africa misses a range of other strategies that are very often important for the poor and marginalised. The consequence is that much research and extension effort misses an important potential set of users. A broader appreciation of the wide range of potential pathways of change would, we argue, allow development efforts to be more effectively targeted. Second, technology development, while clearly essential, often misses the social and institutional processes by which diverse social actors gain access to resources. Prioritisation of research and extension efforts therefore needs to take greater account of the social and institutional settings within which farming and herding take place. In order to respond to these challenges we suggest an approach that takes an understanding of livelihoods as its starting point; one that encourages a recognition of the multiple pathways of change and locates technology development in social and institutional contexts.

The research for this book was carried out between 1997 and 2000 with support from the UK Department for International Development's Livestock Production Programme. For much of this time it was linked to a broader programme of work on sustainable livelihoods being coordinated by the Institute of Development Studies (IDS) at Sussex. Field research was carried out over a period of a year in Mali, Ethiopia and Zimbabwe in a total of nine sites representing different agroecological and socioeconomic settings. With case studies in West, East and Southern Africa a number of important comparisons could be made across very diverse systems both between and within countries.

In all case study areas the work was carried out by teams made up of both IDS-based and African researchers. In Ethiopia links were made with FARM-Africa and SOS-Sahel, NGOs working in the area, as well as the Awassa College of Agriculture. In Mali, the research was associated with the Sikasso and Niono sections of the Institut d'Economie Rurale in the Ministry of Rural Development and Water (MDRE). In Zimbabwe the research was coordinated by the Institute of Environmental Studies at the University of Zimbabwe. We would like to thank all those in these organisations who made the work possible. At IDS the research programme was coordinated by Ian Scoones and William Wolmer, ably assisted by Annette Sinclair, who also helped with quantitative data analysis. Ben Warr, formerly of the University of Reading, carried out time series air photo analysis for all sites. Jeremy Swift and Camilla Toulmin also had inputs to the project at various points. We are particularly grateful to Joshua Ramisch of the University of Wisconsin who, in the final phase, helped with the completion of the Mali work and with the closing chapter. John Morton of the University of Greenwich kindly provided helpful comments on the manuscript. Our greatest thanks, however, should go to all those farmers and herders who participated in the research, patiently answering our questions and sharing their experiences of both past and present cropping and livestock practices.

The arguments in this book have benefited enormously from the inputs made by participants at various workshops held during the course of the project. In 1998 a major workshop was held at IDS to share preliminary results. Comments made then helped substantially shape the analysis of our material and so the contents of this book. Other workshops held in Ethiopia, Mali and Zimbabwe with policy-makers, researchers, extensionists, farmers and herders have also fed into the research and analysis process. While we are happy to acknowledge the contributions of our funders, host institutions, workshop participants and informants, the findings and arguments presented are clearly our responsibility alone.

The book has a simple structure with five chapters. The first provides an overview of the core arguments made in the book, with a review of some of the key literatures informing our research. This is then followed by three case study chapters that respond to these themes. These present the detailed results of the fieldwork, combining historical reflections with analyses, quantitative survey data and more qualitative assessments of differentiated social and institutional processes. In the final chapter, the key themes are revisited with the aim of exploring the implications for development policy and practice.

We hope this book will be of interest to a wide range of people: not only students of farming systems and agricultural change in Africa, but also those more directly engaged in technology development and policy, both in Africa and internationally. Based on the detailed examination of particular cases, we believe our findings present a number of fairly profound challenges for future strategies concerned with the support of small-scale agriculture and livestock production in Africa.

Ian Scoones & William Wolmer

Environment Group
Institute of Development Studies
University of Sussex, Brighton

List of Contributors

Karen Brock is a researcher in the Participation Group at the Institute of Development Studies. She is currently working in Nigeria and Uganda on the policy process around poverty reduction. Other areas of research include a focus on participatory methodologies for research and advocacy, work with civil society engagement in macroeconomic policy frameworks, in addition to long-standing interests in rural livelihoods and pastoralism.

Grace Carswell is currently a Leverhulme Special Research Fellow at the University of Sussex, undertaking research on livelihood change in Uganda. Previously she undertook research at the Institute of Development Studies, focusing on agricultural change in southern Ethiopia. Her doctoral research was on the agricultural history of Kigezi, southwestern Uganda. Research interests include rural livelihoods in Eastern Africa, population–environment interactions and agricultural change under the influence of colonialism.

N'golo Coulibaly is a researcher at the Institut d'Economie Rurale in Sikasso in southern Mali. A sociologist by training he is currently conducting his doctoral research on migration and the constraints of access to land for Malian migrants in the Ivory Coast.

James Keeley is a researcher in the Environment Group at the Institute of Development Studies. He is currently researching policy processes for GM crops in China and Zimbabwe. Other work in recent years has concentrated on understanding the social and political dynamics of policymaking for soils, land management and sustainable livelihoods in sub-Saharan Africa.

Billy Mukamuri is a researcher with the Centre for Applied Social Sciences at the University of Zimbabwe. Previously he was with the University's Institute of Environmental Studies. His doctoral research focused on local perspectives on social forestry initiatives in Zimbabwe. His research concentrates on the social dimensions of natural resource management in Zimbabwe.

Joshua Ramisch is the Social Science Officer of the Tropical Soil Biology and Fertility Institute (TSBF) of Centro Internacional de Agricultura Tropical (CIAT). He is coordinating work in East and Southern Africa on farmer decision-making related to integrated soil fertility management. His research addresses integrating local and scientific knowledge of soil ecology and fertility processes, using social networks for scaling up farmer innovation, and understanding the agroecological impacts of social relationships and transactions.

Ian Scoones is a Professorial Fellow with the Environment Group at the Institute of Development Studies. He works on the relationship between science and development policy, with a focus on natural resource and agricultural issues. Past work has included work on rangelands and pastoralism, wetlands, forestry and soils management. His most recent work is focusing on agricultural biotechnology and sustainable livelihoods in southern Africa and India.

Bevlyne Sithole is a consultant with the Center for International Forest Research (CIFOR) on their Adaptive Collaborative Management Programme. Previously she undertook research on institutions for managing water, wildlife and forest resources. Her doctoral research was on the institutional considerations in the management of wetlands in communal areas in Zimbabwe. Her research interests include: the macro-politics of natural resource management; the impacts of externally derived development narratives and forces on rural livelihood systems.

William Wolmer is a member of the Environment Group at the Institute of Development Studies. He recently completed his doctoral research on perceptions of landscape in southeastern Zimbabwe in relation to conservation and development policy. A geographer by training he is currently working on transboundary conservation in southern Africa and the dynamics of land reform in Zimbabwe.

1

Pathways of Change:
Crop–Livestock Integration in Africa

IAN SCOONES
& WILLIAM WOLMER

Introduction

Increasing agricultural and livestock production is seen by some as one of the major tasks for international development assistance in the new century if food insecurity and poverty in Africa are to be reduced (Pinstrup-Andersen *et al.* 1999). Yet it is far from clear which approaches to the intensification of smallholder farming systems are most appropriate. There are many routes to increasing the average inputs of labour or capital on a smallholding for the purpose of increasing the value of the output per hectare. One route which has often been recommended is the adoption of integrated mixed farming – the cultivation of crops and the raising of cattle, smallstock and/or equines by the same economic entity, such as a household, with animal inputs being used in crop production and crop inputs being used in livestock production (Powell and Williams 1995).

The case for integrating animal and crop systems is based on the premise that by-products from the two systems are used on the same farm, and draught power, use of roughages and low-quality feeds, closed nutrient cycling through the soil, plants and the animals' manure, and improved soil fertility contribute to overall higher outputs per animal and per hectare (Mohamed-Saleem and Mendera 1997). Benefits therefore accrue to cropping in the form of manure and energy (for traction and transport) and to livestock husbandry in the form of fodder from forage crops or crop residues. There are also financial interactions between crops and livestock. Sandford (1989) describes a 'reciprocal buffering effect' in which crop surpluses lead to investment in livestock in good years and subsequent disinvestment in bad years in order to purchase grain for household consumption. Livestock sales can then be used to purchase inputs for crop production. Environmental benefits are also envisaged from such a system, as a closed, household-based mixed farm system enables, it is claimed, a more sustainable management of the nutrient cycle, such that nutrient inputs and outputs can be balanced (Smith *et al.* 1997).

1

But is such a mixed farm model the best solution? Very often the assumption, hidden behind these technical claims, is that mixed farming is somehow at the apex of a natural, evolutionary process, and the challenge for external intervention is to provide a means to support changes towards this end. This book proposes a challenge to this 'evolutionary' view of agricultural change, which sees different standard types of agricultural practice emerging through an inevitable change in land: labour ratios resulting from population pressure. Such a view suggests a linear sequence of crop–livestock interactions moving from limited interactions under low population pressure to an integrated mixed farm model, where crop and livestock production are tightly linked, to more discrete enterprises under more intensive systems.

The case studies from Ethiopia, Mali and Zimbabwe explored in this book show that, while such a pathway of change may well be possible, it will only occur under certain conditions. These are historically contingent and unpredictable and will likely be highly differentiated by both agroecological and socioeconomic setting. Thus, in different places and for different people, the forms of crop–livestock interaction may be radically different, resulting in multiple pathways of change. Assumptions embedded in a deterministic, linear evolutionary view lead, it is argued, to inappropriate policies and technical solutions. By contrast an appreciation of multiple pathways of change, conditioned by institutional arrangements and differentiated by social group, allows researchers, planners and policy-makers to locate interventions more effectively in the real livelihood contexts of poor crop and livestock producers in Africa.

The case studies: Ethiopia, Mali and Zimbabwe

In order to explore the dynamics of crop–livestock interactions in detail, research was carried out in contrasting agroecological zones in southern Ethiopia, Mali and Zimbabwe. Case study sites were located along notional transects stretching from areas with relatively high to low resource endowment (defined principally by rainfall and so agricultural potential). Some of the site characteristics are shown in Table 1.1.

The field research involved a mix of research methods, including rapid appraisals to gain insights into livelihood profiles and agroecological contexts in each case study site, questionnaire surveys of a sample of households to investigate quantitative dimensions of current farming systems, and more qualitative methods to explore historical change and institutional dynamics.[1] A picture of how crops and livestock were linked at the time of the field research was built up through the assessment of a number of indicators relating to soil fertility, tillage and fodder management (Table 1.2). This data shows some important differences in management strategies between the relatively high and low resource endowment sites. But such an aggregate picture tells us only so much. In order to understand the dynamics of change, insights into how strategies are differentiated within sites – among households and individuals and over time – are required. The case study chapters explore some of this detail in depth, illustrating how both across and within the sites there are multiple pathways of

---

[1]The fieldwork was carried out during 1997 and 1998 by teams including British, Ethiopian, Malian and Zimbabwean researchers.

Table 1.1 Site characteristics.

	Ethiopia		Mali			Zimbabwe			
	Admencho	Mundena	Chokare	Dalongué-bougou	Zara-dougou	Chipiriro	Lower Guruve	Ngundu	Chikom-bedzi
Rainfall (mm/year)	1350–2500	900	500	300–450	900–1100	750–1000	350–900	550–800	330–660
Population density (N/km sq)	<500	53	23	11	30	71	c. 20	45	14
Cattle ownership (N)	3.5	3	14.5	20	12	6.5	2.5	1.5	2
Farm size (Ha)	0.6	3	1	18.5	16.5	4.4	5.1	4.6	9.2
Major crops	Enset, root crops, maize	Maize, sorghum, cotton	Maize, sorghum	Millet, groundnut, cowpeas	Cotton, maize, millet, cowpea, fruit, groundnut	Maize, cotton	Cotton, gardening	Maize, gardening	Sorghum
Market access	Good	Recent main roads	Poor	Poor	Good	Good	Fair	Good	Poor

Table 1.2 Indicators of crop–livestock integration.

		Ethiopia			Mali		Zimbabwe			
		Admencho	Mundena	Chokare	Dalongué-bougou	Zara-dougou	Chipiriro	Lower Guruve	Ngundu	Chikombedzi
Soil fertility [% hh]	Manure use	87	91	11	100 (smallstock) 57 (cattle)	75	35	2	50	0
	Fertiliser use	87	83	0	57	81	99	7	39	0
Tillage [%hh]	Use of draught	96	79	79	100	92	91	49	90	45
Fodder [Y/N for practice, or %hh]	Fodder crops grown	No	No	No	No	Some	No	Yes	No	Limited
	Crop residues	Yes	Yes	Yes	Yes	Yes	Yes	Yes	Yes	Yes
	Cut and carry	Yes	Yes	Yes	Yes	No	92	0	15	4
	Rangeland grazing	Yes	Yes	Yes	Yes	Yes	Yes	Yes	Yes	Yes

crop–livestock integration, mediated by a range of social and institutional processes and conditioned by a set of often highly contingent contextual factors.

Through the examination of this data, this book attempts to unpack the underlying assumptions behind the conventional model of crop–livestock integration, exposing some of the strengths and weaknesses of the approach. This chapter sets the scene by examining some of the core assumptions of the conventional model, exploring their origins and assessing their implications. Through this some of the policy conclusions emerging from the conventional model are challenged, and a framework is offered for thinking about crop–livestock integration in ways that encompass new perspectives on ecology, historical dynamics, social differentiation and institutional processes. These themes are subsequently explored in the case study chapters on Ethiopia, Mali and Zimbabwe that follow. The practical and policy implications of these findings are then examined in a closing chapter.

The emergence of the mixed farming approach

The concept of 'mixed farming', which lies at the centre of the conventional view of crop–livestock integration, derives from the 'agricultural revolution' in Britain in the 18th and 19th centuries when a particular package of 'scientific' farming techniques started to be employed. The package included such technical innovations as manure-intensive husbandry, the use of legumes, a reduction of fallows and the integration and mutual development of arable and pastoral husbandry (Campbell and Overton 1993).[2] Coupled with radical state intervention in the form of the Enclosure Acts, these enabled land-owning yeoman farmers to build up soil fertility on intensively managed roughly circular farms centred on the homestead, rather than farming on scattered 'open-field' strips. This new technically informed model for farming was elaborated by soil scientists and others from 1843 onwards with the establishment of the Rothamsted trials by Lawes and Gilbert (see Hall 1905; Dyke 1993). Early in the 20th century, before it fell from favour in Britain (where in the 1940s post-war concerns shifted to increasing production through mechanisation and agricultural specialisation into particular enterprises on large farms), the mixed farming package was exported to anglophone Africa by settler farmers and colonial administrators (Sumberg 1998; see below).

However, this enthusiasm for integrated mixed farming systems did not persist. With the establishment of commodity-based research systems in many African countries, crop and livestock production were often seen to be separate issues. This was reflected in the organisation of research and extension and the focus of policy initiatives. Livestock development, for example, was largely concentrated on beef production from cattle ranching, while the cropping focus emphasised plant

[2]This technological package was known as the Norfolk four-course rotation, which developed after the introduction of clover and turnips to England from Holland. Leguminous fodder crops (clover and beans) were used to restore the soil fertility depleted by cereal growing, and root crops were planted to facilitate the suppression of weeds and to ensure deep cultivation. The clover and root crops were harvested and stall-fed to cattle with straw. Manure and straw from the stalls was ploughed into the arable fields (Astor and Seebohm Rowntree 1946).

breeding and agronomy, often with little attention paid to the implications for livestock. Only relatively recently has there been a return in interest to integrated mixed farming systems, building on the body of work emerging from the 1970s that documented the complexities of real farming systems in the field. This evolved into a new interest in crop–livestock interactions within the farming system (e.g. McIntire and Gryseels 1987; McIntire *et al.* 1992; Powell and Williams 1995; Steinfeld *et al.* 1997). Much of this new emphasis has been driven by concerns for increasing food production without compromising environmental sustainability. Smith *et al.* (1997: 237) comment:

> Rapid growth in human and livestock population in sub-Saharan Africa is creating unprecedented increases in food and feed demands. These pressures on a fixed landbase are likely to promote severe competition for resources and drive agriculture towards intensification. Integrated crop–livestock systems, of the type already common in the highlands, are expected to evolve rapidly elsewhere. Research is required to develop technological alternatives which promote better resource use through synergies from crop–livestock integration.

What are the core assumptions of the conventional approach to crop–livestock integration?

Today, then, the promotion of mixed farming is seen as a key target for external interventions in Africa. But is such a model always the most appropriate? What alternative perspectives are obscured by such an emphasis? In order to explore these questions, we must first examine some of the core assumptions of the conventional approach to crop–livestock integration. Three themes – evolutionary models, social differentiation and agroecological perspectives – are explored in turn in the following sections.

Evolutionary models

At the core of the conventional approach to crop–livestock integration is an evolutionary theory of agricultural change that derives in large part from the influential writings of Ester Boserup (1965; 1981). She saw population growth as the major factor driving an evolution of the agricultural system from one land use to another, with a progressively increasing frequency of cropping on land combined with improvements in agricultural technology. Agricultural intensification was seen in terms of a move from 'primitive agriculture' to a 'higher level of technique and cultural development' via a particular historical sequence of stages characterised by shortening lengths of fallow. Similarly, Ruthenberg's (1980) classification of seven types of production systems implies a progressive evolution from less to more intensive cultivation over time.

Explanations of agricultural change in this mould usually derive from economic theories of 'induced innovation' and focus on the linear relationship between 'drivers' and 'outcomes', with factor substitution and technological change as the two core concepts. As increases in population density occur it is held that the premium on land grows, as does the availability of labour. It therefore becomes profitable for cultivators to shift to more labour-intensive systems based on new technologies. Higher outputs in turn offset diminishing returns to inputs on a fixed land base (Boserup 1965; Binswanger and Ruttan 1978; Hayami and Ruttan 1985). 'The "problem" of population pressure thus gives rise to its own solution; the very scarcity of land, by altering factor prices, results in its more intensive use' (Lele and Stone 1989: 8).

In their study of agricultural mechanisation, Pingali *et al.* (1987) widen their analysis to include market access as a key driver. Improvements in access to markets through better roads and transport facilities are held to have a similar effect to population growth on the intensity of land use, as higher prices and demand encourage cultivation and high rewards to labour encourage in-migration. The model is extended further by Lele and Stone (1989), who distinguish between Boserupian 'autonomous intensification' and 'policy-led intensification', where external investments drive the process of intensification. They argue that the latter are critical to maintaining and preserving resources that would otherwise be degraded though more intensive use.

A number of empirical studies have examined processes of intensification with changing population–resource pressures and confirmed the range of key drivers affecting the dynamics of intensification.[3] However, these variations on the Boserupian model share the assumption that 'structurally and functionally different farming systems ... can be interpreted as being at different phases in an evolutionary space' (Weber 1996: 29). It is this evolutionary metaphor, with implications of progress and advancement over time, which is another important strand in the underlying assumptions of crop–livestock integration models.

Following Boserup much of the literature on crop–livestock interactions talks in terms of the 'inevitability' of rising population density driving the intensification of agriculture towards the greater articulation of crops and livestock. One result of the evolutionary process of intensification driven by population increases is an evolution from extensive pastoralism to intensive mixed farming, which is seen as the most efficient and sustainable means of increasing food production. The Winrock International *Assessment of Animal Agriculture in Sub-Saharan Africa* traces this process in detail:

> Growing competition between crop and livestock farmers for land leads to the evolution of mixed crop–livestock farming systems as the most efficient and sustainable means of increasing food production. When population density is low, specialised crops and livestock production is the most efficient means of producing both crops and livestock. When population densities are high and markets, technology and inputs are not readily available, intensity of land use increases, and mixed crop–livestock production becomes the most efficient and sustainable mode of food production because of complementarities between crops and livestock rising. Key elements in the contribution of livestock to intensification are traction (power), manure (fertiliser), and enhanced income (cash) per unit of land (Winrock International 1992: ix).

This is often characterised in terms of the 'stages' of an apparently unilinear evolutionary sequence (Box 1.1).

---

[3] See, for example, Mortimore (1993) on the Kano close-settled zone of Nigeria; Netting (1993) on the Nigerian Jos Plateau; Tiffen *et al.* (1994) on Machakos District in Kenya; Clay (1998) on Rwanda and Turner *et al.* (1993) for a range of other cases.

Box 1.1   The stage model of crop–livestock system evolution

1.   At low population densities crop and animal production are land 'extensive'. There are few interactions between specialised farming and herding societies other than trade. Specialised and independent crop and livestock systems are more attractive than integrated systems because land is abundant.
2.   Increased population means the demand for arable land increases. Farmers' opportunities for using less labour-intensive techniques of soil fertility maintenance such as fallowing are exhausted, leading to reduced fallow, and encouraging the use of manure as a substitute to maintain soil fertility. Initially manure is often acquired by farmers from herders through exchange contracts.
3.   As population increases further, farmers increasingly own their own livestock and collect, process and incorporate the manure on their crops. Increased population also causes the reduction in pasture at the expense of arable and means livestock owners rely more on crop residues as a source of feed, and encourages pastoralists, who are held to cause too much damage to farmers' crops, to begin to grow their own. This in turn restricts livestock mobility for both seasonal movement and annual transhumance and encourages sedentarisation.
4.   Free grazing of livestock is substituted by confinement and feeding of gathered crop residues and grown forage legumes. This results in more intensive use of both the residues and animal wastes. The high intensity of land use also encourages the replacement of hand labour with mechanisation by draught power. These technical innovations are reinforced by tenure changes – offering secure, preferably titled, individualised tenure over plots of land.
5.   A transition back to specialised commercial farming and livestock production occurs as markets and technologies develop further – tractors replace animals, fertilisers replace manure, and supplements replace fodder crops and pastures. These technical changes eliminate the cost advantages of a mixed farming enterprise and specialisation becomes more profitable.

Sources: McIntire *et al.* 1992; Winrock International 1992; Powell and Williams 1995.

Thus particular practices, such as use of draught power for cultivation, manure for soil fertility supplementation and crop residue for fodder, can be located within this standardised evolutionary scheme. Bound up in this, it is held, are evolutionary changes in the various components of crop–livestock interaction and integration – such as the use of manure, fodder and animal traction and land tenure. These are explored below.

Manure
Within this evolutionary scheme, manuring is generally viewed as the critical technological component driving agricultural intensification in its early stages (Turner 1995). This has been reflected in a large literature on nutrient cycling.[4] Animal manure makes nutrients more immediately accessible to crops than green manure or mulching, and

---

[4]This work frequently focuses on an assessment of the balance of nutrient inputs and outputs on a farm (cf. Smaling *et al.* 1996), and the ratio of arable to rangeland grazing required if the system is to be sustained by manure inputs (cf. Swift *et al.* 1989; Sandford 1989). See also Landais and Lhoste (1993); Powell and Williams (1993); Powell *et al.* (1995); Stangel (1995); Harris (1996); Eyasu *et al.* (1998) for examples of particular cases.

allows the concentration of nutrients from more distant, rangeland sources on farmers' fields. Manure from livestock may contribute as much as 35 per cent of soil organic matter (Steinfeld *et al.* 1997). The evolutionary change envisaged is one from 'open' to 'closed' nutrient cycling systems (i.e. from extensive to intensive farming). Under extensive systems 'long-term fertility of the soil is maintained by periodic fallowing of the land. ... As farming intensifies, more labour-intensive fertilising techniques, such as manuring and eventually composting, evolve' (Pingali *et al.* 1987: 31). Strategies for manure use themselves are held to evolve with increasing farming intensity. This implies a shift from paddocking (where livestock are penned on fields overnight and where they deliver their manure directly to the soil) to keeping animals in the farm compound overnight and collecting their droppings to transport to the field to spread and incorporate them (Powell and Williams 1993).

Fodder
The cropping and feeding of crop residue and other cropland forages to animals is another key interaction between cropping and livestock (see Sandford 1989; Humphreys 1994; de Leeuw 1997; Bayer and Waters-Bayer 1995). The evolutionary schema envisages a shift in feeding strategies from unrestricted extensive grazing on open rangelands, to systems in which animals on private enclosures are fed by a combination of grazing and crop residues, to systems, at a further stage of intensity, in which animals are tied or penned, and fed with crop residues and cut (and often grown) fodder (Tiffen 1995). Intensive management of crop residue is associated with a shift from *in situ* grazing of crop residue to systems in which increasing proportions are harvested and stored for later feeding (McIntire *et al.* 1992; de Leeuw 1997). A shift from communal access to fodder resources to a more privatised arrangement is thus envisaged.

Animal traction
Animal traction is also viewed as a stage in an evolutionary sequence. This is the 'mechanisation ladder' – a technical progression from hand hoeing to the plough to the tractor (Sumberg and Gilbert 1992). Pingali *et al.* (1987), for example, relate the transition from hand hoe to the plough to the evolution in farming systems from 'forest-fallow' (shifting cultivation) to 'annual-cultivation' (permanent cultivation) as a consequence of population growth. The uptake of animal traction with increased population is attributed to its labour-saving role. Animal traction, it is argued, only becomes profitable and labour-saving at higher intensities of farming where, despite higher population densities, the additional labour requirements of intensive farming rise faster than the availability of labour. Under low-intensity, high-fallowing systems, despite the scarcity of labour, animal traction increases the labour requirement per unit of output as labour-intensive operations, such as destumping, draining and terracing fields, weeding, and training, feeding and maintaining the animals, are required if the plough is to be used properly. Therefore the hand hoe is more profitable and farmers are unlikely to accept the costs of ploughing.[5] According to this argument there is thus a distinct point at which the use of the plough becomes economic. However, many

---

[5]It is also hypothesised that in low-intensity 'forest-fallow' systems lack of grazing land and the likely prevalence of livestock diseases such as trypanosomiasis mean the costs of feeding and taking care of draught animals are relatively higher.

argue that, rather than encouraging intensification, animal traction is a spur to extensification in many areas (Raynaut 1984), and more intensive, integrated plough-based systems are associated mainly with cash cropping or high population density areas where markets are readily accessible (McIntire *et al.* 1992).

Land tenure
The assumption that agricultural intensification is bound up with a trend towards individualised tenure is at the core of the Boserupian model.[6] As Platteau (1996: 29) summarises:

> The evolutionary theory of land rights can be considered the dominant framework of analysis used by mainstream economists to assess the land tenure situation in developing countries, and to make predictions about its evolution. A central tenet of this theory is that under the joint impact of increasing population pressure and market integration, land rights spontaneously evolve towards rising individualisation and that this evolution eventually leads rights holders to press for the creation of duly formalised private property rights.

These changes in tenure are assumed to have been accompanied and encouraged by intensification. Individualised tenure, it is argued, encourages investments in land assets, such as soil conservation practices and tree planting. Effective privatisation of arable land in turn may also be followed by the enclosure of grazing land nearby – facilitating the integration of livestock and cropping (Tiffen 1995).

Social differentiation

Underlying these assumptions about shifts in manure use, tillage, fodder management and land tenure are assumptions about the economic behaviour of farmers and herders. Boserupian explanations of agricultural change generally understand this in terms of neo-classical economics' depiction of 'economic rationality', where actors weigh up relative costs and benefits of different actions, in some cases in relation to risk factors. Farmer resistance to new techniques promoted by extension agencies, for example, is explained as resulting from 'sound economic reasoning rather than indolence. It can more plausibly be explained as the result of a quite rational comparison between the additional labour and the probable addition to output' (Boserup 1965: 66). As Morrison (1996: 585) points out:

> The power of [Boserup's] account is that it brings the apparently 'irrational' behaviour of Third World agriculturalists into the fold of neoclassical economics; it 'rationalises' their farming strategies in ways that economists have found appropriate.

Although farmers' behaviour is depicted within the narrow boundaries of cost–benefit trade-offs, the important point about Boserupian analyses is that they recognise that farmers (or herders) are dynamic and inventive. They actively and autonomously adapt and often improve the landscape around them in response to the driving forces of population squeeze or market development. They are neither the passive victims nor rampant destroyers of the environment envisaged by neo-Malthusians, nor trapped by 'tradition' or 'custom' (see, for example, Herskovitz (1926) on the 'cattle-complex').

[6]Boserup (1965); see, for example, Winrock International (1992); Bassett and Crummey (1993); Clay (1998); and Gavian (1993).

However, studies in this mould are less good at recognising that people are far from homogeneous and have widely differing motives and goals. Decision-making is embedded in social and cultural settings, which makes an approach based on independent, individual economic actors problematic. Much of the agricultural economics literature takes the farm household as the unit of analysis (Ellis 1998). This often fails to differentiate strategies within households (reflecting differences in gender, age, etc.), and also often does not set the analysis within an understanding of broader livelihood contexts. A recognition of such factors suggests a less deterministic model where a wider range of outcomes may be possible.

Seur (1992), for example, writing about Serenje District in Zambia, shows that agricultural intensification with increased population density does not necessarily mean that the plough replaces the hoe when the shortening of fallow periods has reached a certain level, as conventionally assumed. Different individuals respond in various ways to land scarcity caused by increasing population density, and the choices and decisions farmers make are not only informed by problems relating to agricultural production and land scarcity, but are also based on other livelihood considerations. The plough has been adopted, not as a necessary response to population pressure, but mainly because this technology enabled farmers to produce more crops for sale. Those living in the most densely populated areas who control very small tracts of land and have no space to extend their fields continue to use the hoe.

Agroecological perspectives

One of the central arguments about crop–livestock integration is that different population densities and different agroecological zones make possible, and even compel, specific interactions between crops and livestock (McIntire *et al.*1992). In the literature, different agroecological zones are distinguished by the amount and distribution of rainfall, and by altitude, principally as it affects temperature (see Jahnke 1982; Mortimore 1991; McIntire *et al.* 1992; Winrock International 1992). This results in different conditions for the realisation of the crop–livestock integration ideal.

The main focus has been on the humid, sub-humid and semi-arid zones, each perceived in different ways to be missing out on the potentials of crop–livestock integration. Thus in the humid zone crop–livestock interactions are seen to be weak or even totally absent owing to pests and diseases. There is, as a consequence, a high potential for greater crop–livestock integration, especially in terms of animal feeding. In the sub-humid zone there are still large areas of thinly settled land where livestock and human population density are low because of disease and poor soils. This zone is the subject of much research, especially in West Africa (see Smith *et al.* 1997, Winrock International 1992; Jabbar 1996). Population increases and increased cultivation and the elimination of tsetse fly are seen as causing the permanent (rather than transhumant) in-migration of pastoralists and hence resource conflicts between farmers and herders. This is also where the mismatch between feed potential and cattle population is perceived as largest and where the greatest opportunity for increasing agricultural productivity through the integration of crops and livestock lies (Winrock International 1992; Powell and Williams 1995; Jabbar 1996). Finally, the semi-arid zone is characterised by lower disease pressure and higher pasture quality than more humid zones. Both production and sustainability benefits are expected from mixed farming options here, as increased use of traction, more sedentary forms of livestock production and improved nutrient cycling are all seen as ways of addressing perceived inefficiencies in current production systems and widespread land degradation.

Agroecology is thus recognised as a key factor, which demarcates the main crop-livestock interactions by influencing comparative advantage (McIntire *et al.* 1992). This can operate across large geographical areas (agroecological zones) or within sites across the catenary sequence, with more intensive systems being expected in the valley bottoms as compared to the interfluve (McIntire, *et al.* 1992; Mortimore 1991). However, while recognising the diversity of agroecological zones in some studies, either explicitly or implicity, there is a slippage from talking about space to talking about time. This is evident in the following quote:

> Different parts of sub-Saharan Africa are at different stages in the evolution of their agricultural production systems. For example, intensive mixed crop–livestock farming is widely practised in the highland agroecological zone. ... Other areas, for example much of the subhumid zone, are in the early stages of transition from slash-and-burn farming and herding of livestock to mixed crop–livestock farming (Winrock International 1992: 47).

This assumes a single pathway of change, with different sites assumed to be at different stages along it and in the process of evolving towards a 'higher' stage. At its starkest this logic involves reading the characteristics of highland farming systems as indicative of the future of sub-humid or semi-arid farming systems. But, as Turner (1994) points out, one should be reticent in inferring the validation of a historical process (in this case the Boserup hypothesis) from spatial correlations. As a result existing systems are deemed inefficient or unsustainable in relation to an evolutionary benchmark, one which may not be remotely appropriate given the agroecological conditions prevailing in the area.

What are the policy conclusions of the conventional approach?

A number of policy conclusions follow from the assumptions made about history and change, social differentiation and agroecology. Three stand out, and are discussed below.

Mixed farming is the most sustainable and efficient system

Current concerns with environmental sustainability have provided an additional spur to the recommendation of mixed farming approaches for smallholder agriculture.[7] For example, Mukhebi *et al.* (1991: 339) argue 'replacing extensive agro-pastoral systems with more intensive crop–livestock systems could lead to more sustainable livestock production'. In a similar vein, Powell and Williams (1995: 30) state 'the greatest opportunity for sustainable increases in agricultural productivity lies in agricultural intensification through the evolution and maturation of mixed crop–livestock farming systems'. Equally, Smith *et al.* (1997: 244) observe: 'in the context of sustainable

[7]See, for example: Landais and Lhoste (1990); Mortimore (1991); Mukhebi *et al.* (1991); Mortimore and Turner (1993); Mohammed–Saleem and Fitzhugh (1995); Harris (1996); Steinfeld *et al.* (1997); Smith *et al.* (1997).

increases in agricultural productivity, there appears to be no alternative to integrating crops and livestock so that synergies are exploited'.

Picking up on these observations, a major multi-donor funded review of Livestock and the Environment coordinated by the FAO and the World Bank notes:

> Mixed farming is probably the most environmentally benign agricultural production system because it is, at least partially, a closed system. ... Because it provides many opportunities for recycling and organic farming and for a varied, more attractive landscape, mixed farming is the favourite system of many agriculturalists and environmentalists. ... The biggest contribution of livestock to the environment is to be seen in providing the main avenue for sustained intensification of mixed farming systems. ... Where there is the potential for mixed farming, policies need to facilitate the transition of grazing systems into mixed farming systems in the semi-arid and subhumid tropics through integrating crops and livestock (manure management, animal draught, residue feeding and fodder crops etc.) (Steinfeld *et al.* 1997: 11, 42)

Thus, it is argued, a 'win–win' scenario is created. Not only can productivity be enhanced through the support for shifts to mixed farming, but also this can be made more sustainable. However, is mixed farming actually more 'sustainable'? Potentially conversion of existing cropped areas to continuous cropping cannot be supported solely by manuring – animals remove greater amounts of biomass and nutrients than they return in the form of manure (Sandford 1989; Turner 1995; van Keulen and Breman 1990). Over the long term, this can result in a combination of reductions in livestock productivity, manure quality, pasture productivity and local livestock presence (Turner 1995; see van der Pol 1992; McIntire and Powell 1995; de Leeuw *et al.* 1995; Campbell *et al.* 1998). Thus intensive mixed farming over a long period is not possible without large areas of rangeland to support the system, or the addition of other external inputs such as fertilisers.[8]

Others also question the productive potential of mixed farming. Many of the benefits of closer integration – in crop and animal productivity, and in improved soil fertility – are inherently limited by the low output response to such high-bulk, low-value inputs as manure, crop residue and animal power. Closer crop–livestock interactions are therefore unlikely to have a major impact on productivity unless they are associated with exogenous technical changes. McIntire *et al.* (1992) conclude from their detailed study of crop-livestock integration in Africa that the gains from integration are small in comparison to those which would be captured from encouraging more radical technical and policy change (cf. Lele and Stone 1989).

Despite such qualifications, most discussion still considers mixed farming as the most sustainable and productive option. The challenge for technical interventions and policies is simply to encourage the plugging of nutrient leaks, the speeding up nutrient cycling and the closing of the nutrient cycle. As Stangel (1995: 53) puts it:

> Crop–livestock systems, if better co-ordinated and more interactive, offer a major solution to the nutrient loss problem through improved efficiency in nutrient cycling by better utilising manures, crop residues and increased use of external inputs (feed concentrates and fertiliser) to stimulate production of crops, livestock or both.

---

[8]Turner (1995: 448), however, cautions that: 'while demonstrating the severe limits of the future of sedentary mixed farming, the high spatial and temporal abstraction of such analyses [of nutrient losses] and the wide variation in their estimates are both cause and effect of the limited awareness of the critical importance of local management practices in affecting the sustainability of rangeland-cropland nutrient transfer'.

Thus, it is argued, development strategies should support, accelerate and help direct the 'natural' process of evolution of agriculture to intensification and integration. A whole suite of technical options are suggested to this end, ranging from developing high-yielding forage legumes and leguminous tree crops to improving the quality of crop residues to improved pasture management to improved feed harvesting and storage to preventing nutrient losses to reducing the feed burden of draught animals to increasing animal resistance to disease and parasites.

In order to encourage this process, Jabbar (1996: 35) argues: 'researchers and policy-makers need to learn from experiences elsewhere and identify appropriate niches for technology development and intervention to facilitate the autonomous process of evolution'. This, he argues, should avoid 'improper intervention and distortion (e.g. tractor subsidies)', which 'has stifled the natural process of development and evolution of production systems' (Jabbar 1996: 34).

Cattle are the most important livestock

The cattle bias in livestock development has often been commented upon (e.g. Sandford 1982; 1993), reflecting an historical bias in research, extension and veterinary services. This is repeated in discussions on crop–livestock integration. In many instances, cattle may well be highly significant, but such an emphasis downplays the importance of smallstock (sheep and goats), equines and poultry. As the case study chapters show such animals may be key components of crop-livestock systems, and may be crucial for access to draught power and manure, particularly for women and poorer farmers (see also Starkey 1990; Starkey and Kaumbutho 2000).

Across the case study countries, and reflected more broadly in international research priorities and funding (see Chapter 5), external support has been concentrated on a limited range of technical options that implicitly assume the mixed farm ideal. Much research effort in draught and traction technologies, for example, assumes the availability of a span of oxen to pull a plough, cultivator or cart. Even when oxen shortages are recognised as a constraint, often the assumption is that available oxen are fit and well fed and able to pull heavy equipment at the end of the dry season. In Ethiopia, for example, much research effort was expended on developing a one-oxen plough in response to recognised oxen shortages, but the uptake was limited, as the oxen in the highland farms, in contrast to those on the research station, were unable to make use of the technology (see Chapter 3). The focus on oxen as draught animals also means that much effort in fodder development has been invested in feed technologies designed for such animals. But where cows, heifers and donkeys are a significant source of draught power, different fodder needs may exist. In terms of soil fertility management, again the main focus of research and extension efforts has been on cattle manure, often ignoring the potential roles of smallstock or poultry manures and the impacts of mixtures.

Ownership of a herd of cattle sufficient to provide mature oxen for draught needs, as well as sufficient manure for a household-managed mixed farm, is limited to very few farmers in the case study sites (see Chapters 2–4). A significant proportion of farmers in the study areas own no cattle at all, and must rely on smallstock for providing manure inputs. Others borrow cattle through a range of lending and sharing arrangements, often making up a span from a variety of different animals, including cows or heifers. Donkeys are a particularly important source of draught power, for instance in Zimbabwe, where recurrent droughts have reduced cattle herds dramatically. Thus in practice the ideal mixed farmer with a viable herd of 10 or 12 cattle is a rarity, making much research and extension effort focused on an unrealisable ideal.

Individualised land tenure should be promoted

The mixed farm model assumes a household farm holding with fixed boundaries and secure, individualised tenure. Often linked to the promotion of mixed farming is a push towards land tenure reform that aims to discourage what are regarded by some as inefficient forms of communal tenure. Individualised tenure, it is held, encourages investment in the farm, resulting in boosts in productivity and efficiency. If land tenure is secured through individualised ownership, it is argued, then more sustainable forms of land management will result as owners can take the long view. In addition, the adoption of mixed farming is seen by some as a means of resolving conflicts between herders and farmers (Jabbar 1993; McCown *et al.* 1979; Winrock International 1992).

The linking of an evolutionary perspective on farming systems with an evolutionary view of property rights results in a number of policy recommendations that are prevalent across Africa. These assume that the ideal state is one where an individualised household plot is granted individualised tenure rights. Such policies thus attempt to mimic the 'natural' process of evolutionary advancement, intervening to speed up the process. Thus land tenure reform that advocates privatisation and titling has long been a major plank of government policies. For example in Kenya, land titling of individualised mixed farms after Independence was a major policy initiative, particularly in the highland areas (Noronha 1988). Many land reform and resettlement programmes assume that new settler households require a fixed plot of land where a self-contained mixed farming operation can be established. The lowland settlement scheme in Ethiopia, the cotton farming zone in Mali and resettlement schemes in Zimbabwe discussed in the case study chapters all have these characteristics (see Chapters 2–4). In a similar way, initiatives for village-level land management (e.g. *gestion de terroirs*), while not necessarily advocating individual land titling, carry similar assumptions about the desirability of an integrated mixed farm system, at least at a village level. Such initiatives have become highly popular in francophone West Africa as a proposed route to encourage more sustainable forms of agriculture and resource management (Painter *et al.* 1994).

Yet, as hinted at earlier, the assumptions of the evolutionary model of property rights (Demsetz 1967) are questionable on a number of counts. While there is little dispute that land tenure security is important for agricultural investment and land management, secure tenure arrangements are not necessarily only associated with privatisation. A wealth of empirical research shows how under a range of complex hybrid tenure systems, often involving mixes of communal and *de facto* private arrangements, security is assured (Bruce 1993). Under common property arrangements the 'tragedy of the commons' (Hardin 1968) is not inevitable unless completely open access situations arise (Bromley and Cernea 1989). Extensive comparative research shows how 'indigenous' tenure regimes in Africa and elsewhere are not a constraint to agricultural productivity (Feder and Noronha 1987;

Bruce and Migot-Adholla 1994; Place and Hazell 1993). Rather than the specific form of property right, it is the array of formal and informal institutional arrangements that determine whether a piece of land is perceived to be secure or not that are important (see Chapter 3 for a discussion of the Ethiopian setting). Under certain conditions – for example in dryland areas where inter-annual variations in resource productivity are high owing to rainfall uncertainties – communal tenure may be the most appropriate, allowing opportunistic movement and flexibile responses to uncertain conditions (Scoones 1995). For much of the time in such settings, it may not be worthwhile investing in the high costs of defending fixed and precise boundaries, and overlapping tenure arrangements may be more likely (Behnke 1994). Indeed, fixing boundaries around village lands that were once vague and negotiated in a more ad hoc fashion may actually result in increased conflict between pastoralists and farmers.

Why has the 'mixed farming model' dominated policy?

These policy conclusions emerging from the conventional model of crop–livestock integration have been at the centre of policy and intervention efforts in Africa for much of the last century. This popularity of the mixed farming model both to colonial administrators and contemporary researchers and policy-makers begs the question of why, despite some evident shortcomings, it has so persistently been invoked as an idealised model of farming practice and had such an impact on agricultural policy? In the following sections we suggest a number of interrelated reasons, exploring the way the mixed farming 'narrative' has become embedded in mainstream policy thinking over the last century.

In policy statements and commentaries, the mixed farming approach advocated for African small-scale farming is repeatedly presented in a simple 'narrative' form – a story with a beginning, middle and end (Roe 1991). The story is appealing and simple (see Box 1.1). In the beginning, the story goes, there is 'backward' and 'primitive' agriculture or pastoralism, often involving shifting cultivation or transhumant or nomadic livestock keeping. Such forms of land use, it is argued, are environmentally destructive. Over time this situation changes through pressure of population and the 'civilising' influences of 'progressive farmers', extensionists and contact with Western modernising influences. Settled farming, with fixed plots, with livestock keeping closely integrated with cropping (through draught power, manure and fodder links) becomes the norm. This is reinforced by tenurial changes that offer secure, preferably titled, tenure over plots of land. This mixed farming ideal is seen to be environmentally benign, and indeed through the application of manure may improve soil fertility over time.

The key point about such narratives is that they provide a framework for action. They help to stabilise and underwrite the decisions necessary for decision-making. Narratives come to play a central role in policy-making by structuring opinions, defining what are to be considered relevant data, and ruling out the consideration of alternative paradigms. They are hard to challenge and slow to change, even in the face of mounting contradictory evidence (cf. Leach and Mearns 1996). Thus the neat, tidy integrated mixed farm model, supported by justifications based on an evolutionary narrative about natural progress, offers a set of clear guidelines for planners and policy-makers in terms of technical interventions and farm planning.[9]

The mixed farming model's 'pleasing symmetry' (Tiffen 1976, cited by Sumberg 1998) fitted well with the technocratic planning approaches of the colonial era in Africa. This remains the case in many contemporary discussions. As Weber (1996: 1) puts it: 'Such an evolutionary perspective offers the opportunity to integrate site-specific systems research and development with strategic ecoregional or discipline-oriented research and provides a common framework for action.'

Science does not emerge independently of the economic, political and social setting within which it is created. A process of 'mutual construction' is evident (cf. Shackley and Wynne 1995) whereby societal values and political imperatives are implicated in the framing and elaboration of scientific questions and technical recommendations. The removal of essentially political aims into the technical realm has often proved highly convenient, especially when contentious decisions can be justified on technical grounds. As a result, apparently objective, scientific justifications for policies and interventions can then be given, without a broader debate about values and priorities being countenanced. Politics and values therefore remain implicit, but, in practice, are intimately bound up in the framing assumptions, underlying arguments and language of the debate.

The mixed farming narrative, for example, has provided a set of justifications for a host of coercive attempts to ban shifting cultivation and settle pastoralists in different parts of Africa. The naturalistic, evolutionary argument proved strategically helpful as it implied that interventions were merely aiding a 'natural' process of sedentarisation and evolution towards mixed farming. Similarly, reorganisations of village residential, arable and grazing patterns along the lines of the mixed farming model in Zimbabwe, owed much to attempts to render citizens visible to surveillance and thus more amenable to segregation, subjugation and administrative control (Phimister 1986; Robins 1994; McGregor 1995). A similar story could be told of the villagisation schemes attempted under the Derg regime in Ethiopia (see Chapter 3) or the establishment of the cotton zone enclave in Mali (Chapter 2). The physical reordering of landscapes through technical measures of land survey and land use planning goes hand in hand with the need to reconfigure society in order to transform agriculture along the lines envisaged. The creation and maintenance of a class of successful small-scale farmers who had modernised their agriculture along the recommended lines was central to the widely adopted demonstration approach to extension (Sumberg 1998). Thus the 'Master Farmers' of Zimbabwe, the 'well-equipped' cotton zone farmers in Mali or the 'Global package' demonstrators in Ethiopia (see Chapters 2–4) all represent attempts to create a social grouping associated with the mixed farming ideal. The creation of a 'yeoman' class of forward-looking, entrepreneurial farmers was seen to be an important way of encouraging the spread of 'civilising' ideals, but also of diffusing dissent and unrest, particularly in the settler economies where land had been taken away following colonial occupation (Ranger 1985).

---

[9]In the same way, the narrative of the tragedy of the commons persists in many quarters, despite consistent challenges to it on theoretical and empirical grounds, as a strong rationale for individualised tenure.

The mixed farming narrative has thus become deeply entrenched in technical, bureaucratic and even political thinking. While there are key national characteristics of the mixed farming debate (see Chapters 2–4), a common set of themes stand out. Key networks of actors support the persistence of the core narrative, institutionalising ideas and practices in scientific and administrative bureaucracies. Such networks cut across disciplinary and organisational boundaries, and stretch from national to international arenas. As we have shown, the evolutionary narrative describing the emergence of mixed farming as an ideal is linked to a variety of other narratives about environmental degradation, land use and tenure. It is around these themes that key actor networks, with major influence over research directions and policy recommendations, have formed over the years.

For example, from the late 1920s a concern for environmental degradation – and soil erosion in particular – was a major spur for the promotion of a mixed farming approach in Africa. Colonial officials from the British colonies made connections in the USA during visits by colonial officials to the US in the aftermath of the 'dust bowl' (Anderson 1984). These were reinforced by training courses held at the University of the Witswatersrand in South Africa supported by the US Department of Agriculture (Tempany 1949). British administrators and scientists such as Lugard (1922), Hall (1936) and King (1939) extolled the virtues of mixed farming, which was expected to increase efficiency and productivity, and resolve some of the worst consequences of environmental damage from 'backward' farming and pastoral practices. Key figures in the British scientific establishment[10] helped promote technical research with the establishment of experimental sites in Serere in Uganda and Ibadan in Nigeria among others (Sampson and Crowther 1943). The aim was the development of what were deemed to be scientifically sound alternatives to native agriculture based on the mixed farming model.

These technical recommendations were translated into land use and farm planning models that became significant elements of rural policy intervention across Africa. For example, in the 1940s a series of unit test farms were established in northern Nigeria to demonstrate the efficacy of the mixed farming model with plough animals, crop rotation and manuring introduced (Tempany et al. 1944). Land use planning approaches, while notionally based on objective measures of land quality and suitability, often carried with them the assumption that the ideal ordering of the agricultural landscape was coincident with the mixed farming ideal. Thus villagisation, settlement and grazing management schemes all provided technically informed routes to encouraging a particular style of crop–livestock production practice. As the case study chapters show, the emergence of this broader concern among colonial adminstrators, scientists and technicians for environmental degradation and the drive to find solutions for smallholder agriculture that emerged had major implications for the direction of policy and intervention in all the case study countries.

In Zimbabwe, for example, the centralisation approach advocated by the Chief Instructor for Native Agriculture, Emory Alvord, was based on a mixed farming model aimed at creating a 'civilised' agriculture in the native areas. This in turn

---

[10]These included Jacks, author of the popular book about soil erosion, *The Rape of the Earth* and director of the Commonwealth Bureau of Soil Science at Rothamsted, as well as Nye, the ex-Director of Agriculture in Nyasaland and subsequently an agricultural adviser at the Colonial Office.

became the basis for a major land reorganisation exercise under the Native Land Husbandry Act during the 1950s, and has continued to inform farm planning, resettlement models and extension advice in the post-Independence era (Wolmer and Scoones 1998; see also Chapter 4). A similar set of concerns emerged in the French colonies, including Mali, dating from Aubreville's influential work on 'desertification' (Aubreville 1949). Village-level resource planning and management (which later became popularised as the *gestion de terroir* approach in the 1980s) attempted to create fixed, ordered village spaces amenable to external intervention and planning (Chapter 2). While Ethiopia was not colonised in the same way as Mali or Zimbabwe, broader debates in the international scientific community had a major influence. US support, for example to the establishment of the Imperial Institute of Agricultural Research, had an impact on the way technical options were thought about, as did the establishment in Addis Ababa of the International Livestock Centre for Africa (ILCA) in 1973. Models used elsewhere have informed interventions over many decades, whether in the form of the package programmes, integrated rural development programmes or land use planning associated with settlement schemes and villagisation (see Chapter 3).

Through publications, during meetings and as a result of informal connections, highly influential networks were established that linked scientists and administrators both internationally and in Africa. In the colonial era, close linkages between scientists, planners and administrators were established, often stretching between countries within anglophone and francophone areas. Since then, while networks have become larger and sometimes more diffuse, a coherence can still be identified, with particular types of technical scientific advice often being closely bound up with aid programmes or government initiatives. Key 'policy entrepreneurs' – often pivotal people in particular networks – have been vocal advocates for a particular approach. Thus in Mali, the work of Henk Breman and colleagues on the importance of soil fertility in the savanna areas has provided an important impetus for policy responses to encourage intensive mixed farming. In the same way, the raising of the prospect of massive land degradation through soil erosion in the Ethiopian highlands by Hans Hurni and the Soil Conservation Research Project in the Ethiopian Ministry of Agriculture has resulted in considerable investments in mechanical soil protection measures. Since the 1970s Henry Elwell has similarly been a keen advocate of radical reform of the smallholder farming system in Zimbabwe in order to encourage a more sustainable mixed farming system that prevents soil erosion.[11]

Thus over time, the ideas of such policy entrepreneurs have become embedded in mainstream policy thinking, and, through the activities of the often well-connected networks of actors associated with such ideas, have been institutionalised into the regular routines and patterns of administrative practice, in government bureaucracies, donor agencies and, very often, NGOs. There are clearly variations in emphasis. Thus, at particular times and particular places, different elements of the mixed farming narrative may be emphasised depending on wider contextual conditions. For instance, in the 1930s–40s, and again in the 1980s–90s, a major concern with environmental degradation was at the forefront of the debate. At other times, a more

---

[11]See Keeley and Scoones (2000a, b, c, d) for a discussion of agricultural and environmental policy processes in Ethiopia, Mali and Zimbabwe.

productionist concern has been evident, particularly following periods of food production failure in the smallholder sector. Given the food security challenges of Ethiopia, it is not surprising therefore that the benefits of efficient mixed farming for food production have been given a major emphasis over many years. In other situations, the assumed benefits of individualised land tenure on a homestead farm have been particularly highlighted. However, despite these variations in pitch and emphasis, a broadly common stance can be discerned that sees the route to improved productivity and environmental protection as one based on an evolution towards a mixed farming model, a natural process that can be assisted in various ways by technical or policy intervention. In the following sections we explore some of the problems with this underlying model.

What's wrong with the evolutionary model of crop–livestock integration?

Evolutionary paradigms are a well-grounded intellectual tradition in the social sciences.[12] Indeed, Darwin's use of the term evolution derived from the writing of the social philosopher Herbert Spencer, who associated it with a trend in human society of 'universal progress' towards 'modern values' (Gould 1996; Bowler 1989). Victorian social thought derived, in part, from pre-Darwinian 18th-century ideas about the progress from 'savagery' to 'civilisation' (Stocking 1987).[13] After Darwin's *Origin of the Species*, the term became explicitly concerned with the 'cultural evolutionary ladder'. Tylor (1873), for example, in *Primitive Culture*, arranged 'cultures' into a 'scale of civilisation' associated with 'race'.[14] Bowler (1989) argues that, in a turbulent context, the Victorians sought reassurance through the belief that social evolution was moving in a purposeful direction. The idea of 'progress' became central to their thinking because it offered the hope that current changes might be part of a meaningful historical pattern.

Darwin's work had a revolutionary impact on Western intellectual thought, with the *Origin of the Species* being a key intellectual reference point (Stocking 1987). The term evolution also became a particularly powerful metaphor. Using this biological analogy in the social sciences confers a sense of 'naturalness' on particular patterns of change, and implicitly or explicitly imbues them with notions of 'progress' and advancement. The latter is particularly evident where writers have used metaphors such as ladders, levels and stages. One example, taken from economics, is Rostow's model of stages of 'development' (Rostow 1960). Development is thus associated with progress towards a modernised ideal.

However, Gould (1996) argues forcefully against the notion that biological evolution represents linear 'advancement' or 'progress' along an ascending ladder of complexity from bacteria to human beings. Indeed, this teleological argument has

[12]Including sociology (Comte 1875, Spencer 1972), anthropology (Tylor 1873), philosophy (Popper 1972) and economics (Veblen 1919; Schumpeter 1934).

[13]Good examples of this include the writings of Thomas Malthus, John Stuart Mill and Auguste Comte.

[14]For Morgan cultivation was one of the key elements in the transition from savagery to barbarism, and he, anticipating Boserupian stage-models, speculated on a development from tillage of patches of open land, to cultivation of enclosed gardens, to use of the plough on open fields (Netting 1974).

been used to justify the arrogant assumption that humans represent the apogee of evolution. This reductionist viewpoint ignores the fact that Darwin's more appropriate metaphor for evolution was a branching bush – with many pathways and outcomes. Such linear understandings of evolution essentialise one individual trend at the expense of variation in a total system that has no main line and no predetermined goal.[15] Gould argues that 'using the same term – evolution – for both natural and cultural history obfuscates far more than it enlightens' (1996: 219). This tension between biological and social interpretation has been consistently problematic from Social Darwinism to Sociobiology. Yet despite associations with racism and eugenics, theories of cultural evolution have repeatedly resurfaced in the social sciences (e.g. Steward *et al.* 1977).

The point is that 'evolution' is not a neutral term. Implicitly or explicitly its use carries assumptions about the nature and pattern of change. It tends to imply a gradual, historical progression along a single pathway, ignoring the potential for more rapid change, resulting in multiple pathways and outcomes. This general critique of the evolutionary paradigm in the social sciences points us towards various problems with the evolutionary model of crop–livestock integration. Three of these are drawn out below.

It contains assumptions about 'progress'

As we have seen, the term 'evolution' carries baggage in the form of assumptions surrounding patterns of change – mixed farming is portrayed as a 'progressive' step along a ladder of advance to a 'higher' state of more efficient crop–livestock interactions. Boserup (1965), for example, describes agricultural intensification as an evolution from 'primitive' agriculture towards higher levels of technique and cultural development. This is more than simply a matter of linguistic importance. Significant policy recommendations follow directly from such assumptions. As already discussed, many evolutionary accounts contain the assumption that individualised tenure is necessarily the only way that effective intensification of agriculture is going to be encouraged, and tenurial reform must be part and parcel of the parallel transformation of technical practices.

It ignores diversity and variability

Models by definition simplify complex patterns. The question then is whether such simplification enables improved understanding or whether, by defining away diversity and variability, they actually obscure and mislead. Morrison (1996: 583), for example, describes Boserup's model as a 'unilineal and universalising cultural-evolutionary stage typology'. The problem is that 'at the heart of the Boserup model is a set of propositions about the nature of economic organisations and of change, propositions that find expression in a series of quasi-historical stages that falsely sequentialise

---

[15] Historians have also long recognised the dangers in the study of the past for the sake of the present. Butterfield (1963), for example, describes the 'Whig interpretation' of history where past phenomena, which seem to resemble those of concern in the present, are identified, then lineages are traced up to the present in simple sequential movement. If informed by a normative commitment this linear movement is 'progress'.

modal agricultural strategies' (1996: 583). But spatial, temporal and social diversity and variability are critical aspects of both the structure of agricultural production and the process of agricultural intensification, and their analysis is not well served by 'rigid typological constructions of stepwise cultural evolution'.

Thus, as Gass and Sumberg (1993) point out, the 'theory of the evolution of farming systems' is used to explain not only the causal factors of change in farming systems, but also the direction in which they change, and the series of logical, orderly and predetermined stages through which they pass. Many evolutionary studies of crop–livestock interactions also analyse a cross-section of farming systems, with the implicit assumption that they represent points along a particular trajectory of change from extensive herding and cropping to mixed farming (e.g. McIntire *et al.* 1992; Winrock International 1992; Bourn and Wint 1994). Evidence for this presumed trajectory of change over time is drawn from the spatial conjuncture of different 'stages'. As already noted, there are serious dangers in reading spatial environmental differences as evidence of historical change (Turner 1994).[16]

A linear, deterministic evolutionary model therefore leads to policy conclusions that discount the possibility of diversity and variability. The influential Winrock report, for example, states that 'interventions should target components of the natural process of evolution in ways that will accelerate intensification and make crop–livestock systems more productive' (Winrock International 1992: 48). But, as the case study chapters that follow amply show, there exist multiple pathways of agricultural change. Integration of cropping and livestock systems may result from a wide variety of forms of herding, manure and fodder supply contract; rather than a single evolutionary 'ladder', a veritable 'bush' of alternative possibilities is evident (cf. Gould 1996).

It ignores process

Most analyses of crop–livestock change derive principally from an agricultural economics perspective. They focus on the quantifiable drivers of such change, showing how differences in factor proportions (e.g. of land, labour and capital) are correlated with changes in technical practice. But such studies often fail to examine the underlying social and institutional processes of change, embedding the analysis in historical dynamics. Morrison argues that:

> Concern for process takes us into consideration of specific trajectories, into history. The challenge, then, is to construct historically informed analyses of change that ... recognise the contingent and transformative nature of change. ... [We] are not well served by simplistic typological schemes that distort the recognition of such regularities and lead us away from a genuine concern for the processes of change (Morrison 1996: 585, 597).

An emphasis on processes of change points to the need to understand historical contingency and conjuncture. Change does not always happen smoothly, gradually, predictably. There are often sudden shifts and reconfigurations. These may arise from a set of highly contingent circumstances, the result of a combination of events

---

[16]Similarly, Fairhead and Leach (1996) provide a good example of how inaccurate assumptions about the past can be inferred from misreading contemporary landscapes.

occurring at a similar time. Thus the coincidence of a major drought period and the implementation of structural adjustment policies in Zimbabwe in the early 1990s resulted in major shifts in agricultural practice (see Chapter 4) that could not have been predicted from a gradualist model of evolutionary transformation.

The case studies presented in this book therefore challenge this linear, evolutionary view of crop–livestock integration. While such a pathway of change may well be possible, it will only occur under certain conditions. These may be historically contingent and unpredictable and will likely be highly differentiated by both agroecological and socioeconomic setting. Our aim is not to reject out of hand the possibility of a Boserupian pathway of change. Indeed, as the case studies show, such a pattern is important in many settings. Instead, our aim is to highlight that this is not the only option – and for some also not the most desirable. In practice there is a wide potential range of pathways of change, many of which are ignored by a focus on a single dominant model.

New perspectives on crop–livestock integration

As already noted, the analytical focus for the majority of studies on crop–livestock integration has been on the relation between a set of 'drivers' (e.g. changes in population and market access) and a set of 'outcomes' (e.g. mixed farming). While telling part of the story, this approach obscures the processes linking drivers and outcomes: the role of contingent events and institutional dynamics in pushing pathways off their presumed 'evolutionary' course, and thereby the fact that alternative pathways lead to different outcomes for different people. The case study chapters that follow take these issues as analytical starting points. Clearly, the analysis of drivers and outcomes remains an important part of the research task, but this must be significantly extended.

In our research this has required new disciplinary perspectives and field research methodologies that go beyond the conventional reliance on agricultural economics and household surveys to more qualitative analysis of historical, geographical, anthropological and sociological perspectives. When effectively combined, these approaches provide a set of new insights into crop–livestock interactions, which, in many instances, suggest a fundamental challenge to the conventional model. These in turn suggest new directions for technical intervention and policy in this area (see Chapter 5).

The following sections highlight some of the key themes of the approach taken in this research. Four are highlighted: understanding agroecological and livelihood contexts; history and the dynamics of change; social differentiation; and institutional processes.

Understanding agroecological and livelihood contexts

The conventional model of mixed farming and crop–livestock integration often fails to take account of broader contexts. The focus on the farm household assumes an integrated farm family unit, where crop and livestock farming is effectively the sole activity. But of course this is not the case in the majority of settings across Africa.

While agriculture or livestock production may be the dominant activity, livelihood portfolios are often made up of a range of other activities. An understanding of livelihood diversification is therefore critical (cf. Reardon 1997; Ellis 1998).

If broader livelihood contexts are understood, patterns of crop–livestock change in particular locales can often be interpreted in a new light. Thus in Mali the growth of the market economies in the coastal states of West Africa has had a huge impact on migration possibilities. In Zaradougou, one of the Mali case study sites, farmers have long invested in cocoa farming in Côte d'Ivoire as a diversification strategy, and thus divert labour and capital from cropping and livestock enterprises in their home village (see Chapter 2). Similarly in Zimbabwe, the importance of circular migration to generate remittance incomes has been of major significance to rural livelihoods since the 1930s. This remains the case, although, with economic reform and cross-border migration restrictions, opportunities and returns are lessening. Again, as Chapter 4 makes clear, this has major implications for the dynamics of crop–livestock integration in the Zimbabwe study sites.

In many parts of Africa a process of 'deagrarianisation' (Bryceson et al. 2000) and 'disintensification' (Connelly 1994) has been observed, even in the context of rising population densities. This is not accommodated by Boserup's model because it contains the implicit simplifying assumption that populations are self-contained and subsistence-oriented. It ignores the possibility that farmers, faced with declining yields and deteriorating environmental conditions, reduce their labour inputs into farming in favour of other economic activities that promise to be more remunerative or less risky. Rather than a simple population-driven process, explanations of shifts in agricultural practices must be linked to an understanding of the broader political economy, and changing policy priorities, sometimes emanating from other countries.

In addition, growing numbers of livestock and increasingly intensive forms of agriculture may not be coincident with a move towards the typical mixed farm model. Again, an understanding of livelihood contexts and the underlying rationales for changes in production strategies is required. So, for example, accumulation of livestock by sedentary agriculturalists does not necessarily stem from a desire to integrate crops and livestock through draught power or manure. It might instead be that livestock are being kept as a source of capital that can be tapped for a range of expenses not necessarily linked to agriculture (Turner 1995). Such livestock may not be owned by the same people who are investing in farming. A pattern of absentee livestock ownership is evident across Africa (cf. Sutter 1987; Anderson 1988), with richer, often urban-based, investors buying up animals as a relatively secure investment. Resident agriculturalists may benefit to some degree from such livestock, but may be required to pursue a different suite of agricultural practices if they do not actually own the livestock.

The agroecological context may also be highly significant in setting the boundaries of what forms of intensification may be pursued in particular places. The mixed farm model takes very little account of the variability over space and time of agroecological conditions. While broad agroecological zones are recognised (see above), somehow it is assumed that the end point in all settings must be the integrated mixed farm; it is just that different constraints apply. But, as the case study chapters demonstrate, agroeocological contexts may be much more influential. For example, in dryland areas, where rainfall is variable and uncertain, livestock production based on cultivated fodder, fixed plots and delimited grazing areas is often unviable. Owing to the spatial and temporal variability in rainfall and so grassland productivity, flexible, opportunistic movement is required if livestock herds and flocks are to be sustained (Behnke and Scoones 1993). In the same way dryland cropping strategies must respond opportunistically to variable and uncertain rainfall, with different plots, crop mixes and agronomic strategies being made use of in a flexible and responsive fashion (cf. Scoones *et al.* 1996 for Zimbabwe). Under such conditions, a neatly integrated, stably defined mixed farm is clearly inappropriate.

Spatial variation within an area also disturbs any generalisation. Different pathways of change may be evident along the catena, with more intensive investments seen in the valley lands where agroecological conditions are more stable and certain, while more opportunitisic, extensive systems are more likely in the drier toplands (cf. Pingali *et al.* 1987; see also Mortimore 1991; Scoones 1991). Within a village area – or even within a farm – different patterns of intensification may be evident, with different degrees of crop-livestock integration required. For example, on Zimbabwean farms in Ngundu, Chivi small patches – often around the homestead, but also capitalising on relatively favourable soil and water conditions in small niches (such as former cattle kraals or settlement sites) – may be cultivated highly intensively, following the model of the mixed farm (intensive tillage and cultivation, manuring, etc.). On immediately adjacent areas a much less integrated system is apparent, with relatively little manuring and less intensive tillage and cultivation systems (Scoones 1997).

History and the dynamics of change

Setting such insights into livelihood and agroecological settings in an historical context has been central to our approach. Historical analysis of archival records, air photos, reports and other documentary sources was complemented by interviewing key informants in all case study sites. This allowed us to develop a time line of crop-livestock change and, most importantly, to identify key events that had shifted the broad pathway of change at key junctures. Such analysis also showed how current practices are often influenced by past actions. As Morrison (1996: 587) points out: 'Diversity in the course of [agricultural] intensification follows from the historically contingent nature of agricultural land use, human transformations of the environment work to create new environments which confront later peoples.'

Steps taken at one point tend to frame the next set of possibilities. In the language of economics 'path dependence' shapes and constrains options, and both the positive and negative legacies of past practice influence future generations. This implies contingency without determination. Thus rather than seeing the observed patterns of crop-livestock interaction as determined simply by ratios of land or labour availability, they can often be best explained as the result of the accumulated practices over time, conditioned by particular, contingent circumstances.

Major transformations in cropping and livestock practice may be triggered by particular events, or combinations of events acting together. The case study chapters show how events such as drought, disease episodes, currency devaluations and land policy interventions have influenced crop-livestock integration patterns, either singly or in combination. For example, in Zimbabwe the combination of structural adjustment and drought in the early 1990s resulted in major shifts in the crop–livestock system, with the growth of hoe-based gardening systems that responded to emerging market opportunities and the lack of draught power. In Mali, the devaluation of the CFA franc in 1994 had a major impact on the relative profitability of different cropping options. In the cotton zone, this resulted in increasing investment in cotton, but, with major fertiliser price hikes, the soil fertility strategy to support this had to increasingly rely on integrated options, including a rise in demand for manure. In Ethiopia, uncertainty over tenure rights has been a major feature over the last decades. With land reform and villagisation in the Derg period, the pattern of settlement and agriculture in the study area changed significantly, with major implications for who controlled land and resources. Change is thus very often non-linear, uncertain and the result of the contingent interplay of multiple events, and not predicated on a simple evolutionary model.

Social differentiation

Another key aspect of our approach has been the recognition of the importance of social differentiation and power relations. Not all individuals have equal access to all production options, and so agricultural and animal husbandry possibilities are mediated by structures of social difference and power relations, as well as economic, demographic and ecological parameters. The opportunities and constraints for differing farming strategies (or the perceived opportunities and constraints) depend on farmers' wealth, gender, age, class and ethnicity.[17] As Gass and Sumberg (1993: 5) point out, there is a risk that:

> … the renewed emphasis on the integration of crop and livestock production through mixed farming systems will result in a minimisation of the importance and potential of other pathways for the intensification of livestock production. … These alternative pathways are particularly – and will likely become increasingly – important for women and other marginalised groups who generally have limited access to high quality land and other productive resources. For these people the intensification of livestock production outside the mixed farming model may be a critical element of a viable livelihood strategy.

In our work, a differentiated analysis across socioeconomic groups highlighted how mainstream policy efforts are often focused on a relatively small proportion of the whole population. The detailed analysis of the questionnaire survey, together with a range of individual case study profiles of farmers and farm families, highlighted how gender, age, wealth, ethnic and other differences are key to understanding how different people integrate crops and livestock. For example, in Mali ethnic differences in the Sahelian study site between Bambara farmers and Fulani and Maure pastoralists result in highly differentiated strategies. In Ethiopia, wealth differences reflected in access to land and draught power allow very different options to be pursued by different households. In Zimbabwe, gender differences are important, with women's strategies for managing smallstock as part of both an individual and household farming enterprise often underestimated.

Inappropriately aggregated descriptions of agricultural change may therefore miss important differences within and between areas. For example, the now-classic study

---

[17]Berry (1984); David and Ruthven (1993); Seur (1992); Morton and Mathewman (1996); and Wolmer (1997).

of Machakos district in Kenya, which demonstrated that overall increased agricultural output through intensification was achieved at the same time as improved environmental management (Tiffen *et al.* 1994), has been criticised for not paying sufficient attention to social differentiation within the area (Murton 1997) and for taking too narrow a geographical focus, ignoring different dynamics evident in the drier, lowland parts of the district (Rocheleau 1995). Thus while a trend towards intensive mixed farming – associated with investments in land management – is evident for some people in some places, this is, it seems, not universal.

Institutional processes

A final analytical theme of our work has been the investigation of the social processes that mediate particular pathways of change. What is the social fabric that has intersected with technology, ecology and socioeconomic differentiation to create particular patterns and pathways? Our focus has been, in particular, on the institutional arrangements, both formal and informal, and often acting in combination, that shape the ways in which actors access, use and derive well-being from resources essential to crop and livestock management (such as land, livestock, draught power and manure) (cf. Berry 1993; Leach *et al.* 1997). As Berry (1993) points out, understanding resource access and use is not just about responses to relative factor prices and property right rules. Farmers' access to and uses of key resources for production have also been shaped by power relations and the terms in which rights and obligations are defined.

Unfortunately, where research on crop–livestock integration has considered institutions at all it has often been in a very functionalist manner (e.g. Jabbar 1993). Other work has adopted an institutional economics perspective explaining, for example, farmer–herder manure exchange contracts or draught sharing from a 'transaction cost' point of view. McIntire *et al.* (1992: 39–40) explain the appearance and disappearance of farmer–herder contracts thus:

> Where demand for animal inputs into arable farming is weak and costs to obtain them are low, contracts among herders, stock owners, and farmers govern exchanges of land, crop residue and manure. Where the demand becomes greater, costs rise correspondingly and contracts or markets for interaction become less efficient. Farmers then have incentives to integrate crop and livestock production on the farm and abandon contracts or market solutions, while herders have incentives to settle and begin mixed farming themselves.

In our analysis we take a broader view of institutions, where power relations governing the definition of rights and obligations are seen as centrally important. Institutions can be defined, following Giddens (1984), as regularised patterns of behaviour that persist in society. They are better conceived of as dynamic process than static entities (Mehta *et al.* 1999). Table 1.3 is a highly schematic representation of the way different institutions, across different domains, might mediate access to key resources required for crop–livestock production (Davies 1997). This matrix necessarily simplifies the fuzzy, messy, complex nature of these institutional relationships and processes. Any institutional arrangement is the result of negotiations between actors with different amounts of bargaining power, and so cannot be understood separately from power relations and social networks. For example, as the case of Dalonguébougou in Mali shows,

Table 1.3 Institutional arrangements mediating access to resources central to crop–livestock integration.

	Land	Labour	Draught power	Livestock	Manure	Feed	Credit	Capital equip't	Info
Intra-household	Inheritance Subdivision	Family labour	Teaming/pairing Borrowing/loaning	Inheritance Loaning	Gifts	Family labour, gifts and loans	Borrowing	Borrowing	Seasonal migration networks
Inter-household groups and practices	Customary access arrangements Sharecropping	Work parties Herding contracts Exchange for land	Work parties Teaming/pairing Sharecropping Exchange for labour	Bridewealth Loaning Herding contracts	Farmer–herder exchange contracts	Communal grazing Exchange agreements	Savings clubs Farmer groups	Plough–sharing Well-digging teams	Seasonal migration networks Farmer groups
Inter-household cash transactions	Local land sale and rental	Hiring	Hiring draught animal power Hiring tractors	Local markets		Local markets	Money lending	Local markets	
Formal organisations	Land tenure legislation	Church work parties	State schemes	NGO/state restocking Formal markets		Commercial feed markets	NGOs Co-ops Banks Parastatals	NGOs State aid	Extension services Vet depts NGOs Parastatals

farmer–herder contracts have not simply been abandoned in the face of rising costs (as McIntire *et al.* predict above), but have persisted and been continually renegotiated in response to changing circumstances, to the extent that the majority are now water–draught rather than water–manure exchange contracts (see Chapter 2).

Comparisons between sites, across social groups and over time show how institutional arrangements are both highly differentiated and dynamic. In some settings dense, overlapping – sometimes competing, sometimes complementary – institutional arrangements exist; in others there is a remarkable absence of institutional processes mediating access to particular resources for particular people. A close analysis of the institutional matrix – differentiated by site and by social group – therefore provides an opportunity for identifying ways in which interventions focused on institutional issues might result in greater access to key resources, and so positive shifts in strategies that reduce poverty and improve sustainable livelihoods (see Chapter 5). Thus, for example, for women farming goats in Zimbabwe it may not be a technical intervention that would result in desired outcomes, but an institutional intervention that focused on credit and so allowed poorer women to purchase a first female goat and build up a flock. Similarly, an emphasis on land tenure security in Ethiopia may be important if particular technologies are to be adopted that require long periods to result in a significant return, especially given the long history of disruptive policy intervention in this area. For those without any access to certain resources, an emphasis on supporting sharing and loaning systems may be important, rather than emphasising a technology that assumes a particular level of asset ownership (such as two-oxen ploughs, for example). A key aspect of assessing priorities for institutional interventions is the interaction between local, informal and more meso/macro formal institutional arrangements. The case study research highlights how, in a range of cases, such interactions were too often ignored, with external interventions either contradicting or undermining local institutions, with sometimes detrimental consequences for poor and marginalised groups.

As the case study chapters show, a complex array of institutions – formal and informal, local and more macro – interact in mediating access to resources for different people. The processes of negotiation, bargaining, contest and conflict are all significant factors influencing the outcomes of crop–livestock practices observed. Pathways of crop–livestock change are therefore intimately bound up with social and institutional processes. Despite similar agroecologies or comparable demographic patterns, in different sites institutional arrangements governing access to resources can widely differ, resulting in quite different pathways of crop–livestock change. Pathways of change are therefore not deterministic, but affected by a range of institutional factors, which are historically located. An understanding of this, often complex and messy, institutional matrix, we suggest, is critical if processes of agricultural change are to be understood, and interventions to support particular pathways of change are to be effectively directed.

Conclusions: implications for policy and practice

Across the case studies therefore a range of pathways of change are evident, differentiated both within and between sites. While the classic mixed farm option is important in some settings, this is only one among a variety of other possibilities.

What emerges in a particular place is conditioned by a range of contextual and institutional factors that can only be understood by looking at the complex, and often highly particular, interactions of agroecological and livelihood contexts, historical dynamics, social differentiation, power relations and institutional processes. A uniform, linear, deterministic evolutionary model proves highly limiting. Such a simplistic model hides from view a range of other possibilties which, for particular people in particular places, may be key. Table 1.4 offers a highly schematic summary of some of the major pathways of change observed across the case study sites. The chapters that follow examine these in more depth.

We have explained some of the reasons why the mixed farm model has emerged as the dominant mode of explaining crop–livestock change, and why this has persisted as a guide to intervention and policy. This, as we have seen, has long historical roots, with evolutionary ideas from the 19th century implicitly – and sometimes explicitly – informing interpretations. The neat, tidy formula proved appealing to planners and

Table 1.4   Pathways of change: some examples from the case study sites.

Pathway	Key contexts	Significant institutions	Case study examples
Towards the 'mixed farm' model, with integrated crop–livestock subsystems on one farm unit	High potential zones, relatively low land pressure, available labour, individualised tenure	Household labour organisation, land tenure	Bolosso, Ethiopia
Towards the integration of communal rangelands and individualised arable production	High-medium/low potential, low land pressure, available grazing, mixed tenure systems, inc. functioning common property regime	Land tenure, 'community' organisations, supra-household labour organisation	Bele, Ethiopia; Chipuriro, Zimbabwe; Zaradougou, Mali
Towards specialisation and the separation of extensive livestock and arable crop production	Proximity to extensive arid/semi-arid rangelands, differentiation, occupational specialisation, conflict negotiation mechanisms	Pastoral/agricultural 'traditions', 'community' organisations, procedural legal frameworks	Chokare, Ethiopia; Chikombedzi, Neshangwe, Zimbabwe; Dalonguébougou, Mali
Towards the separate intensification of crop and livestock sub-components, based on external inputs	High potential areas, high production returns, good input/output markets	Markets, individualised tenure, household organisation/labour task specialisation	Chipuriro, Zimbabwe; Bolosso, Ethiopia; Zaradougou, Mali
Towards the abandonment of cattle production, with a focus on smallstock and hoe-based garden agriculture and off-farm income	Recurrent drought/disease, availability of river bank/lowland agricultural sites, available labour	Off-farm migrancy networks, labour markets, natural resources legislation	Ngundu, Zimbabwe; Bele/Bolosso, Ethiopia

policy-makers, and the social and political implications were often compatible with broader policy objectives both in the colonial era and since. But does it matter? Does this concern go beyond mere academic interest? What are the implications for policy and practice of taking a different view?

Based on the empirical research presented in subsequent chapters of this book, we argue that it does matter. And particularly so if an emphasis on poverty reduction and sustainable livelihoods is to be taken seriously. A narrow focus on the mixed farming model, and a continued attachment to the simplistic, unilinear evolutionary paradigm that underlies it, is deeply problematic for a number of reasons. A focus on one pathway of change as the 'natural', 'optimal' and desired outcome diverts attention from other potentially important alternatives. Too often, other pathways, while recognised, are deemed to be undesirable and in need of transformation. But, if we avoid making normative assumptions about the desirability of one option over another, and open up our enquiry to exploring the potentials of alternatives, then – as the case study chapters amply show – a range of other alternatives may be equally appropriate, and often highly effectively adapted to particular agroecological, economic and social conditions.

Such diverse pathways of change are mediated by a complex interaction of social and institutional factors played out over time. Understanding the social and institutional basis for agricultural change represents an important complement to conventional technical research. By identifying institutional constraints and opportunities, a range of other entry points for development intervention are identified, which can potentially assist in the reduction of poverty and improvement of the sustainability of livelihoods. While particular technologies and management techniques of course remain vitally important, a key lesson is that the institutional challenges must also be considered alongside these. To date these have been almost completely ignored in the development of research and development priorities around crop–livestock issues, with by far the largest investment going into technical interventions (see Chapter 5).

The assumption that only one relatively limited pathway of change is desirable has had major consequences for the overall direction of agricultural research and extension investment. Most recommendations relating to crop–livestock integration across the three case study countries remain informed by a mixed farming model. As we have seen, this may not be relevant to many farmers and livestock keepers, particularly more marginalised groups without the capital assets to invest in the presumed ideal. Technical recommendations thus focus on cattle manure, draught oxen and improved fodder management, and so favour the relatively better-off farmers following the recommended practices. Yet, as the examples from our findings show, many farmers are following strategies that diverge from this standard pattern, and usually for very good reasons.

If research and development policy is to engage with those following these diverse pathways, and so assist in alleviating rural poverty, it needs to take account of such diversity and complexity. As explored in Chapters 2–4 for particular case study countries, and in Chapter 5 more generally, an acceptance of multiple pathways of change and a rejection of a universal evolutionary model moving inexorably towards a standard form of mixed farming has major implications for thinking about strategies for technology research and development around crop–livestock integration.

2
Crop–Livestock Integration in Mali: Multiple Pathways of Change

KAREN BROCK, N'GOLO COULIBALY,
JOSHUA RAMISCH & WILLIAM WOLMER

Introduction

Cropping and livestock husbandry are integral components of rural livelihoods in Mali. The two activities have rarely been the exclusive concerns of specialised farmers or herders, rather they are combined in varying ways over time by agro-pastoral 'farmer-herders' or 'herder-farmers' (Toulmin 1983; Bosma *et al.* 1996; Ramisch 1998). However, policy-makers in Mali, and West Africa more broadly, have typically sought to order the diversity of ways in which agro-pastoralism fits into local livelihoods by seeking to aid a progression from pastoralism to an integrated system. This more integrated system – 'mixed farming' – is conceived of as fully exploiting the complementary and mutually reinforcing potential of crop and livestock production activities through applying manure, using draught power and feeding crop residues to animals (see Chapter 1). Such a search for order, however, underplays the importance of already existing interactions between crop and livestock systems. This chapter examines the dynamics of crop–livestock interactions in two contrasting sites in central and south Mali. For the actors involved, crop–livestock integration is not something pursued in its own right, but as a part of larger efforts to improve household and livelihood security. This chapter traces the history of crop and livestock management in the two sites, and presents the multiple pathways that diverse actors have followed. In particular, it focuses attention on the role that institutions have played in shaping those pathways. The adoption of technological innovations has been non-linear and much more diverse than simple models would predict. This focus on diversity and institutions challenges certain assumptions underpinning attempts to encourage the 'natural progression' from pastoralism to integrated systems and thus has important implications for policy.

The existing crop and livestock research and extension policies in Mali, as in much of sub-Saharan Africa, have favoured cattle over other livestock and cash crops (especially cotton) over other crops. Household crops have been favoured over individually managed crops like gardens, orchards or women's rice. Donor support and research has been compartmentalised into agricultural, forestry and veterinary livestock concerns, with interdisciplinary integration a usually elusive ideal. The institutions that mediate access to livestock – to draught power or manure, for example – and their dynamics in shaping agricultural change have not been a focus for crop and livestock development efforts. Because of these biases, the currently promoted mixed farming model may benefit some farmers, but it is not necessarily suitable for all farmers, in all areas. Because of the multiplicity of development pathways being followed by different 'actor groups' in each site, many peoples needs are ill served or excluded.

The chapter begins by introducing the case study. It then addresses the state of crop–livestock interactions in the two sites. The next section then outlines the key events that have shaped their agricultural histories and identifies the pathways of agricultural change that actor groups are presently following. The institutions that mediate access to the resources needed for those pathways are described in the following section. The final section concludes by examining how the interaction of cropping and livestock systems are differentiated within each site, and suggests more effective ways that policy could engage with more marginalised groups.

The case study sites

The two villages – Zaradougou in southern Mali and Dalonguébougou in central Mali – were chosen to represent contrasting agroecological zones (see Fig. 2.1). The intention was to examine relatively high and low resource endowments and the contrasting economic opportunities of each to reveal something of the diversity of experiences of crop–livestock integration in Mali. Dalonguébougou was chosen as the semi-arid site because of a comprehensive study conducted in 1980–2 (Toulmin 1992), which gave the work greater historical depth. Fieldwork was conducted during 1997–8, evaluating activities and practices from the 1996–7 season just concluded and from the 1997–8 season that was still ongoing.[1] The methodology combined conventional survey tools and qualitative methodologies, including: rapid rural appraisal methods, a census, structured and semi-structured interviews, field and yield measurements, key informant interviews, oral histories, group discussions, analysis of aerial photographs and extensive use of secondary materials from the Malian National Archives.

Zaradougou is situated 27 km northeast of the major regional town of Sikasso on a paved, all-season road. This southern region (known as Mali Sud) is relatively wealthy in contrast to the drier, northern zones of the country. Agriculture is dominated by the production of cotton and the wetter environment favours a broad range of crops and agricultural livelihoods. The parastatal, cotton marketing body, the Compagnie Malienne de Développement des Textiles (CMDT), is a powerful local presence in the region. It is the principal source of cotton and improved cereal seeds, inorganic fertilisers and pesticides, as well as agricultural extension advice more generally. As part of its operation at the village level, the CMDT has created

[1]For discussion of the methods used, see Brock and Coulibaly (1999) and Brock (1999).

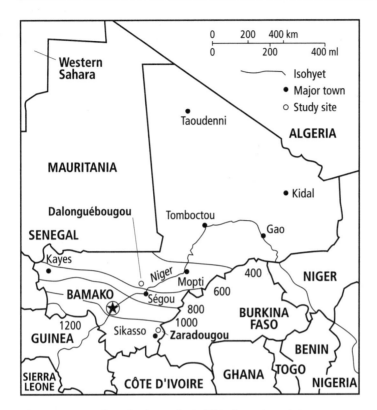

Figure 2.1   Mali study sites and rainfall isohyets (mm/yr)

Associations Villageoises (AV) that organise collective labour, credit and the distribution of agricultural inputs.

Zaradougou was founded in the 1880s, under the reign of the last pre-colonial king of the Senoufo kingdom, Kénédougou. Since the Sahelian droughts of the 1970s and the 1980s, the region has experienced a large-scale immigration of cattle and people searching for grazing and land for cultivation, attracted to the area from drier regions by the relatively high rainfall and more sophisticated infrastructure. One result of this is that Mali Sud is now the most important producer of livestock in the country. Sharing borders with Burkina Faso to the east, Côte d'Ivoire to the south and Guinea to the west, Mali Sud is an important crossroads for trade and population movements. However, Zaradougou, unlike other villages in the Mali Sud region, is not on a seasonal route of transhumant Fulani pastoralists (cf. Ramisch 1999; Bosma *et al.* 1996). The proximity of Côte d'Ivoire has also prompted most Zaradougou households to invest in coffee and cocoa plantations[2] there, as a key component of livelihoods beyond their cotton and cereal fields in Mali.

---

[2]The people of Zaradougou refer to their farms in Côte d'Ivoire as 'plantations', but it should be emphasised that these are essentially farming camps cleared in forested areas for the purpose of cash crop cultivation. They are not large-scale, commercial operations.

By contrast, Dalonguébougou is a more ethnically diverse Sahelian village with a longer, more complicated settlement and agro-pastoral history. Transhumant herds of mixed livestock move across this semi-arid, drought-prone zone in search of grazing and water, and many come to the millet production areas in the south during the dry season, even from Mauritania 200km away across Mali's northern border. The region is not as well served with roads and markets as Mali Sud. Dalonguébougou is 35 km from the nearest paved road and the regional market town, Dougabougou. To the south and east of the dryland areas lies the irrigated rice production zone of the Office du Niger. Here a series of canals divert the water from the Niger River to farmers living along an 80km axis running north-northeast from Ségou, the regional capital, to Niono, a large market town that is an important centre for the cultivation and trading of rice, as well as livestock.

In Dalonguébougou, ethnicity and duration of residence form the bases of social and economic differentiation. They also influence farming and herding practices by determining access to both land and water, which are central to viable livelihoods of both villagers and transhumant herders. Although the stress of a low rainfall year has always presented a significant threat and risk for all, the majority of households have developed complex coping systems, and the agroecosystem is resilient. The increasing numbers of land users in Dalonguébougou means that this situation is in a state of flux and adaptation, although the key factor defining Dalonguébougou's production system remains the low and unpredictable rainfall.

Policy environment

The principal facilitator of agricultural intensification in southern Mali has been the CMDT, and its predecessor before nationalisation in 1974, the Compagnie Française de Développement des Textiles (CFDT). Since its formation in 1949, its activities have resulted in both the expansion of the area under cotton and in an intensification of cotton production with consistently increasing yields. The 'mixed farm' model, introduced by French colonists, at the start of the 20th century, continues to be advocated as the most efficient and sustainable way of maintaining and increasing the production of cotton. This model of intervention hinged largely on the promotion of draught animal power (supported by research on improved ploughs and donkey carts), as well as a secure supply of fertilisers for cotton, improved seed varieties, and improved technologies for weeding and sowing. The CMDT's model (Table 2.1) has a strong emphasis on the integration of crops and livestock, especially through the use of manure and 'modern' livestock management. The components of 'modern' livestock management emphasise the management of livestock to benefit crop production, and include supplementary feeding of oxen (including the extension of fodder crops), animal health care measures and improvements to stabling and corralling.

The CMDT uses a four-level classification scheme to evaluate the level of equipment in a household. It is intended to be a descriptive typology, a diagnostic tool to help CMDT agents determine what technologies are appropriate to a given household or village. It ignores questions of access to livestock or equipment in favour of ranking households on the basis of the ownership and mastery of ox-ploughing technology. The scheme distinguishes at its top end between 'fully equipped' Class A

Table 2.1   CMDT model of agricultural intensification.

Elements of CMDT intensification model	Technology extended
Mechanised agricultural production	Principally ploughs and oxen, but also tractors since the 1980s, as well as seeders and wheeled tool-carriers (*multiculteurs*). Consistent credit provisions for equipment (including donkey carts) since late 1960s; gradually phased out in established cotton-producing areas
Use of external inputs	Improved cotton and maize seed; credit available for industrial fertilisers, herbicides and pesticides, together with information on optimum doses
Improving nutrient cycling within system of production	Extension packages concerned with demonstrating different techniques of manure and crop residue management – improved *parcs* (corrals), composting methods, etc.; methods to prevent soil erosion; application of industrial fertiliser, rock phosphates, pesticides, herbicides and (recently) Integrated Pest Management
Integrated management of livestock	Extension of fodder crops; supply of industrially produced cotton-residue fodder; improved animal varieties/artificial insemination; credit for donkey carts; training in animal health care; manure management/composting/use of crop residues

households, with more than two pairs of oxen and a full set of ploughing and weeding tools,[3] and 'partially equipped' Class B households with at least one pair of oxen and at least a plough. 'Under-equipped' Class C households have either oxen without a plough, or a plough without oxen. They are considered to have experience with animal traction, but not yet the equipment for it. Class D households cultivate entirely by hand, have no experience with animal traction, or have not yet mastered it.

This hierarchy is clearly a prescriptive, normative one, and not one that can adequately describe the existing complexities of crop–livestock integration. It focuses on describing the ideal end point of a 'Class A' mixed farmer, with livestock integrated into supporting cotton production, even though relatively few households qualify as Class A households. This classification stresses the equipment and knowledge that households do not have, or that they will need to be successful, but does not acknowledge the skills, networks and access to equipment already gained. The vast majority of households growing cotton are left largely undifferentiated in the very broad Classes B or C. This risks over-generalising the situation of these 'partially-' or 'under-' equipped households and fails to anticipate the divergent opportunities and constraints that shape their crop–livestock integration pathways.

Agricultural and livestock service provision in Dalonguébougou, being far from the cotton zone, is under the responsibility of the Ministère du Développement Rural et de l'Eau (MDRE). The section of MDRE responsible for agricultural extension is the Direction Régional d'Appui au Monde Rural (DRAMR). Extension agents are responsible for delivering 'training and visit' messages on agriculture, livestock and the environment to between seven and ten villages.

---

[3]In the Koutiala region, Class A households are also expected to have a herd of at least 10 cattle, to provide the cotton field with sufficient manure (Kleene *et al* . 1989).

However, regional funds are concentrated within the Office du Niger, since this is an area where production of important food and cash crops (rice and vegetables) can be intensified and expanded. Support for lower potential activities (such as Dalonguébougou's extensive, rainfed production of millet and livestock) are under-funded and minimal, and extension visits are rare. Formal extension has been much less important to households in Dalonguébougou than information brought by migrants returning from travels in other regions of the country.

Agroecological dynamics

The broad, agroecological characteristics of the sites are presented in Table 2.2. The greatest difference between the sites is rainfall, which accounts for the greater abundance of valley bottom (*bas fonds*) soils in Zaradougou, as well as its more densely wooded savanna vegetation.

On average, Zaradougou receives between two and four times as much annual rain as Dalonguébougou. However, rainfall variation in both sites is considerable – between years, between months of a given year and across scales of even a few kilometres at the local level. In Zaradougou, the rainy season is typically between June and October, with a peak in August. In Dalonguébougou rainfall is more erratic, and the rainy season sometimes starts as late as mid-July. There is also often a dry period of several weeks with little or no rain in late August, which constitutes a major threat to the millet harvest. The rainy season in both sites is followed by a cooler dry season until March, when temperatures begin to rise until the next rains approach. During this hot dry season, temperatures can reach the high forties. For most of the year, evaporation rates are high and humidity low.

Figure 2.2 shows clearly the drought years 1973 and 1984, and a general decline in rainfall over the last 70 years. Although the contemporary debate over the nature of climate change warns us about making generalisations concerning trends such as these,[4] the graph reflects the opinions of farmers in both villages who say that, during the course of their lifetimes, they have seen a decline in rainfall. In Zaradougou, this has led

Table 2.2 Agroecological characteristics of the two sites.

	Zaradougou	**Dalonguébougou**
Average rainfall (mm/yr)	900–1100	300–450
Average temperature °C	27	28
Soil types	Well-drained sands, finer valley bottom soils	Light sands, small patches of clay
Vegetation types	Wooded savanna. Dominant species: *Vitelleria paradoxa, Parkia biglobosa* and the perennial grass *Andropogon gayanus*	Lightly wooded. Trees include the baobob *(Adansonia digitatata)* and kapok *(Bombax costatum)*; annual and perennial grasses include *Schoenefeldia gracilis* and *Diheteropogon hagerupii*

[4]Analysis of climatic change in nine dryland zones across the world has shown that the African Sahel is the only one that has demonstrated 'a significant drying trend' (Hulme 1996: 61).

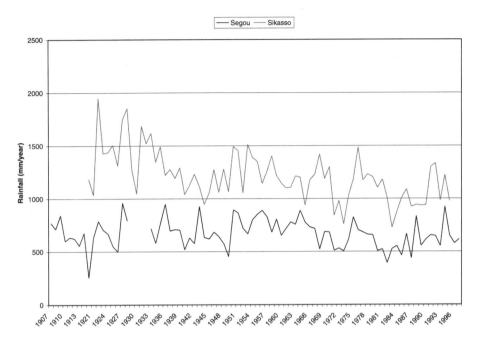

Figure 2.2 Rainfall at Sikasso and Ségou, 1907–96 (from Agrhymet, Sikasso and Département National de la Météo)

to the drying up of local rivers: a 1925 map of the Sikasso region shows the village covered by an area of *rizière inondable*, where rice could be grown without irrigation.

Socioeconomic dynamics

The two sites also differ substantially in their socioeconomic character (Table 2.3). Zaradougou is a much younger settlement than Dalonguébougou, with good market access and infrastructure, and a much more homogeneous ethnic composition.

'Actor groups': Ethnicity, livelihood and social differentiation

Rural communities are highly differentiated by many criteria – including gender, age, wealth and ethnicity. The strategies and negotiating power of different 'actor groups' are bound to differ, with implications for the patterns of agricultural change associated with each. Given this multiplicity of criteria of differentiation, we have chosen to illustrate our argument by focusing on one key axis of difference in each site. In Zaradougou we explore who gets access to which resources and how they do it with respect to community-defined classes of 'livelihood sustainability'. In Dalonguébougou 'actor groups' are defined with respect to socially important differences in ethnicity and duration of residence.

Ethnically, Zaradougou is virtually homogeneous: the vast majority of its 566 inhabitants in 1997 were Senoufo. Zaradougou is unusual, both within its local area and within Mali Sud, in having only two immigrant households, both of whom have arrived within

Table 2.3 Socioeconomic descriptors of the two sites.

	Zaradougou	**Dalonguébougou**
Age of settlement	Established late 19th century	Continuous inhabitation since 17th century
Ethnic composition	Homogeneous settled population Senoufo (+ recent Gana and Dogon immigrants)	Diverse settled and transhumant groups Bambara, Fulani, Maure
Population density	30/km²	11/km²
Infrastructure	Good (paved road, near to markets)	Poor (poor roads, market access)
Village population, 1997	566	774 village Bambara 1826 total population
Number of households	16	35 village Bambara★

(★Most of the analysis has been conducted for the village Bambara households only)

the last five years. A 'livelihood sustainability' ranking exercise conducted in the village[5] generated a set of three 'actor groups' differentiated by their wealth in livestock and material assets, their management ability, and the complexity of their households (Table 2.4). The 'sustainability class' of a household reflects the villagers' own assessment of how effectively that household could maintain a viable livelihood, and is used throughout this chapter to differentiate practices and attributes within Zaradougou.

Although such a ranking exercise was carried out in Dalonguébougou as well, research showed that the most significant social differences in the community were

Table 2.4 'Actor groups' in Zaradougou.

Livelihood sustainability class	Number of households	% of households	% of population
I – Highest	5	31	48
II – Intermediate	3	19	28
III – Lowest	8	50	24

[5]Over several months households were asked to rank themselves and their neighbours according to locally defined criteria of 'sustainability', with Class A the most sustainable and Class C the least. In Zaradougou the criteria were *moyens, gestion* and *structure*. *Moyens* (lit.: means) refers to the equipment owned by a household – in this case tractors, oxen, ploughs, carts and donkeys. *Gestion* (lit.: management) refers to the skill of the household head in assuring the day-to-day running of the household. Finally, *structure* refers to the demographic structure of the household: not only the number of members, but the distribution of age and gender and the position of the household within its reproductive cycle. This categorisation is thus about much more than wealth alone, although it does correlate well with livestock ownership (often a good proxy for wealth).

Similar sets of criteria were used in Dalonguébougou, but the ranking exercise was only possible within the village Bambara 'actor group'. The methodology was similar in the two villages, but the starting points (i.e. the number of cattle, the types of equipment, etc.) were not equivalent so there is no comparable 'poverty line' between the two.

defined by ethnicity and the relative permanence of their residence in the village. In view of the key importance of this differentiation, these actor groups are defined in detail in Box 2.1. These highlight how it is no longer possible – if it ever was – to talk of separate 'farmers' and 'herders' *per se*. The agro-pastoralist 'farmer-herders' or 'herder-farmers' of Dalonguébougou coexist in a context of overlapping and continually renegotiated institutional arrangements.

Box 2.1   'Actor groups' in Dalonguébougou

- **Village Bambara** are those households who live in the central settlement of the village. This community includes descendants of the original settlers of the territory and those households that have in-migrated and been permitted to settle permanently.
- **Fulani** are the small group of households whose presence in the village depends on at least one member of their household having a herding contract with a village Bambara household. They live in the village all year round and farm small fields in addition to their herding activities; some households have lived in the village for more than 20 years.
- **Maure** are the group of households who farm fields at the edge of the village territory. Although visiting Maure herders have been coming to the village territory to water their animals during the dry season since at least the early 1900s, this group is now resident in the village all year round, and has grown in size considerably since the first Maure household was permitted to cut a field in the early 1980s.
- **Visiting Bambara** are those farmers whose villages of origin are found close to the irrigated rice zone, where during the 1980s their crops were persistently destroyed by birds from a sugar cane plantation. They are resident in the village territory of Dalonguébougou only during the cropping season, arriving in late May/June with the first rains, and leaving between December and February when their crop is harvested. They spend the dry season in their villages of origin.
- **Visiting herders** are those people (mostly of Maure and Fulani ethnicity) who spend part or all of the dry season in the village in order to water their animals at the wells of the village Bambara, which they pay for with the manure their animals deposit on the fields.

Households
There are significant differences between Senoufo, Bambara, Maure and Fulani traditions in terms of the way in which households reproduce and are managed. Members of a household, as defined here, 'cultivate a common field and eat from a common granary' (Toulmin 1992: 30), and are related by patrilineal kinship. The responsibilities and powers of a household head pass from the oldest male member to next youngest living brother or eldest son, who also inherits the former head's personal wealth and his wife or wives. Every member of a household has certain obligations to fulfil in terms of labour to produce adequate food and necessary goods to secure their mutual livelihoods. In return, the household meets their basic needs in terms of food, the payment of taxes and the funding of marriages. The amount of time and energy that household members can devote to their own individual activities varies greatly from one household head to another.

The Senoufo households of Zaradougou and the Bambara households of Dalonguébougou are relatively large and complex, but the Maure and Fulani households tend to be much simpler.[6] In all cases women leave their household of origin when they marry and become incorporated into another household, while men either stay with their household of origin or leave to establish a new, independent unit. No households were female-headed in either study site.

The households of the Fulani are generally the smallest of the three groups (mean household size = 8), being basically nuclear in structure. A father is obliged to find a wife for his sons and, upon marriage, most sons (as herders or artisans) seek to establish their household independently. This means that Fulani families often divide geographically as well as structurally, although social and economic links between parents, sons and brothers remain strong. If the son of a household finds work in the village, the two households will often live side by side, sometimes sharing the work of cultivating a field, but owning separately herded animals. Fulani are polygamous, but second wives among the Fulani in Dalonguébougou are far less common than among the village Bambara, and tend to be the widow of a deceased elder brother.

Maure fathers are also obliged to find wives for their sons, but unlike the Fulani these sons will stay in their father's household until their own children reach maturity, at which point they will leave to establish their own household. The youngest son, however, does not leave his father's household. Despite a relatively recent history of transhumant herding, many of the sons of households, who lived in the village in 1980/1, have remained in Dalonguébougou after their departure from their father's household.

The break-up (*éclatement*) of the traditional complex household and the relation-ships of production and labour it incorporated has provided a major dynamic of social and economic change in Mali, particularly in the south. As later sections will show, the start of these changes in Mali Sud is associated with the advent of colonialism in general and the introduction of cotton in particular (Coulibaly 1979; Diabaté 1986; Rondeau 1980; Sanogo 1984). The processes of *éclatement* did not stop when the French departed in 1960. Nor have complex households followed a simple, linear path of decomposition into several simple units.

Zaradougou is somewhat unusual in the context of Mali Sud in that the vast majority of the population (94 per cent) still lives in complex households (see Table 2.5). Eight households have broken up in the past, of which six, since the 1960s or 1970s, have grown into complex, extended households themselves. A further three are currently in a prolonged and acrimonious process of breaking up. Similarly, the village Bambara of Dalonguébougou represents another exception to the national trend of household break-up. The largest household in the village has 86 members, and 90 per cent of the population is part of complex households. Comparing data from 1980/1 with 1997, there did not appear to be any increase in the frequency or prevalence of *éclatement* among the village Bambara of Dalonguébougou.

The large, extended household typical of Bambara and Senoufo society is the central institution through which people gain security, pool resources and share risk. When managed well, it provides a remarkable framework within which people can negotiate a degree of independence and possibilities for accumulating their own

---

[6]Complex households are defined here as households where there is more than one married man. Simple house-holds are those where there is either a single married man, or several unmarried men with a widowed mother. Large, complex households are taken here as those which contain more than 35 people.

Table 2.5 Distribution of population over household types, Zaradougou and Dalonguébougou, 1997/8.

Type of household	Zaradougou		Dalonguébougou (village Bambara only)	
	% of households	**% of population**	**% of households**	**% of population**
Complex (1+ married man)	69	94	71	90
Simple (≤1 married man)	31	6	29	10
Total number of households	16		35	

assets. However, such management requires a judicious balancing of private versus group rights and duties. The frequency with which households break up suggests that it is not everyone who can master these tensions to good effect.

Organising labour: work groups and individual fields
The production of cotton in Zaradougou, and the need for strong social cohesion in a variable environment like Dalonguébougou, promotes numerous forms of collective labour. The CMDT in particular has promoted Associations Villageoises (AVs) to deal with the relationship between cotton farmers and extension agents. The original functions of the AVs were to mediate the supply of basic agricultural equipment to villages and to manage agricultural credit for the commercialisation of cotton production (Diabaté 1986). AVs are likely to have a central role in the process of decentralisation in Mali Sud, and are seen as a relatively sophisticated, 'modern' institution in contrast to other areas of the country where agriculture is not so commercialised.

Traditional work groups (*ton* in Bambara) exist in both sites, and are organised principally along lines of age and gender. These groups not only provide labour for cultivation and weeding (especially important in Zaradougou's cotton fields), but also organise village festivals, provide informal credit and other forms of mutual aid. The power and status of *ton* were bolstered following independence by the socialist regime of Modibo Keïta, which also gave official sanction to the formation of special youth *ton* in Malian villages. The youth *ton* can be hired to provide extra labour for household fields. Young, unmarried women in Dalonguébougou also often hire their labour out collectively or individually during the millet season as *namadé*, to raise money for their wedding. Hunters, musicians, water pump management and various other committees are also active village groups.

Despite the pooling of labour for so many endeavours, fields cultivated by individuals for generating secondary sources of income also exist in both sites.[7] The role and extent of these individual activities has varied over time and across households. These are predominantly women's fields, although this has not always been so. For example, before the 1960s, individual fields of groundnuts for both men and women

[7]The names of these fields (i.e. *jonforo* – 'slave field' or *bolofeforo* – 'side activity field') reflect their subordinate status with regard to the household fields.

were common in Dalonguébougou. Toulmin (1992: 32) speculates that a shift away from individual production was related to the declining groundnut yields and, with the growing investment in plough teams, carts and wells, sufficient capital could only be generated by pooling of labour and other resources at the household level. There may also have been a shift in social values among the village Bambara, who began viewing production by men outside the joint household as divisive and likely to lead to the household's competitive destruction. In 1997/8, 93 per cent of married or widowed women and only 31 per cent of adult men (all retired) cultivated individual fields in Dalonguébougou.

Women in both sites gain access to small parcels of land upon marriage through their husband's household. In Zaradougou, women's fields are found in four distinct spatial locations, corresponding to the locations of the household fields of the four major lineages. Among the village Bambara in Dalonguébougou women are given fields from old fallows in the village field zone, or the former fields of women who have died. Often women's fields are on soil that is identified as barely suitable for cultivation. The area cultivated is a function of the amount of time available to the woman after she has fulfilled her other obligations of domestic work and agricultural labour in the household field, as well as the number and age of the children she can call upon to assist her. Most women in Dalonguébougou have a single, fixed plot where they grow millet and other cereals, and a series of tiny, shifting plots where they grow groundnuts. Women in Zaradougou grow groundnuts, cereals and cowpea, but never cotton. Women's crop production, although the only source of independent income open to most women apart from making shea nut butter,[8] does not play a significant role in the economy. For this reason, women's agricultural practices have been largely ignored by external interventions.

Migration, plantations and off-farm income
It is impossible to discuss rural livelihoods in West Africa without mentioning the importance of migration. Although migration was not unheard of in the pre-colonial period, it was unusual; becoming a soldier, a hunter or a bandit was risky (Rondeau 1980). Seasonal and long-term migration, from rural hinterlands to urban centres or neighbouring countries has, however, been characteristic of the Sahel since the 1920s. Under the French, forced labour and military conscription also took young men away from their villages, often during the season when their labour was most in demand. It was during the 1930s that young men from Dalonguébougou first began to make dry season migrations in order to earn money to pay taxes, walking to Senegal to work on the groundnut harvest. This necessity came about in large part owing to extremely poor Malian harvests throughout the 1930s and persistent plagues of locusts.

Young men of Zaradougou were more likely to seek their fortunes in the relatively more prosperous economy of what is now Côte d'Ivoire. Their migration was predominantly during the dry season and was also motivated by the need to raise money to pay taxes. An especially important episode for the village, dating from just after the Second World War, established connections to cash crop plantations in Côte d'Ivoire that remain crucial to village livelihoods to this day (see Box 2.2).

---

[8]A versatile cooking oil, condiment and ingredient in local medicines or beauty products. It is extracted from the fruits of the shea tree, *Butyrospermum paradoxum*, known in French as '*karité*'.

Box 2.2   History of Zaradougou's Ivorian plantations

Birama Bengaly, a maternal cousin to one of oldest lineages in Zaradougou, had been sold into slavery by his family to pay colonial taxes in the 1940s. When in 1948 he returned to Mali, the tales of the cocoa and coffee plantations on which he had worked and earned his freedom were enough to impress the young Aly Traoré (now the head of one of the largest and wealthiest households in Zaradougou). Birama returned to Côte d'Ivoire and, by 1953, was able to invite Aly to join him. That first plantation was forest land in the village of Aboisso, which (being near the border of Côte d'Ivoire and Ghana) was a disputed territory and not land that the local villagers could sell. Installing the Malian strangers was a way for the people of Aboisso to secure the land at minimal risk to themselves. The coffee and cocoa plants that Aly Traoré cultivated there also permitted his household to greatly increase its wealth and influence back 'home' in Zaradougou. Not surprisingly, the earliest pioneers of these plantations were the households with the highest 'livelihood sustainability rankings' in 1997/8, and had invested much of their income in livestock and agricultural improvements.

Since the 1950s, there have been two other principal waves of plantation settlement in Côte d'Ivoire. By 1985, when new land became scarce in coastal Aboisso, other households tried their luck near the western town of Daloa. This land was purchased, not cleared from virgin forest, but relations with the local population have not been easy. Considerable portions of the plantation revenue are used to bribe and placate the locals. The third wave of plantation establishment (in the late 1980s) has been in national forests (*forêts classée*) near Divo. The Malians have had the support of local people in setting up these illegal settlements, but again substantial portions of the plantation revenue must go to bribes to pay off forestry agents. Two of these plantations have also been burned in enforcement of the national forest protection law.

Other sources of off-farm income that are important to Zaradougou include a rental property in the town of Sikasso, and remittances from household members holding professional jobs in other major cities of the country. Migration remittances were responsible for financing some of the first purchases of ploughs and draught oxen in the study sites. Migration also introduced many households to new technologies and practices that were subsequently adopted in their home villages, especially in places like Dalonguébougou where extension agents were sparse. The revenue raised from off-farm sources nowadays is typically channelled toward home building or agricultural improvements. Examples of the interchange between Malian and migrant livelihoods will be discussed below.

Despite conditions of tenure insecurity, households in both sites have shown a willingness and commitment to investing in soil fertility improvement, perhaps an attempt at asserting ownership through use. One of the possible motives explaining the adoption of ox ploughs and the subsequent expansion of cultivated land is that cultivation is a means of laying claim to potentially contested land.

Land, water and farming systems

The field sizes cultivated by households in the two study sites are relatively large compared to the areas found in either Zimbabwe or Ethiopia. The total cultivated area accounts for 24 per cent of Zaradougou's landscape and 15 per cent of Dalonguébougou's. The remaining land, not all of which is even potentially arable, is sylvo-pastoral bush used for grazing and collecting common property resources. Soils are relatively diverse at the local, landscape scale, and local knowledge evaluates soils on how well they produce under different rainfall regimes. A feature common to both sites is that founding lineages have established themselves on the best soils, and have attempted over time to regulate access to these soils as immigrants have arrived.

Nevertheless, households have positioned their fields to exploit the soil and agro-ecological diversity available to them (Table 2.6). Households in Zaradougou are relatively unconstrained for space, and often have large fields that cover several soil types along the catena. Several households have secondary fields located on the wetter, valley bottom land (*bas fonds*), allowing vegetable and rice production through the dry season. By diversifying their livelihoods to include Ivorian plantations they are exploiting an exceptionally broad set of agroecological resources.

In Dalonguébougou, the power in determining regional land use is vested in the village Bambara council of elders: the best soils have long ago been appropriated by the village Bambara and are cultivated on a permanent basis as 'village' fields near their homes. The village Bambara also have shifting 'bush' fields in the wider sylvo-pastoral landscape. The Fulani have been allocated fields within the village field zone, while the visiting Bambara are allowed to cultivate only in the 'bush' field zone. The Maures now cultivate several kilometres away from the village, deep in the 'bush' zone, after their expulsion from the village fields. The Maures would not be unhappy with this shift in field location if they were permitted to dig a well at the site of their fields, but this is strongly opposed by the village Bambara. The Maures and the visiting Bambara, although restricted in terms of where they can cultivate, experience no restrictions on the size of their fields. The Fulani, however, are more constrained because their fields are surrounded on all sides by the fields of the village Bambara.

While relatively abundant in Zaradougou, water is a key resource in Dalonguébougou. Water for human consumption and dry season watering of animals comes from subterranean sources, accessed by pumps and wells. Five hand-pumps were installed in the village centre by NGOs in the 1980s and are used by all groups for domestic and drinking needs. This can represent a round-trip journey of 14km for some Maure. Additionally, 56 wells (54 of which are privately owned) have been dug

Table 2.6 Types of fields cultivated by households in the two sites, 1996–8.

	'Village' field	'Bush' field	Plantation (Côte d'Ivoire)
Zaradougou	✓	No	✓
Dalonguébougou			
• Village Bambara	✓	✓	No
• Fulani	✓	No	No
• Visiting Bambara	No	✓	No
• Maure	No	✓	No

in the village field zone by village Bambara, who regulate access to them for watering livestock in the dry season. Before Independence in 1960, only the village chief had the authority to dig wells. After 1960, all Malians had the nominal right to freely exploit land and water resources, but in fact village Bambara still retain a *de facto* veto on any other group wishing to dig a well in the village territory. This stance has become a considerable source of conflict, particularly between the village Bambara and the Maures, as human and animal populations have risen.

The differences in rainfall regime and market access are particularly apparent when contrasting the farming systems of the two sites (Table 2.7). Mean land holdings and labour force are roughly equivalent in the two sites, but the crops produced using these resources are quite different. The sub-humid climate and more developed market access of Zaradougou favours a cash crop-oriented (cotton–maize) system, while the semi-arid Dalonguébougou's fields are more geared towards subsistence production, with long and short-cycle millets planted to cope with rainfall variability. Livestock holdings also differ between the sites: in Dalonguébougou livestock are central to most of the livelihoods of all actor groups, with smallstock, cattle and donkeys abundant. In Zaradougou, by contrast, only draught oxen and donkeys are prevalent, with only the wealthier households owning cattle beyond draught animals. The opportunities for livelihood diversification are higher in Zaradougou than in Dalonguébougou, meaning that cotton or livestock are important investments, but not unique ones, when orchards or *bas fonds* in Zaradougou, Ivorian plantations or other off-farm properties vie for attention. In Dalonguébougou, however, the crop and livestock systems represent the paramount activities for virtually every household. As a result, a greater diversity of crop and livestock livelihoods and inter-actions can be found in Dalonguébougou.

Crops

The agroecosystem in Zaradougou is principally based on the production of cotton, cereals, fruit and cattle. Although maize is the staple food, most households focus their resources on the production of cotton, which is cultivated in rotation with cereals. Fertiliser (organic and non-organic) is mainly applied to cotton, with cereals receiving the residual benefit in the following year. Maize is the most common cereal cultivated, but sorghum and millet are also found, and cereals are frequently inter-cropped with legumes such as haricot beans or cowpea.

Through the efforts of the CMDT, the process of agricultural intensification in Zaradougou is now largely cotton-led. The availability of credit and inputs depends on the cultivation of cotton. Although both fertiliser and credit are available on the open market, no households in the village have stepped outside the CMDT system, preferring the security of input supply, transport and a guaranteed price that comes with the use of credit and inputs for cotton. In this respect intensifying the production of any other crops – such as maize – is intimately linked to cotton.

Groundnuts are grown in small quantities by some households, sometimes double-cropped to try to take advantage of the demand for fresh groundnuts in Sikasso. They are the principal crop grown by women on their individual fields. Some households have very small plots in the *bas fond* area close to the river where they are able to

Table 2.7 Overview of the farming systems in the two sites,[9] 1997/8.

	Zaradougou		Dalonguébougou	
Cropping system	Cotton dominates. Maize and some sorghum/millet. Also cowpea, beans, fruit and some groundnuts		Millet dominates. Also groundnuts and cowpea	
Livestock types	Cattle, donkeys (few goats, sheep)		Cattle, goats, sheep, donkeys, camels	
Cattle per household	0 – 50		0 – 152	
mean herd size	12		20	
median herd size	3		8	
Smallstock per household	0 – 11		0 – 143	
mean flock size	2		32	
median flock size	1		22	
Average farm size (ha)	16.5		18.5	
Number of workers/ household	11.4		12.7	
Average area cultivated/ worker (ha)	Cotton	0.82	Village field	0.41
	Cereal/groundnut	0.63	Bush field	1.05
	Total	1.45	Total	1.46
Households growing major crops	Cotton	81%	Long cycle millet	100%
	Maize	100%	Short cycle millet	71%
	Millet	92%	Cowpea intercrop	100%
	Sorghum	17%	Bambara groundnut	100%
	Groundnut	67%	(Groundnut[10])	
Tillage methods	Ox-plough	92%	Ox-plough	100%
	Hoe	8%		
	Tractor-plough	38%		
	(in all cases, tractor ploughing is a supplement to oxen ploughing)			

[9]Sampling and weighting of the measures varies between the sites. A) Livestock data are for all village Bambara households in Dalonguébougou and *all* households in Zaradougou. B) Crop data are for seven out of 35 village Bambara households, in a stratified sample across the range of sustainability ranks. Crop data are for a sample of 12 out of 16 households in Zaradougou, based on those who were willing to share information. (Exception: % of households growing major crops is based on *all* households.) C) Dalonguébougou field areas were measured with a GPS unit while Zaradougou field areas are those given by the CMDT. D) The 'Worker index' is based on Toulmin (1992), where: Adult man aged 16–45 = 1.0; Men over 45 = 0.8; Women over 15 = 0.6; Girls and boys 12–15 = 0.7.

[10]Groundnut is an individually cultivated crop in Dalonguébougou and not recorded in household production figures.

cultivate vegetables in the cool dry season, after the rains have ended but before temperatures rise and the river dries. Small orchards of fruit trees (mango and orange) are also found principally in the *bas fond* area, where the presence of the river allows tree seedlings to be established through irrigation. There is no unclaimed land in the *bas fond* area, and some households have planted orchards on fields normally used for cultivating cotton and cereals.

The agroecosystem in Dalonguébougou is principally based on the production of millet and livestock (cattle and small ruminants). Although millet is the staple food, most households produce adequate surplus to trade for other goods. Millet, usually intercropped with cowpeas, is grown on heavily manured fields close to the village where there is no rotation or fallow, and largely without external inputs on large shifting bush fields further away from the village. Two varieties of groundnuts, largely produced for sale, are the most important of several secondary crops and are grown on household fields, individual fields and in some case on fields farmed by a sub-group of a particularly large extended household. Dah, maize, sorghum, calabashes, okra, tomatoes and tobacco are grown on individual fields, although millet dominates the agricultural activities of individuals.

Livestock

Animals, particularly cattle and donkeys, are important to livelihoods in both sites (Table 2.8), providing milk, meat, manure, draught power, income, savings, transport and status. In both sites, ownership of many cattle is an indicator of wealth, but access to (and preferably ownership of) at least one pair of draught oxen is central to most livelihoods: oxen are usually the primary investment priority of poorer households. Donkeys are common in both sites as well, for transporting workers, manure and crop residues, as well as goods to market. However, they are more common in Dalonguébougou where they are essential to the drawing and trans-porting of well water, as well as the seasonal migrations of the visiting Bambara, and Fulani and Maure herders.

Smallstock are also much more common in Dalonguébougou. They are the prin-cipal assets owned by many individual men and women, although they are also owned in a few cases at the level of the household. They are not abundant in Zaradougou, in part because of a recent disease outbreak, but also because they are perceived to be difficult to manage when grazing, and because in Senoufo culture

Table 2.8 Ownership of livestock in the two sites, 1997/8.

Households owning...	Zaradougou	Dalonguébougou
• at least one ox	69%	80%
• cattle other than draught animals	38%	75%
• no cattle	25%	20%
• donkeys	81%	94%
• smallstock	44%	97%

sheep are associated with the end of a person's life. Where they are kept by Senoufo households, they are typically the personal possessions of the household head.

The few horses in Dalonguébougou are proud relics of the area's 18th- and 19th-century military history and are prized as status symbols by older men. Only the Maures own camels, using them for transport, drawing well water and occasionally ploughing. Finally, individually owned chickens are common in both sites, used for meat or sold.[11] However, they are not typically fed or housed, and infectious diseases frequently destroy entire flocks, such that chickens living to maturity are seen almost as a bonus, rather than as a useful investment of time or energy.

Although livestock diseases like trypanosomiasis are endemic to Mali Sud, animal populations in the region have generally experienced a consistent growth since the 1960s, when the first wave of herders from more arid areas further north turned south in search of grazing for their animals and land to cultivate. This trend continued through the droughts of the 1970s and 1980s, and the growth in livestock populations it caused was amplified by an increase in the livestock holdings of indigenous farmers (Bosma *et al.* 1996; Ramisch 1998). In Zaradougou, even a few decades ago, the ownership of cattle was not so widespread, being concentrated in the hands of only a few, wealthy owners. Today, cattle have become important sources of investment for cotton and plantation income, and the agroecosystem now relies heavily on manure inputs to maintain soil fertility. The widespread adoption of draught power, and the toll of drought and disease on the larger herds, have also served to make the holdings somewhat more equitably distributed over time: the total numbers of animals in the village may be comparable, but more households now own at least an ox or two to serve as plough animals.[12] However, only the higher 'livelihood sustainability class' households are likely to own cattle beyond those used for draught (see Table 2.9). Class II households are also more likely to invest their incomes in smallstock rather than cattle.

Overall livestock populations are much greater in Dalonguébougou, and are perceived to have increased considerably over the last few decades. The Maures (who often own extremely large herds of cattle, and 100–200 sheep) are generally perceived to be responsible for most of this increase, both through immigration and natural increase

Table 2.9 Livestock holdings by sustainability class of households, Zaradougou, 1997/8.

Sustainability class	Average number of animals / household			
	Oxen	Other cattle	Smallstock	Donkeys
Class I	6	22	2	1
Class II	3	8	5	1
Class III	0.75	0.26	2	0.5
Village total	**58**	**125**	**45**	**12**

[11]Eggs are never eaten; according to the Bambara, 'a boy who steals an egg will grow into a man who steals cows'.
[12]Similar trends have been observed elsewhere in Mali Sud (Ramisch 1998; Sanogo 1989).

of their herds already present in Dalonguébougou. Actually determining the size of the livestock population in Dalonguébougou was much harder than in Zaradougou. Neither Maures nor Fulani (for whom livestock management is the main livelihood activity) were willing to discuss directly the size of their herds. However, village Bambara animal holdings can be compared with data collected in 1980/1 (Table 2.10).[13]

Particularly striking is the low growth of draught oxen, which increased by a much lower factor than the rest of the cattle population. This was attributed to an outbreak of cattle disease in the early 1990s, from which many households said they were still recovering. A second possible explanation can be found in the changing relationships between the village Bambara and the Maures. The latter used to be the principal source of oxen for the village Bambara to buy, but with the changes in the terms of water exchange contracts (discussed below), many Maures are now paying for watering their animals in the dry season with a loan of oxen at ploughing time. Thus it is now in the interests of the Maures to hold on to their oxen, rather than sell them. These figures from the two sites should be placed in the context of available regional figures shown in Fig. 2.3. At a regional level smallstock are more abundant than cattle in Ségou, while in Sikasso cattle are more common than smallstock. The shorter reproductive cycle of small ruminants gives them a comparative advantage in terms of recovery following disease or drought, and their growth curves are somewhat steeper than those of cattle in either site. Upward growth trends for all types of livestock are interrupted only by a brief downturn in 1987 for Ségou (a year of particularly low rainfall) and a more pronounced drop in cattle numbers in the Sikasso region in 1991 following an outbreak of contagious bovine pleuro-pneumonia (CBPP). Although the major regional losses happened in 1991/2, the disease did not have a large impact on Zaradougou until 1994. Once it had arrived, however, its highly infectious nature meant that many cattle were lost over a relatively short period of time. Numbers of cattle lost by farmers in Zaradougou ranged from one villager who previously had 80 cattle and was left with 20, to one who had 100 and was left with 30, to another who had 90 and was left with 40. Villagers cited 1994 as the worst year for the disease, which was also said to affect donkeys and smallstock.

Table 2.10   Changes in animal holdings, village Bambara, Dalonguébougou, 1981–97.

	Population 1981	Population 1997	Growth factor
Human population (village Bambara)	550	774	1.4
Draught oxen	120	144	1.2
Other cattle	482	1870	3.9
Smallstock	698	1021	1.5
Donkeys	45	111	2.5

[13]The information gathered from this census was triangulated as far as possible through conversations with Fulani herders, through observation of cattle-watering at wells and through clandestine head counts of small-stock. In most cases, the observations more or less matched the census; exaggeration and downplaying tended to be only in terms of four or five animals. The data in Table 2.10 should therefore be regarded as a reasonable

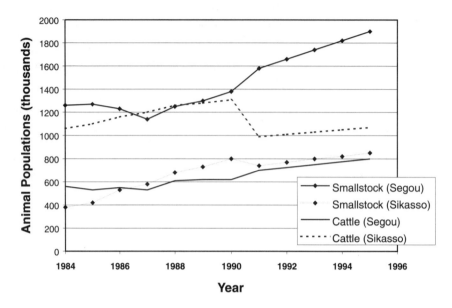

Figure 2.3 Populations of cattle and smallstock in Ségou and Sikasso regions, 1984–5 (OMBEVI, Annual Reports 1984–95)

Tenure

Tenure reform and decentralisation have been major issues pursued by the democratically elected Malian government that succeeded the 1991 Revolution. Land rights throughout the country are being contested, especially as established authorities feel themselves threatened either by younger, democratically minded generations or growing immigrant populations. Issues of tenure insecurity are present in both study villages, where land rights are based on traditional authorities granting usufruct rights. Such insecurity accentuates tensions between livelihoods competing for the use of land. As examples, the village Bambara were prompted to expel Maure households from the core fields of Dalonguébougou as the Maure population expanded rapidly in the mid-1980s. In Zaradougou, recent immigrant households have been intentionally settled on lands that are also claimed by the neighbouring village of Diassadian. Indeed, the households of Zaradougou also experience tenure insecurity in their Ivorian plantations. The plantations in Aboisso were cleared from virgin forest and are held without legal title, while those in Divo are completely illegal clearings in national forests. Even in Daloa, where plantation land has been purchased, the Malians' status as outsiders has led to considerable local tension, and significant portions of the plantation revenue have to be paid as bribes to placate local residents and officials.

As in the rest of Mali, land in both villages is not owned, bought or sold. Tenure rests on the principle of settlement: the earliest-settling lineage maintains *de facto* power over the distribution of land and access to well water (which in Dalonguébougou is as valued as land). The founding lineage, represented by the person of the village chief, has the authority to grant land to immigrants, which is 'paid' for symbolically with an offering, usually of kola nuts. In Dalonguébougou, a council of elders representing all village Bambara households has a powerful advisory role to the chief. Although any Malian citizen has a legal right to cultivate land and use water in any location outside protected forest areas, access to land and water for outsiders depends on negotiation with this centre of power. Immigrants must find support for their wish to cultivate from within the village with a sponsor[14] who will make their case to the village chief or *chef de terre*. The relationship with this sponsor may be based on kinship, as in the case of visiting Bambara, or economically based, in the case of Fulani and Maures who herd village Bambara cattle. The negotiated nature of tenure security for the different actor groups is summarised in Table 2.11.

Table 2.11   Tenure security for the different actor groups, Dalonguébougou, 1997/8.

	Village Bambara	**Fulani**	**Visiting Bambara**	**Maure**
Tenure security	Secure	Moderately secure	Insecure	Mixed
Access to land contingent on...	Inherent through customary rights of settlement	Herding contracts with village Bambara households (most are long-term and stable)	Kinship and social obligation networks (must be constantly reaffirmed and renegotiated)	Integration into local economy through manure- or draught-for-water exchanges; undermined by conflicts over crop damage and watering rights

Crop–livestock interactions

In both sites, cropping and livestock husbandry interacts to varying degrees (Table 2.12). Crop land is prepared and weeded using animal draught power, crop residues are grazed in the field by animals (and in some cases stored as fodder), and some quantities of livestock manure are applied back to the crop land. Donkeys and carts are crucial to the transport of harvests, manure and water in both sites. Livestock also represent an important investment and store of wealth: acquiring plough teams of oxen was identified as the highest priority livestock investment in both sites. The pastoral traditions and opportunities in Dalonguébougou mean that smallstock and cattle also figured highly as stores of individual as well as household wealth. The largest herds and flocks were made up of over 150 animals. In Zaradougou, more investment opportunities present themselves, but ownership of cattle herds (of 20–50 animals) is still considered a sign of wealth.

In general, the interactions found in Zaradougou involve greater and more labour-intensive manure applications, combining the manure with harvested crop residues

---

[14]In Bambara, *jatigi* or 'the one responsible for being hospitable'. Known in French as *tuteur* or *logeur*.

Table 2.12   Indicators of crop–livestock integration by site, 1997/8.

	Zaradougou	Dalonguébougou
Manure	75% cattle manure 0% smallstock manure Applied to cotton fields, used in combination with inorganic fertilisers; some mix manure with crop residues	57% cattle manure 100% smallstock manure Applied to village fields and some individually cultivated fields (millet); deposited *in situ* by herds using wells in the dry season
Inorganic fertiliser use	81%	57% (village Bambara)
Draught power (cultivation)	92% oxen teams 38% tractors 8% cultivate by hand	100% oxen teams (camels used by some Maures)
Draught power (transport)	81% own donkey(s) + cart	94% own donkey(s) + cart
Fodder	Free grazing of residues; stored crop residue fed to animals in dry season, some manufactured feed used (cottonseed cake)	Free grazing of crop residues in dry season. Some use of stored groundnut and cowpea residue as fodder in the dry season
Investment	Plough team = priority	Plough team, donkeys = priority for households; smallstock and cattle = principal asset of many individuals

and applying manure in conjunction with an inorganic fertiliser regime. In Dalonguébougou more energy is devoted to securing access to water, and adequate fodder or grazing for animals during the dry season, although manure plays an important role in maintaining the soil fertility of the 'village' fields of village Bambara and Fulani households.

Manure

Various studies in Mali have drawn attention to the perceived risk of soil nutrient depletion (Maïga *et al.* 1995; van der Pol 1992). Prolonged monoculture causes depletion of nutrients, and it is held that farmers do not use sufficient fertiliser to offset the underlying decline in soil nutrients fully, and the application of manure and crop residues is inadequate to maintain soil structure (Maïga *et al.* 1995; McIntire and Powell 1995).

At the village level in Zaradougou, expansion of cultivation on to new land is still taking place but, simultaneously, there has been some uptake of technologies designed to improve soil fertility. The principal methods adopted by farmers in relation to improved nutrient cycling concern organic fertiliser and crop residue use. All organic fertiliser produced, whether manure, compost or household waste, is applied to cotton fields. The types of organic fertiliser used relate to both the number of animals owned by a household and the institutions that mediate access to manure and transport (see below).

In Zaradougou cattle manure is gathered and processed in a number of different ways. During the wet season, when crops are growing in the field, cattle are taken to pasture outside the cultivated area in the charge of a household member, often a child, and kept in a *parc* (corral) close to the compound during the night. The manure is transported to the field during the dry season to fertilise the soil for the following season. In 1996/7, owing to an unexpectedly early rainfall, many households did not have time to utilise their manure. Mixing cattle manure in the *parc* with crop residue is common among those households with larger herds, and is a technology extended by the CMDT to improve organic fertiliser quality. Some households add crop residue to manure immediately after the harvest; some store it to be added gradually throughout the season. Some households also compost this mixture, removing it from the *parc* to a compost pit or heap. During the post-harvest period of the dry season, cattle are released to graze crop residues left on the fields. The manure they deposit directly is incorporated into the soil without processing. Crop residues remaining after grazing and gathering[15] are often burned *in situ* – also recommended by the CMDT – leading to important losses of nitrogen from the nutrient cycle.

Compost heaps are constructed and added to gradually throughout the cropping season. Composted organic manure contains a range of components, which varies from household to household – animal manure, crop residues and household waste such as compound sweepings, chicken manure and food waste. Although villagers would differentiate 'compost' piles from the unmanaged 'household waste' that accumulates in the compound, the efficacy of most composting in Zaradougou is doubtful. Apart from one exceptionally well-managed compost pit, they are not layered or watered, and there is no apparent knowledge of composting technology.

While all the groups of Dalonguébougou use cattle and smallstock manure to some extent, the rates of application are on average much lower than those seen in Zaradougou. Manure is typically the only soil amendment, since inorganic fertiliser applications are also much lower than in Zaradougou. Cattle manure is accessed across all actor groups either through having a well where animals will water in the dry season, or through ownership of cattle that can be corralled on harvested land. Manure that collects in wet season *parcs* in the bush is also collected by the cattle owners. The manure of donkeys or smallstock is collected by their owners where they are tethered (in the compound or near to the hut or tent), and transported to the fields in those cases where the human dwelling is not located on the field. Although manure is concentrated around wells, temporary herder dwellings and under trees, a certain amount is also spread over the whole village field area. All households that cultivate in the village field zone thus gain some manure during the dry season when animals graze crop residues freely, regardless of crop boundaries.

Draught power

Draught oxen are central to the CMDT's model of agricultural intensification, and the role of livestock in agricultural intensification in the Mali Sud region has been consistently emphasised in research and extension (Bosma *et al.* 1996). Only one household

---

[15]In addition to gathering for addition to *parcs* as bedding, small quantities of residues are collected for artisanal activities and for the production of potash, which women use in small quantities as a sauce ingredient.

in Zaradougou cultivated by hand with hoes in the 1997/8 season, while the rest all use oxen or tractors for tillage. In Dalonguébougou all households used animal draught power. The fact that more people use draught power than own draught animals can be explained by the existence of institutional arrangements by which people without their own draught animals gain access to draught power (see below).

Data from the 1995/6, 1996/7 and 1997/8 agricultural seasons in Zaradougou reveal a general tendency for households to increase the areas cultivated under cotton, consistent with trends observed across the region. Thus, despite adopting many of the techniques of intensive crop and livestock management, many farmers actually rely on agricultural extensification, rather than intensification in the manner envisaged by the mixed farming model, to maintain or increase agricultural productivity. Households with a higher livelihood sustainability ranking are better able to increase manure and inorganic fertiliser inputs to match this expansion in area of cotton cultivated. Nevertheless, an extensification strategy often appears related to lower yields per hectare: keeping pace with the labour demands for weeding, in particular, is difficult on increasingly larger fields (Pieri 1992).

Fodder

In Zaradougou during the rainy season, animals find all their food through grazing, but during the dry season many also use stocked crop residues (groundnut and cowpea foliage) and industrially produced cotton seed cake (*torteau*) to supplement grazing, particularly for draught animals. Although only two of the 14 cultivating/animal-owning households (17 per cent) said they used *torteau* during the 1997/8 season, 11 households (79 per cent) ordered some from the CMDT for the 1998/9 season.[16]

Feeding forage crops to animals kept tethered in the compound – donkeys, and occasionally oxen and smallstock – has become an accepted practice in the relatively recent past, as has the purchase of supplementary feed, but no animals are purely stall-fed. Most farming households produce cowpea, a crop traditionally cultivated as a grain for human consumption, but now increasingly valued for its leaves, which are used as fodder. The foliage of groundnuts is also used as fodder but, unlike cowpeas, groundnuts are never grown simply for fodder.

Although farmers say that rangeland is under pressure from larger herds of animals, they do not see this pressure as critical. Adama Diourthé, who owns the largest herd of cattle in Zaradougou (50 head), said that before the CBPP outbreak, finding adequate grazing during the dry season was becoming extremely difficult. Although he was angry at having lost so many of his animals to disease, he conceded that the reduction in overall cattle numbers was not altogether a bad thing.

Innovations in other areas of animal management are rare. One household has a *parc ameliorée* (improved corral) on their land, constructed by the CMDT for demonstration purposes in 1993. The wire-fenced *parc* has certain advantages – it is harder

---

[16]This discrepancy is typical of most cotton-producing villages in Mali Sud. The demand for *torteau* usually far exceeds the supply available for various reasons: for example, in 1997/8 one of the three CMDT factories, which usually produce it, failed to do so. The CMDT also often prefers to sell to commercial buyers who then resell the *torteau* at an inflated price on the open market. Such complications often frustrate households that are attempting to improve their livestock's nutrition and waste the potential benefits of cotton residue.

for animals to escape, and can hold more crop residue, as the sides are more solid – but it is also immobile and requires expensive materials for construction. Traditional *parcs*, wooden and mobile to allow rotation if necessary, remain the norm and the *parc ameliorée* has not been adopted by other farmers. The same household was also involved in trials of a *hache paille*, a manually operated shredding machine, which turns maize residue into easily digestible fragments that can be mixed with molasses to make supplementary feed. Aly Traoré abandoned this experiment when it seemed that his cattle did not find the resulting feed palatable.

In Dalonguébougou, cattle are pastured in the village territory throughout the year, and corralled in moveable *parcs* at night in the bush. Livestock graze freely on crop residues on the village fields after harvest. Millet stalks are gathered and stored for use in building furniture, fences and roofing material, but no millet residues are stored for animal feed. However, cowpea hay and sometimes groundnut foliage are gathered and stored on hangar roofs and used to feed principally donkeys, horses and sick or pregnant smallstock and cattle. The method of storage leaves crop residues open to the sun, wind and rain, which is not conducive to lengthy storage. Crop residues are not used to feed draught oxen before ploughing time because any not consumed by then would have deteriorated too badly to be of any feed value.

Patterns of crop–livestock integration: an overview

Farmers in Zaradougou have adopted many of the CMDT's recommendations, especially the use of inorganic inputs and animal traction. However, the uptake of its technologies to improve organic fertiliser management and livestock husbandry has been patchy and limited to households that have available human and animal resources to invest in changing their practices. So long as pastures remain adequate to support existing herds with little apparent difficulty, and the supply of industrial fertilisers remains secure and affordable, farmers in Zaradougou see little incentive to change their practices further.

Agriculture in Dalonguébougou can be characterised as labour-intensive and low in external inputs. Changes to the agricultural system have been bound up with crop–livestock interactions and have also been characterised by an interaction between two subsystems that use resources in different ways: the relatively intensive permanently cultivated village field subsystem, which relies heavily on manure application to maintain soil fertility and yields, and the bush field subsystem, which relies on shifting fallow and some external inputs. The relationship between the investment of resources in these two spatially defined subsystems has changed over time for the village Bambara, the only group who cultivate both 'village' and 'bush' fields. These changes in resource use are central to the process of agricultural intensification, as well as to understanding the roles of other actor groups who rely on agriculture as a secondary (if integrated) livelihood strategy.

This overview of the agroecological characteristics and farming systems in the case study sites has drawn attention to some contrasting experiences of cropping and livestock husbandry interactions in Mali. It has also hinted at the importance of a variety of social arrangements in mediating access to the resources at the core of crop and livestock interactions. Since the crop and livestock systems described above are embedded in a wide portfolio of livelihood strategies, this overview necessarily hides a great deal of internal diversity. Patterns of crop–livestock integration are differentiated by household size and structure, ethnicity, gender, wealth and age. It is also true that such snapshot pictures say nothing about the pathways of change pursued by different actors over time. It is to these issues to which we now turn, tracing the key events that have influenced crop and livestock interactions in Mali, and in Zaradougou and Dalonguébougou in particular, and then investigating the strategies and institutional arrangements employed by different actors in gaining a livelihood from crops and livestock.

Key events influencing crop–livestock integration in Mali

Several themes emerge from the markedly contrasting historical experiences in Zaradougou and Dalonguébougou (Table 2.13). Beyond certain major events that had impacts on both sites (most notably the creation of colonial French Soudan in 1898 and Malian independence in 1960), central and southern Mali differ markedly in their experience of colonial and post-colonial state intervention in agriculture. Zaradougou, in what was deemed a higher potential region, was from the start more enmeshed in the colonial and international economies. As a result, agricultural change there has been deeply influenced by state intervention, prevailing economic and land administration policies, as well as migration and other off-farm opportunities. Dalonguébougou, on the other hand, has been at the periphery of these policies, and its history of agricultural change has been shaped more by its changing demography and by ecological dynamics.

State extension policies and technologies

Cotton, taxation and the forced adoption of ploughs
Although local varieties of cotton were grown in Mali Sud, and were part of an artisanal economy, colonial policy in Mali Sud focused on producing 'improved' varieties of cotton for export to replace the American imports that dominated the French market (Roberts 1996). Farm households had to pay a tax in cotton between 1912 and 1947 (Rondeau 1980).[17] Farmers were further forced to cultivate communal fields of cotton on land belonging to village and canton administrators. Work on these fields followed a strictly ordered timetable and caused considerable resentment when communal obligations prevented farmers from working their own fields. Although forced cultivation on communal fields was abandoned in 1926, the cultivation of cotton as a cash crop was established, and the extension service, which was formed in 1923, was principally designed to 'modernise' cotton production.

This extension service advocated a range of technologies that owed much to the European notion of crop–livestock integration on 'mixed farms', where all of the components were controlled by a single owner-operator (Ramisch 1999; Sumberg 1998; Landais and Lhoste 1990; Curasson 1947). The ox plough was introduced and

[17]For example, each household had to pay a tax of 10 kg of cotton in 1924.

advocated, along with the use of manure and compost pits, the use of chemical fertilisers, the complete clearance of trees and sowing in straight rows. Farm schools, such as Zamblara near Sikasso, were established to test, develop and disseminate these new technologies and 'indigenous farms' in villages functioned as demonstration plots, allowing villagers to see the new methods first-hand. Yet some of these technologies, particularly the plough, were unpopular with farmers because of the coercive way in which they were initially extended.

In Mali Sud, households, where a member had trained at 'farm schools' as well as those households that already owned oxen, were forced to accept ploughs on credit. Accepting a plough also meant accepting a quota of crops that had to be cultivated with it each year. Farmers with oxen who refused could have their animals confiscated and given to someone more willing to take the plough (Rondeau 1980). However, the ploughs were heavy and required four oxen to pull them. Farmers were understandably concerned about the health and safety of their animals, and also anxious about the impact that the heavy ploughs would have on the soil. This forcible introduction of ploughs was associated with a reduction in cattle populations in Mali Sud during this period. Rondeau (1980) attributes this decline partly to a lack of oxen that led some farmers to plough with cows, which were unable to support the strain of heavy work and often died.

Not surprisingly, it was a common practice throughout Mali Sud for farmers to disperse their livestock holdings (entrusting animals singly or in pairs to relatives) to avoid having to adopt ploughs, train in Zamblara during the cultivation season and take on the debts entailed (cf. Sanogo 1989; Ramisch 1998). Zaradougou resident Adama Diourthé described how, under such coercion, 'a large, rich family in a neighbouring village felt obliged to give away cattle for fear that they would be chosen as an experimental family for the introduction of the plough'.

The first households to obtain ploughs in Zaradougou did so in 1958, while the most recent did so in 1993. The gradual replacement of the hoe by the plough through the better part of the 20th century was initially concentrated on household fields. However, this has only occurred relatively recently. As ploughs became more common, however, the sizes of individual and sub-household fields also began to expand. At the same time, the cash economy grew alongside the availability of manufactured goods, and individual and sub-household fields often took on increasing importance as the means of meeting personal needs for cash, which the household was not always able to provide, given the financial demands of tax, marriage and inputs to agriculture. Sub-household fields were usually cultivated by groups of sons of the same mother, and many complex households eventually divided along these lines (Diabaté 1986).

Colonial policies of taxation and forced labour had a huge impact on Senoufo culture and social organisation, particularly on the structure of the household. Household heads had to manage not only labour and social relations for subsistence production, but also a household-level cash economy where the allocation of labour to work outside the household (to fill forced labour quotas and to allow young men to migrate to earn cash to pay household taxes) had become centrally important. This increased the power of individual household heads, a power which some abused, causing particular resentment among young men (Rondeau 1980; Sanogo 1984). These factors did much to move many complex households towards *éclatement*.

Table 2.13 Chronology of events shaping agricultural change in the two sites.

Date	Event	Site	Impact on cropping and livestock
1898	Creation of French Soudan within colonial French West Africa	Both	Taxation drives adoption of cash crops; forced labour builds roads, buildings; colonial 'peace' makes long-distance migration feasible
1912	Cotton and 'cotton tax' introduced	Zdg	Cash economy broadens powers of household head, increases intergenerational tensions → *éclatement*
1912–43	Forced introduction of the (4-ox) plough	Zdg	Expansion of cultivated areas, many households sell/give away cattle to avoid having to take ploughs
1923	Introduction of agricultural extension	Zdg	New cereal varieties (maize), veterinary services become available
1929/30	Plague of locusts	Dgb	Famine, cattle herds depleted, out-migration
1929	Wall Street crash/global economic crisis	Both	Dramatic fall in cotton prices, leading to an increased French interventionism in agriculture
1939	Rosette virus epidemic	Dgb	Groundnut harvest wiped out – livestock sales support households but out-migration common
1946	Post-war economic crisis in France; abolition of forced labour	Both	Direct intervention in Malian economy stops; precipitous drop in use of ploughs/export of cotton
1949	Establishment of CFDT	Zdg	Large-scale cotton promotion, input supply becomes more stable; rainfed Mali Sud replaces irrigated Niger delta as main cotton region
1950s	Recovery of groundnut production	Dgb	Village Bambara rebuild livestock herds
1953	First wave of Ivorian plantations	Zdg	Virgin forest cleared in Aboisso (secure tenure)
1960	Independence; promotion of 2-ox ploughs	Zdg	Gradual return to ploughing, expanding cultivated areas
1960	Independence; end to chiefly monopoly on well digging	Dgb	Well-digging gradually undertaken by nearly every village Bambara household
1960s	Unusually good rainfall continues	Both	Cultivated areas expand, herds grow larger
1962–7	Mali outside of CFA zone	Zdg	Input prices increase, their use declines
1967	Moussa Traoré's military coup (state control of maize market)	Zdg	Low maize prices for urban markets shift crop rotations away from maize to millet
1972/3	Major drought	Both	Major losses of livestock; movement of pastoral populations from the north to the south of Mali; increase in cropping by Fulani and Maure

1974	CFDT nationalised as the CMDT; restructuring of maize markets puts CMDT in charge of pricing	Zdg	'Maize boom' of good, stable prices begins, encourages planting maize instead of millet/sorghum
1981–5	*Quelea quelea* birds devastate crops	Dgb	Visiting Bambara use kinship ties with 'village Bambara' to occupy bush field areas
1983–4	Major drought	Both	Major losses of livestock; movement of pastoral populations from the north to the south of Mali
1983–6	'Cotton crisis' (US floods market)	Zdg	Cotton prices collapse, input use drops
1984	Structural adjustment programme initiated	Zdg	CMDT removed from maize market, maize prices slump again
1985	Second wave of Ivorian plantations	Zdg	Land purchased in Daloa but tensions with locals
1987	Third wave of Ivorian plantations	Zdg	Illegal occupation of *forêt classée* near Divo
1991–4	Contagious bovine pleuro-pneumonia	Zdg	Loss of oxen, cattle
1994	Devaluation of CFA franc	Zdg	Increased price of agricultural inputs leads to reduction in use of inorganic fertilisers, expansion of crop area; increased exports of cereals and livestock to Côte d'Ivoire
1999	Decentralisation	Both	Uncertainty about land tenure, increased negotiations over land use

The Depression, groundnuts, the end of direct intervention and the creation of the CFDT

The export of cotton marked the integration of Mali Sud into the world economy, and tied its fate to global commodity markets. However, the economic crisis of the 1930s provoked a disastrous fall in cotton prices. Between 1934 and 1947 in the *cercle* of Sikasso, total cotton sales only met an average of 27 per cent of the total demand for taxes, prompting much migration to Côte d'Ivoire, Senegal or the major Malian cities to raise money (Rondeau 1980: 414).

The French response was to increase taxes, and replace cotton with the obligatory cultivation of groundnuts. The attention to groundnut production in the 1930s was one of the first national-level policies to have a direct impact on Dalonguébougou, which until then had been a neglected hinterland to the Office du Niger irrigation area. Societés Indigène de Prévoyance (SIP) grain bank cooperatives had been in operation throughout Mali since the turn of the century, but were now established both in Dalonguébougou and Zaradougou. Farmers had to contribute to these 'famine reserve' granaries: 2 kg per taxable person in 1937, which rose rapidly to 30 kg per person by 1941. The SIPs also provided credit for the supply of animal-drawn ploughs and carts to farmers (Toulmin 1992). However, the grain bank function of the SIPs was enormously resented. This, combined with the cultural reluctance of the Bambara to become indebted to outsiders, meant that in Dalonguébougou no-one took up the credit offered for ploughs and carts. It was not until the 1950s that the first ploughs, paid for outright with migration earnings and livestock sales, arrived in Dalonguébougou (Toulmin 1992).

A large balance of payments deficit in France and domestic turmoil brought on by the Second World War led to a shift in French policy after 1943 away from direct intervention. Forced labour, the forced introduction of ploughs, as well as the obligatory cultivation of cotton were abandoned. The use of ploughs diminished immediately and did not become widespread again until after Malian independence in 1960. Demonstrative of this decline is the fact that there were more ploughs in the Sikasso region in 1934 than there were in 1986 (Diabaté 1986). The immediate result of the abolition of compulsory cotton cultivation was also dramatic: in 1946 82,000 tonnes of cotton were produced for export, a quantity which by 1947 had fallen to 1,800 tonnes (Anon 1947). The period of direct state manipulation of agricultural production was coming to an end, to be replaced by the parastatal intervention of the Compagnie Française de Développment des Textiles (CFDT). This body was established in 1949 with the objectives of improving France's post-war negative trade balance (Fok 1994), and ensuring a secure supply of cotton to metropolitan France. The CFDT model of the 1950s involved achieving increased productivity through stability. This stability comprised not only a reliable supply of inputs, equipment and training for farmers, but also achieving annual and inter-annual price stability through the purchasing and stockpiling of reserves.

Independence: changing economic policies and the global economy
The period immediately following Independence was also one of favourable rainfall. The euphoria of post-colonial freedom was matched by bountiful harvests, and the first president, Modibo Keïta, promised to help both the rural peasantry and the urban population. One step was the establishment of the Office des Produits Agricoles du Mali (OPAM), which administered a system of purchasing grain quotas from every village at a price fixed by the government. OPAM had (at least in theory) a legal monopoly on all grain sales in the immediate post-harvest period, and the power to set producer and consumer prices for cereals. However, combined with a lack of investment in agricultural research and infrastructure, OPAM had to resort to force to secure its deliveries and attempt to uphold its monopoly. Producer prices were low throughout the 1960s, and Mali's small cereal export surplus had disappeared by 1966 (Simmons 1987).

Despite a brief period in 1969 when OPAM's legal monopoly was abolished by the Traoré regime, which had seized power the preceding year, it was quickly re-established and low prices to cereal farmers, stagnating production and lack of investment in research and extension continued throughout the 1970s (Simmons 1987). It was during this period that the first wave of migrations from Zaradougou to Côte d'Ivoire took place: young men recall wanting to escape from the repressive atmosphere and lack of opportunity they found at home. In the cotton sector, the CFDT was nationalised in 1974, and the CMDT continued to provide equivalent services to farmers.

Changes to cereal production in Mali Sud came in the early 1980s when donors, increasingly unwilling to subsidise OPAM[18] (which was also responsible for distributing food aid), reached an agreement with the Malian government to restructure the marketing of cereals. The immediate effect of the PRMC

---

[18]OPAM's deficit at the end of the 1976/7 agricultural season was US$ 80m (Staatz *et al.* 1989: 705).

(Programme de Restructuration des Marchés Céréalières) in Mali Sud was that the CMDT was given responsibility for promoting cereals as well as cotton. The result of this shift was a brief maize boom in the early 1980s, when farmers enjoyed a relatively high fixed price from the CMDT and an assured supply of inputs. This period, however, was merely the transition phase of the PRMC, which always aimed to move through the stage of mixed public and private support to the cereals sector to complete liberalisation, in line with the first Structural Adjustment Programme (SAP) that was agreed in 1984. The maize boom ended in 1986 when price guarantees were removed and the CMDT withdrew from providing credit for inputs to maize. Unfortunately, this also coincided with a collapse in the world price of cotton between 1983 and 1986. The price of inputs increased dramatically, especially relative to incomes, and farmers say their profits declined rapidly. Unsurprisingly, the second and third waves of migration to Côte d'Ivoire to establish more plantations occurred at this same time.

Mali's first SAP focused on policies of selective liberalisation, attempting to encourage domestic markets for agricultural products while maintaining import controls in an attempt to turn around the chronic deficit in Mali's balance of trade (INRA/IRAM/UNB 1991). Measures during this early period of adjustment included limits on rice imports, increased technical assistance to cash crop producers, support to cereals traders to stimulate the export of grain and credits to Village Associations for storage facilities in surplus years. The SAP was accelerated in 1988, with an emphasis placed on reforming parastatals, the institutional structures of state rural development institutions, and the relationships between them. For example, the Ministry for Rural Development (MDRE) was gradually reformed and a process of decentralisation to the regional level was undertaken, which continues to the present.

The liberalisation policies culminated in the devaluation of the CFA franc in 1994, undertaken in the context of restoring Francophone Africa's fiscal balance, and immediately altering Mali's terms of trade with its West African neighbours and world cotton markets. It had a direct impact on Malians by doubling the price of many consumer goods overnight before any benefits in the form of increased income had trickled down. For CMDT farmers, the cost of fertiliser doubled, and its use fell dramatically in the season immediately after devaluation. It recovered slowly in subsequent years as the devaluation and other reforms raised the prices received by producers for their cotton (Giraudy and Niang 1996). The higher prices of inorganic fertilisers helped stimulate greater interest in livestock manure and composting. Devaluation also served to increase the export of both cereals and livestock to neighbouring countries, especially Côte d'Ivoire.

1991's Revolution, decentralisation and demographic changes
Decades of political frustration with the dictator Moussa Traoré culminated in a popular Revolution in 1991, establishing a democratic government under Alpha O. Konaré. One manifestation of the Revolution in even the smallest Malian community was the turning of the populace on the local government forestry agency (*Eaux et forêts*) agents, with many reports of evictions, physical assaults and even lynching. These agents were the most visible and despised instruments of the overthrown regime for most villagers; they had been responsible for enforcing unpopular restrictions on clearing forest and also the ban on bush fires. Since the Revolution, it

has been much easier to expand cultivated areas since forestry agents have been reluctant to fine people who clear bush without their permission. One response to democracy, therefore, has been an unwillingness to listen to local representatives of the state, and a greater likelihood that disputes are resolved spontaneously through local means. This is particularly true where actors with different livelihoods are in competition for the same resources, as in the case of farmers in the zone of Kadiolo who dismantled a Fulani herders' hamlet in a dispute over grazing rights.

In this context, the new regime (backed by significant donor support) has been implementing decentralisation of administration to the local level. Decentralisation promises to change the balance of power between different actors at the local level. Non-citizens, such as the Maures of Dalonguébougou, who do not pay taxes to the Malian state (or indeed to Mauritania, their place of origin), may be important local actors who will be further disenfranchised in the new institutions. The debates around establishing new *communes rurales* that combine several existing villages into a single new government layer, as well as a new Forest Code determining rights of land use, have excited considerable discussion over land tenure, the rights of immigrants and natural resource management more generally.

The increase in land under cultivation in Mali Sud in the 1990s has been seen by some as a response to growing immigrant pressure on available land. Expansion of cultivation is one way for local farmers to demonstrate occupancy of land and prevent others from using it (Hesseling and Coulibaly 1991; Fok 1994). In Zaradougou this expansion of cultivation has been manifested in two ways. First, indigenous households have been steadily expanding their areas under cotton cultivation since 1978, thanks to the spread of draught power and the availability of fertilisers to maintain yields. This process was accelerated by the devaluation of the CFA franc in 1994 when inorganic fertiliser costs doubled and increasing crop yields through extensification became much more attractive and feasible than through intensification. Second, the two recent non-Senoufo immigrant households in Zaradougou have been intentionally given land at the village boundary to assert a claim to land that is also contested by a neighbouring village.

Questions of land rights in Dalonguébougou have been much more complicated, and reflect the shifting power relationships between the various actor groups. The village Bambara were once the uncontested masters of the area, but their power has diminished because so many other people have settled in the *terroir* over the last twenty years. The large growth in Maure and visiting Bambara populations represents in-migration in addition to the natural growth of the Maure community that already existed in 1981. Although the Fulani community has absorbed new households since 1981, it has also lost others, and the total number of households has remained largely stable (Table 2.14).

The most conspicuous population increase is that of the visiting Bambara, who are settled each rainy season in 11 informal hamlets (*hameaux de culture*) between 5 km and 14 km from the village itself. The first households arrived in 1982, escaping plagues of *Quelea* birds from a neighbouring sugar cane plantation that had destroyed their crops. The majority of families arrived between 1985 and 1990, although the last arrivals completed their first season during 1997/8. Before the 1980s, the village Bambara obliged Bambara newcomers to settle definitively in the village, to be absorbed into its social life and networks. Their goal was to prevent strangers from

Table 2.14   Changes in human population, Dalonguébougou, 1981–97.

	Population 1981	Population 1997	Growth factor
Village Bambara	550	774	1.4
Village Fulani	85★	106	1.2
Village Maure	34★	136	4.0
Visiting herders	108★	57	0.5
Visiting Bambara	0	753	–
Total settled population	669	1016	1.5
Total visiting population	108	810	7.5
Total population	**777**	**1826**	**2.4**

★denotes estimate based on interviews and average household sizes.

farming their land, returning to their home villages with the harvest, and leaving the Bambara of Dalonguébougou with ever greater constraints on expanding bush fields in the future (Toulmin 1992). However, the visiting Bambara are legally entitled to farm Dalonguébougou as migrant farmers, and their settlement has taken place in a political context of increasing awareness of the formal institutions that govern natural resource allocation and management.

The relationship between the founding Bambara lineage and the council of elders has become increasingly complicated, as the demands of outsiders for access to land have grown more numerous. Opinions differ hugely within the council about how best to address the increasing scarcity of land for farming and the rights of others to dig wells. Consensus is seldom achieved. The role of the founding lineage is to somehow steer a path that satisfies friends and neighbours, puts the best interest of the Bambara community at the centre of decisions, is actually enforceable and unlikely to attract official attention.

A decision in 1996 to expel all Maures from the village territory, after a particularly tense dry season, failed. It was especially divisive for the Bambara community, because of the benefits many had been gaining from the Maures' presence (access to draught oxen, manure and milk to name a few). It was therefore unenforceable, as well as being technically illegal. Conversely, a decision to stop welcoming visiting Bambara households, also made in 1996, has been successfully enforced. This may have succeeded because, despite kinship ties between Bambara communities, the visiting Bambara offered few new resources or opportunities and were largely perceived as burdensome.

Ecological dynamics: pests, diseases and droughts

The past century has seen a host of ecological fluctuations in the Sahel and diverse natural disasters like pest outbreaks, disease and drought. Generally, disasters have stimulated out-migration and conversion from livestock to more cropping-based activities, and have often reversed moves towards crop–livestock integration (especially with the deaths of draught animals). Drought and livestock disease have left their mark on both sites, but Dalonguébougou (with its lower and more variable rainfall) has been the more vulnerable of the two to catastrophic natural events. Table 2.13 outlined some, but by no means all, of the ecological shocks that had repercussions on changes in agricultural practices. Droughts and plagues of locusts that had dogged the region from the turn of the 20th century culminated in a serious attack of locusts and widespread famine in 1929/30, just as the global economy fell into turmoil. Locust-related crop failures of the 1930s were met by the French with a programme to promote root crops and various anti-locust measures. However, these strategies did not reach 'low potential' areas such as the north bank of the Niger, where the impact of plagues of grasshoppers was hunger, out-migration and a depletion of cattle herds (Toulmin 1992). The promotion of groundnuts as a cash crop in Dalonguébougou was also dealt a blow when rosette virus swept the Sahel in 1939. The total devastation of the groundnut crop again provoked considerable consternation, and forced many young to migrate out of the village in search of alternative sources of income.

The most notorious droughts were the major Sahelian droughts of 1972/3 and 1983/4. The 1970s and 1980s were generally periods of low rainfall in contrast to the relative abundance of the 1950s and 1960s. The 1973 drought was preceded in Dalonguébougou by several years of heavy rainfall, which allowed many households to survive the drought on the grain they had stored. Although some people remember leaving the village to seek paid work in towns at this time, by far the majority recall the kinship networks that allowed them to stay in the village to see them through the worst of the drought.

One impact of the 1973 drought was a change in the balance of cattle ownership across actor groups and a resulting shift in the relationship between agricultural and pastoral livelihoods.[19] Many farmers were well placed to expand their herds immediately after the droughts, and grain prices were high compared to low livestock prices, as herders were forced to sell their animals to survive (Toulmin 1992). Several Maure herders recalled that it was after the 1984 drought that many of them began cultivating in the village because they no longer felt that transhumant pastoralism could provide an adequate livelihood for their households. This shift in the distribution of animals towards richer, settled farmers owning larger herds of cattle and herders beginning to farm took place within the context of a fall in overall livestock numbers.

Those whose livelihoods depended on livestock have experienced far greater difficulties in periods of drought; many recall the total or near-total loss of herds that took years to build up again, and long periods of mobility as they searched for work to earn money for restocking. The mix of agricultural versus pastoral activities within a given household is also responsive to environmental factors. The death of livestock during the droughts of the 1970s and 1980s meant that for many households the proportion of 'farming' increased relative to 'herding' just to maintain a viable livelihood. This agro-pastoral flexibility has long been a characteristic of Sahelian societies, despite strongly felt cultural identities as Fulani or Maure 'herders' or Bambara 'farmers'. Households that still identify as 'herders' will name very definitely the moment they began to cultivate, and this moment is often drought-related. However, within Dalonguébougou, many of the village Bambara have larger herds than their Maure or

---

[19]See Hampshire (1998) and Guillard (1993) for parallel processes among Fulani in Burkina Faso.

Fulani neighbours, and several Maure households have been growing millet for nearly three generations. The actuality of agro-pastoral livelihoods is not entirely reflected in people's ethnic identities.

Finally, the persistence of livestock diseases in both sites has meant that crop–livestock integration has not proceeded in a linear fashion. Fig. 2.3 showed how drought and disease in both sites have been responsible for important losses of livestock in the early 1990s. Households that have lost their oxen have had to resort to negotiating access to others' plough teams if they are to maintain cultivation on the increased areas that ploughs have provided them. Losses of herds to disease also have the effect of undermining intensification strategies that were reliant on animal manure for soil fertility maintenance. In this way, disease and drought play roles akin to the economic shocks described above in that they sabotage farmers' abilities to improve soil fertility or to broaden their range of crop–livestock integrations.

Land use change
Changes in land use reflect the impacts of increasing human and livestock populations, ecological dynamics and technological change. Air photo analysis of both sites over the last half century shows that the cultivated area has increased at the expense of the sylvo-pastoral 'bush' that surrounds the villages (Table 2.15a and b).[20] This change has lowered the rangeland to cropland ratio (RCR), with important consequences for livestock producers and for farmers using livestock to manure their fields. Using the areas delimited by the air photos (which is not necessarily the total extent of the grazing ranges), it is possible to show that the RCR in Zaradougou has dropped from 13: 1 to barely 3: 1, while in Dalonguébougou the decline has been from 30: 1 to roughly 6: 1. A RCR of 20: 1 is often suggested as sufficient to maintain fertility under fallow conditions (Ruthenberg 1980), but such a ratio does not account for seasonal variations in the grazing ranges, nor does it adequately address the number of animals the range is supporting. The large areas of uncultivated bush clearly have a decisive role to play in supporting both herds and manure-related nutrient transfers in the study area, but will also need to be supplemented by feed from elsewhere – either crop residues from the cultivated areas or grazing outside the ranges identified in the aerial photos. This suggests that fertility maintenance through the use of manure is an option really only for a relative minority of households, unless substantial reallocation of manure takes place within the region.

The different settlement histories are also evident from the air photo analyses. Over a 38-year period, the cultivated area in Zaradougou grew by a factor of 3.2. In Dalonguébougou, where immigration has been an important element in adding to the population, the factor of increase was 4.8 over a 37-year period. In 1952 and 1975, the village Bambara were the only group farming land in the area, but by 1989 the immigrant Bambara farmers and the settled Maure herders had also been granted land. This is reflected in the expansion of the total bush field area by 1989. However, in keeping with the declining demographic and political power of the village Bambara described in preceding sections, Table 2.16 shows that the land holdings of the average village Bambara household themselves declined over the 1981 to 1997 period.

---

[20]Based on analysis undertaken by Ben Warr as part of this project.

Table 2.15a   Expansion of agricultural land use, Zaradougou, 1952–90.

Year	Estimate of land use type as % of total village territory			Rangeland[21]: cropland ratio
	Cultivated fields	Fallow	Sylvo-pastoral land	
1952	7.46	11.61	80.18	13 : 1
1975	18.93	11.29	68.10	4 : 1
1990	23.66	10.98	62.95	3 : 1

Table 2.15b   Expansion of agricultural land use, Dalonguébougou, 1952–89.

Year	Estimate of land use type as % of total village territory			Rangeland[21]: cropland ratio
	Village fields	Bush fields	Fallow/Sylvo-pastoral land	
1952	0.58	2.48	96.94	30 : 1
1975	0.89	4.30	94.81	18 : 1
1989	2.77	11.78	85.45	6 : 1

Table 2.16   Change in average household land holdings (village Bambara only), 1981–97.

Year	Village fields (ha)	Bush fields (ha)	Total household land (ha)
1980/1	5.0	22.5	27.5
1997/8	5.2	13.3	18.5

Key events and historical dynamics: change in Zaradougou and Dalonguébougou

As we have seen, a multitude of factors has influenced agricultural change in the two sites. The policies of the colonial state, the succeeding Malian administrations or indeed of international donors have had both intended and unintended results in shaping crop–livestock integration and agricultural intensification. Idiosyncratic events, such as those leading to the establishment of Ivorian plantations by the households of Zaradougou, have also had important repercussions. Individual households have thus had to negotiate their responses to changing economic and ecological opportunities, development approaches and institutional contexts.

External interventions have especially marked the history of crop and livestock production in Zaradougou. While the regional economy is now dominated by cotton,

---

[21]Rangeland here indicates all potential grazing land (i.e. fallow fields plus the sylvo-pastoral bush land) identified within the photographed areas.

within Zaradougou cotton is but one valued diversification strategy among several other good options (the Ivorian plantations, but also orchard production and urban livelihoods based in Sikasso). Despite these diversification options, farmers in Zaradougou have been vulnerable to a significant degree to the decisions of external actors. These include the CMDT, Ivorian villagers and state agents of both Mali and Côte d'Ivoire, all of whom can be seen to be working to different agendas. With respect to patterns of crop–livestock integration it has been the interplay of often coercive agricultural extension measures, macro-economic reforms, and drought and disease events that have fashioned the broad pathway of change in Zaradougou. The adoption of the plough, for example, was not a linear, evolutionary process of uptake in response to increasing population density (cf. Pingali *et al.* 1987), but rather a much more fluctuating pattern in reaction to external interventions and opportunities.

Dalonguébougou, on the other hand, has remained relatively insulated from the direct impacts of state interventions and the global economy. Innovations like improved cereal varieties or draught implements arrived in the village not by dint of official policy but along with returning migrants who had encountered them elsewhere. In general, ecological forces of drought and disease have had greater impacts than any external policy in shaping the pathways of crop–livestock integration in Dalonguébougou. The arrival of new ethnic groups following drought or crop devastation elsewhere have strained and reoriented the old power relationships between the village Bambara and the settling immigrants. Well-digging, which once assured access to the manure of herds, is no longer perceived as a viable option, and the water table is declining from heavy exploitation.

A variety of different possible pathways of agricultural change is evident in the two sites (Table 2.17). These pathways can be grouped together by their reliance on expanding or intensifying resource use, the relative concentration on livestock or cropping, or whether production has been subsistence-focused. A fifth group of pathways, usually followed by individuals if not entire households, is those who have exited from agriculture locally altogether.

These pathways will be discussed in greater detail in the following sections. We first turn to the specific ways in which crops and livestock are currently integrated by different people in Zaradougou and Dalonguébougou and the institutions that mediate these strategies. We will then describe the social differentiation related to the different pathways of agricultural change, and what these differences imply for policy.

Institutions mediating access to crop and livestock resources

Village life is characterised and organised by multiple institutions, from intra-household arrangements, through inter-household groups, practices and cash trans-actions to formal organisations. Table 2.18 presents the institutions from both sites that influence crop–livestock integration. The diversity of arenas in which access to crop and livestock resources is negotiated is quite striking. Loaning, borrowing and hiring relationships within and between households are important means of complementing the resources that households actually own. As we shall see, many of the pathways introduced have been the result of negotiating means to supplement insufficient household labour, inputs or draught equipment.

Table 2.17   Pathways of agricultural change presently followed in the two sites.

	Zaradougou	Dalonguébougou
1. Extensification	Expanding common maize/cotton fields with a) animal draught or b) tractors	Expanding millet fields with animal draught (bush field zone only)
2. Intensification	a) 'Mixed farming' (draught and fertilisation) following CMDT model b) Cotton production supported by revenue from Ivorian plantations c) Labour intensification of individual gardens, *bas fonds*, or orchards	a) Use of manure and fertilisers on village fields b) Extensive livestock producers intensifying bush field production with herd manure
3. Livestock-centred	(Some individual investment in smallstock for seasonal markets)	Extensification of livestock production supported by watering exchanges (Cattle replaced by smallstock in many herds)
4. Subsistence / marginal	Cotton/maize production supported by manure and draught-sharing arrangements	Seasonally distinct cropping and livestock livelihoods (Visiting Bambara)
5. Diversification	Purchase/maintenance of Ivorian plantations Migration within Mali or to neighbouring countries	Migration within Mali or to neighbouring countries

Zaradougou

The most important institutions for crop–livestock integration in Zaradougou regulate access to three key resources: draught power, manure and Ivorian plantations. The relative success of a household in negotiating and maintaining access to each of these resources determines in large part the nature of the household's dominant pathway of recent agricultural change (Table 2.19). Water, arable land, grazing and animal feed (as grazing land) are all felt to be relatively abundant, and thus, unlike Dalonguébougou, have not become grounds for negotiation or tension.

The balance between access to sufficient draught power and the means to maintain soil fertility, for example, determines to what extent extensification or intensification strategies are pursued. Similarly, the viability of plantations, and of social networks in Côte d'Ivoire or elsewhere in Mali, will determine whether cotton, plantation or some other off-farm migratory activity represents the focus of a household's (or individual's) livelihood. Those whose poverty and overall lack of social capital limit their sustained access to all three crucial resources are most likely to be unable to pursue any strategy except marginal, subsistence production. The following sections demonstrate some of the complexity of the institutions facilitating access to the key resources of draught power, organic fertiliser and carts, and Ivorian plantations.

Draught power

In Zaradougou, 13 of the 16 households own at least one plough and/or a pair of oxen. Of the three households that have neither, one is an immigrant household that cultivated a hectare of cotton by hand in the 1997/8 season. The remaining two

Table 2.18 Institutions mediating access to resources required for crop–livestock integration

	Land	Labour	Draught power	Livestock	Manure	Water*	Feed	Credit	Capital equip't	Info
Intra-household	Inheritance; Subdivision	Family labour	Teaming / pairing; Borrowing / loaning	Inheritance; loaning / entrustment	Gifts	Well ownership inherited*	Family labour, gifts and loans	Borrowing	Migration earnings; borrowing	Seasonal migration networks
Inter-household groups and practices	Customary access arrangements	Ton (work parties) namadé *; Herding / ploughing exchanges; seasonal labour exchanges	Work parties; Teaming/ pairing; exchange for labour (or for water*)	Bridewealth; Siringoro sharing of animal offspring Loaning; Herding contracts	Farmer–herder exchanges* (water or draught for manure)	Free access to hand pumps; manure or draught for water exchanges*; tuteur agreements for drinking water*	Communal agreements for drinking water*	Kin-based loans; Savings clubs; Farmer and women's groups	Plough sharing; Well-digging teams *	Seasonal migration networks; farmer groups**
Inter-household cash transactions		Hiring (herding and farming)	Hiring draught animal power; hiring tractors**	Local markets		Some water-cash exchanges being discussed*	Local markets	Money lending	Local markets	
Formal organisations	Land tenure legislation (decentral-isation)	Association Villageoise (AV)**	State schemes**	NGOs; Formal markets		NGOs (built hand pumps)	CMDT and commercial markets for Torteau (cotton seed cake)**	NGOs; Co-ops (Kafo jigineu); Banks; CMDT**	NGOs; State aid	Extension services; Ag.&Vet. Depts.; NGOs; CMDT**

(Institutions marked * are for Dalonguébougou only, ** are Zaradougou only)

Table 2.19   Relationships between pathways of change and institutions regulating access to key resources in Zaradougou.

Pathway of change	Institutional and resource conditions [Key resources = access to draught power, manure, plantations]
1. Extensification	Access to manure / inorganic fertilisers < access to draught power
2. Intensification	Access to manure / inorganic fertilisers ≥ access to draught power
3. Livestock-centred	(Individual strategy: access to markets, labour to care for livestock)
4. Subsistence / marginal	Poor access to draught power, manure and plantations

5. Diversification
  a) Plantation
  b) Other off-farm
	Limited access to draught power, manure in Zaradougou…
	= Good access to plantation labour with tenure risks ≤ cocoa or coffee income
	= Poor access to plantations, but social networks strong elsewhere

households do not cultivate at all: one is supporting itself from the profits of an Ivorian plantation, and the other from an orchard in Zaradougou.

Ownership is the most common means of accessing ploughs and oxen. Of those owning ploughs, the majority fall into the category described by the CMDT as 'partially equipped'. In real terms, this often means that the equipment they own is not adequate to allow them to utilise fully their available labour for agricultural production. However, this designation assumes that ownership of equipment and oxen (not available labour) is the limiting factor for production and ignores the importance of various institutional arrangements that allow households to gain access to draught power.

Two such arrangements are loaning and hiring, which were quite common despite the widespread ownership of ploughs and oxen. The number of households across each 'livelihood sustainability class' entering into these arrangements is shown in Table 2.20.

The propensity to borrow or hire oxen or ploughs seems strongly related to the livelihood sustainability class of a household. While households in all classes appeared ready to lend or rent out their equipment and animals, only the Class III households were hiring or borrowing tools or oxen that they lacked. However, even Class I and II households reported that they sometimes hired and borrowed equipment from others (including the village's only tractor) if they wanted to finish a field quickly, or their own animals fell sick or lame.

The relative ease with which households are able to hire or borrow equipment (and the range of options available for payment) suggests that the availability of equipment is not a key factor restricting either intensification or extensification. Loans are usually, but not always, related to kinship networks, and hiring seems purely related to an ability to pay. Households in the highest class appeared to be the most likely to expect cash payments, while loans that were free or paid for with household labour were more common when lower livelihood sustainability class households' equipment was being borrowed. Unlike Dalonguébougou, where market transactions for oxen hire now prevail, in Zaradougou draught exchanges freely given by neighbours or kin are still relatively common.

The major disadvantage of borrowing or hiring either ploughs or oxen is the delay caused to the start of the agricultural season, as equipment is usually only available for

Table 2.20 Hiring and borrowing of oxen and ploughs, Zaradougou, 1997/8.

	Total number loans/hires	Livelihood sustainability class		
		Class I – Highest	Class II – Intermediate	Class III – Lowest
Borrow/hire in				
• oxen	14	0	0	14 (6 for cash, 8 for labour)
• plough	3	0	0	3 (all cash)
Lend/hire out				
• oxen	15	7 (all for cash)	6 (2 for cash, 2 for labour, 2 free)	2 (both free)
• plough	5	2 (both cash)	2 (1 for cash, 1 for labour)	1 (cash)

hire once the owner's cultivation needs have been met. Since cotton (and millet) are photo-period sensitive, households relying on borrowing strategies to intensify production of these crops run the risk of lowered yields if access to oxen and ploughs comes late. Higher livelihood sustainability class households, merely topping up their existing holdings with others' equipment, are less likely to miss the ideal planting moment, and may indeed benefit by planting more of their cotton during the crucial periods of late May and early June.

The *éclatement* of households has had important consequences for the institutions that allow access to draught equipment, especially those indicated as 'loans' in the table. The resources acquired and controlled by a large household are typically divided among heirs, sometimes with unfortunate consequences for livelihood security or accumulation strategies. The household of Kassim Sylla, for example, inherited a single plough and a pair of oxen when a large household split in three. The other two households shared two plantations between them, as well as the majority of the cattle herd. The fortunes of Kassim's household took a further turn for the worse when the oxen succumbed to disease. This descendant of a once well-off family must now resort to borrowing equipment, and does not have ready access to the means to re-equip itself to the level of the previous generation, showing that gaining the equipment necessary for mechanised agriculture is not necessarily a straightforward 'upward' path.

A further potential difficulty in the adoption of mechanised agriculture is changing terms of credit for basic equipment from the CMDT. The long-established Crédit Premier Equipement programme, which had allowed many households to take up mechanised agriculture, recently ended. For the many 'partially equipped' households who often struggle under enormous debts taken out for fertiliser and past livestock purchases, the removal of this credit decreases the chances of acquiring the basic tools for mechanised agriculture.

Organic fertiliser and carts

Twin factors determine the use of organic fertiliser (manure, compost or household waste) by cultivating households. The first is the ownership of animals or access to manure of animals not owned by the household. The second is access to labour and means of transport. For wealthier households, the latter is likely to be in the form of hiring the tractor; for the poorer, it is likely to be the loan of a cart.

Not surprisingly, the use of organic fertiliser varies with the livelihood sustainability class of a household (Table 2.21). Class I households make the greatest use of livestock manure, Class II households are the most likely to compost their organic matter, and Class III households are relying predominantly on unmanaged household waste piles as their organic fertiliser. The greater ownership of livestock by Class I and II households explains their greater use of manure. Class II households appear to be composting their manure and other wastes to improve fertilising quality: their herds are smaller than those of Class I households, but they have access to sufficient household labour to manage a compost pile. All three organic fertiliser types require investments of transport and labour in the late dry season, which are most notably lacking in Class III households. Such households also typically have very few animals: the majority of the manure that they use, in fact, comes from others. For example, three Class III households that split from the same large household now share the manure from seven cattle inherited by one of the households. The manure is not composted, a situation that illustrates the impact of *éclatement* on the management of labour necessary to carry out composting.

Simple abundance of organic manures must be matched with access to labour and means of transporting manures. Elsewhere in Mali Sud, where the ownership of carts is less prevalent than in Zaradougou, cart owners often hire their carts to labour-poor/waste-rich households at exorbitant rates that ensure either a large share of the manure transported or considerable sums of cash come their way (Ramisch 1998). The importance of having secure access to means of transport can be shown by the fact that in 1997/8, 13 of the 16 Zaradougou households owned at least one donkey and a cart.

Nevertheless, as with cultivation equipment, household ownership was supplemented by loans and hires (Table 2.22), which again display a pattern based on

Table 2.21   Use of organic manures by household, Zaradougou, 1997/8.

		Livelihood sustainability class		
	All cultivators (n = 14)	Class I (n = 5)	Class II (n = 3)	Class III (n = 6)
Average TLU[22]/household		29.2	12.6	1.7
% using animal manure	79	100	100	50
% using compost	43	40	66	33
% using household waste	85	100	66	83

[22]Tropical livestock unit (TLU) is 250kg live weight. Mature cattle = 1.0 TLU, calves = 0.5, smallstock = 0.2.

livelihood sustainability class. Two cart-less Class III households entered into the only borrowing relationships for donkey carts, while the tractor was hired from its Class I owners by households whose own labour and equipment were insufficient to deal with their manure transport needs. The Class I households that hired the tractor were transporting manure from the wet season *parcs* of relatively large (20+ head) cattle herds. The Class II and III households hiring the tractor are fragments of a large household that split some years ago; the two smaller resulting households retain access to a proportion of the manure of the formerly common cattle herd.

Table 2.22 Hiring and borrowing of donkey carts and tractors, Zaradougou, 1997/8.

	Total number of loans/hires	Sustainability class		
		Class I	**Class II**	**Class III**
Hire tractor in	6	4 (cash)	1 (cash)	1 (cash)
Hire tractor out	6	6 (cash)	0	0
Borrow cart	2	0	0	2 (free)

Ivorian plantations
The role of the plantations in Zaradougou's pathways of agricultural change has been extremely serendipitous and, as the earlier section showed, has led to continuing interest in finding new plantation sites in Côte d'Ivoire over the last four decades. The pioneering households are today among those with the most sustainable liveli-hoods, by the village's own classification scheme, while more recent entrants into strategies using plantations have faced problems of tenure security, corruption and rising input costs with fewer rewards.

For the households of Zaradougou access to the plantations in Côte d'Ivoire has been a source of power and opportunity akin to that offered to the village Bambara of Dalonguébougou by their control of well-digging. For some households their plan-tations constitute a more important source of income even than cotton – surprising in the much-lauded CMDT cotton zone (Table 2.23).[23] Orchards, and the hiring out of the tractor, are also rivals to cotton, suggesting that, despite the CMDT's emphasis on a single pathway to agricultural intensification and success, livelihood strategies based on 'non-cotton' paths remain important and viable in the zone.

Remittances from Ivorian plantations are thus key to livelihoods in Zaradougou. This strategy can act either as an alternative to investing primarily in cotton production or to support the latter. Many also choose to invest plantation revenues in cattle and further integrate crops and livestock to intensify cotton production. Those who can successfully integrate crops and livestock beyond the adoption of mechanisation are those who have invested successfully in migration. However, the status of these plan-tations is relatively insecure, so that, while returns are high, they are also very risky.

---

[23]In other areas of Mali Sud, similar external flows of capital come from a range of diversification activities: see Crole-Rees (1997).

Table 2.23   Most important sources of household income, Zaradougou, 1997/8.

Most important source of household income	% of households
Cotton	50
Ivorian plantation	31
Orchard	12
Tractor	7

Dalonguébougou

The more complex array of actor groups in Dalonguébougou makes a discussion of institutions and their relationship to the pathways of change more difficult than in Zaradougou. Clearly, the most important resource, water, is the one around which the most negotiations and institutions exist. These are the water–manure and water–draught contracts enacted between village Bambara well-owners and herders in other actor groups. However, other arrangements are also made to gain access to manure, and to draught power, and institutions regulating access to fodder are important for those pursuing more livestock-centred strategies.

As in Zaradougou, the pathway of a household's recent agricultural changes is related to the relative success of negotiating institutional arrangements (Table 2.24). The most notable difference between the two villages is the relatively restricted range of arrangements that lead to an intensification pathway (essentially only found on the village fields of well-owning village Bambara, the bush fields of Bambara households with access to inorganic fertilisers and labour, and the heavily manured bush fields of large herd owners). Extensification strategies of cultivation are much more common, given the widespread ownership of draught oxen and the relative availability of bush fields. Only the village Bambara are in a position to intensify some of their bush field production. Indeed, while yields on the intensively managed village fields have declined over the last twenty years, village Bambara bush field yields have been increasing (Brock and Coulibaly 1999). Many village Bambara households now see that their best option for maintaining or increasing harvests is to concentrate investment (of labour particularly) in bush field cultivation, where maintaining soil fertility relies on shifting fallow and some use of inorganic fertilisers. At the village scale the capital-led intensification of the village field subsystem, which was seen in the 1980s, has given way to an intensification of labour inputs into the bush field subsystem.

Livestock-centred strategies are also more common than in Zaradougou. Herd owners with secure access to water (through contracts with village Bambara) and grazing land are able to devote more energy to extensive livestock-oriented strategies, while individuals and households can concentrate on smallstock production if they have secure access to water in the dry season (i.e. through contracts with well-owning village Bambara). A few village Bambara households have also successfully concentrated on smallstock production, although this strategy requires capital to buy stock and to pay a herder. Bambara individuals can specialise in smallstock if they can buy the stock, pay for a herder (or are already part of a household that has a large herd of smallstock that their animals can run with) and make arrangements with a woman to carry water to the animals. Households that owned many smallstock also typically stored crop residues, although the quantities involved were minimal relative to flock size.

Those households with poor access to any key resources are likely to be restricted to the most marginal of subsistence production activities. Many of the visiting Bambara would fall in this last category: unable to settle permanently in Dalonguébougou and unable to sustain themselves year-round in their villages of origin, they are presently stuck in seasonally-distinct livelihoods that appear to offer little hope of improvement. Village Bambara households that were ranked as 'low' sustainability also struggled to support their millet cultivation through draught-sharing arrangements similar to those seen in Zaradougou, and by collecting manure where possible from more livestock-wealthy households in the village.

Table 2.24   Relationships between pathways of change and institutions regulating access to key resources in Dalonguébougou.

Pathway of change	Institutional and resource conditions [Key resources = access to water, land, manure, draught, fodder]
1. Extensification	Access to draught power Watering contracts support livestock extensification

2. Intensification
   a) Village fields
   b) Bush fields
	Well owners: manuring contracts and/or water–draught contracts
	Large herd owners: access to manure, watering contracts and pasture
	Village Bambara: access to labour, draught, inorganic fertiliser

3. Livestock-centred	Capital for initial investment, access to herding and watering labour
4. Subsistence/marginal	Poor tenure security (seasonally distinct dry and wet season livelihoods), poor access to water, land, manure or draught
5. Diversification	Common to all – varies with skills, access to labour, markets, social networks

Water

Access to water, and the changing institutional relationships surrounding it, are central to understanding different pathways of change in Dalonguébougou. The village Bambara may have lost their grip on controlling access to land, but they remain united in limiting access to water, which is still a scarce and highly contested resource. Their intransigence with regard to others digging wells in the village territory reflects the importance of the issue.

The early 1980s were a time of remarkable levels of investment in wells by the village Bambara. Despite the considerable investment involved in digging a well, it became a priority for all but the poorest households. In 1980/1, 'the main reason why a household digs a well is to gain access to the dung of animals watering there' (Toulmin 1992). The returns to well-digging were high, whether it resulted in an expansion of the area of the village field or a more intensive application of manure on an existing area. Both resulted in significant gains in per hectare short-cycle millet yields. At that time, contracts whereby village Bambara farmers exchanged their well water for the manure of a transhumant herd in the charge of a visiting herder were the norm. This situation has changed substantially since, as is demonstrated by Table 2.25 and Fig. 2.4.

In 1980/1, the visiting herders were transhumant agro-pastoralists who cultivated fields in villages further north in the Sahel and came south during the dry season to water their animals. Many had been coming to the village for many years, sometimes for several generations. The composition of this group of visiting herders has changed dramatically. Many of the households now classified as 'village Maures' were former visiting herders who, since the early 1980s left their rainy season camps further north to cut fields and settle in Dalonguébougou's territory year-round. Almost half of the 'visiting herders' who arrived during the 1997/8 dry season were not on long-range transhumance, but, like the village Maures, have settled in villages near to Dalonguébougou. However, these herders lacked secure access to dry season water in the villages where they have settled, and come to Dalonguébougou as an alternative. The remainder of the visiting herders are still predominantly transhumant agro-pastoralists, as well as two Mauritanian herders who follow purely pastoralist livelihoods.

The exact terms of these watering contracts, and the relationships that surround them, are variable. The Maures make no secret of the fact that they prefer water–draught to water–manure exchanges if they can find them, as this allows them to take their animals farther afield in search of good grazing during the dry season. If a herder is exchanging draught rather than manure, there is no obligation to stay on the farmer's field overnight, which, during the hot dry season, provides the opportunity for his animals to arrive at pasture before the heat of the day.

The growth in the number of water–draught exchange contracts can also be explained by the loss of village Bambara cattle to disease and a growing tendency towards the expansion of bush fields among the village Bambara. Many households have experienced a loss of soil fertility on their village fields following this shift in watering contracts from dung to draught. Individual accounts of specific contracts, however, show the importance of inter-household relations in determining particular outcomes (Box 2.3).

Table 2.25 Distribution and type of dry season water exchange contracts with village Bambara well owners, 1997/8.

Partner in exchange contract	Exchange of water for manure	Exchange of water for draught
Visiting herder	11	0
Visiting Bambara	1	0
Village Fulani	1	0
Village Maure	5	12
Total	**26**	**12**

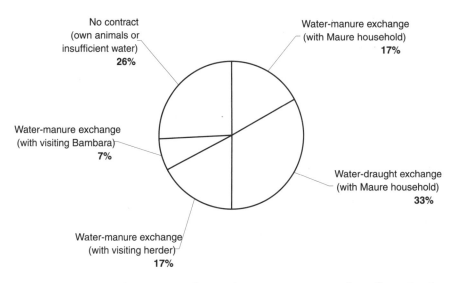

Figure 2.4   Types of dry season livestock watering contract for village Bambara, Dalonguébougou, 1997/8

Box 2.3   Changing terms of water contract – Soungho Diarra

In 1980, Soungho Diarra's household dug their first and only well. They were a long-established, middle-ranking household. The then head of the household, Koké Diarra, negotiated a water–exchange contract with a Maure household already living around the village. At the start of the 1990s, Koké fell ill, and the family was forced to sell two of their oxen to pay for medical care. At the same time, another ox fell ill and died, reducing the household's draught power from two teams to a single animal. At this point, Koké forbade all the young men of the household from migrating for a single dry season. Instead they were to concentrate their efforts on deepening the well to increase its capacity to attract herds. At the end of that dry season, he died, passing his responsibilities on to his young son Soungho.

From that time onwards, the well has been able to support three herds for the duration of the dry season, but all three exchanges have been against the use of an ox at ploughing time. The contract with the Maure household still stands, 18 years since it was first established, and despite the fact that the terms of the contract changed from manure to draught after Koké's death, the Maure continues voluntarily to establish his tent, and tether his animals, on the household's fields during part of the dry season. The household, having secured access to draught power and having a young male workforce, has been able to expand its bush field considerably. Their unusually strong relationship with the Maure household has helped them maintain their village field soil fertility and thus their livelihood through a difficult period.

The case of Soungho Diarra's well illustrates not only the process behind the changing terms of water exchange contracts, but also the importance of a good relationship in helping maintain the fertility of village fields. Close relationships between village Bambara and other households are not uncommon, and many

Maure households have a granary in the compound of the village Bambara household with whom they have a water contract. Economic relationships between village Bambara and Maure households can also be very close; the Maures use the shops and mills of the Bambara and often trade livestock for grain.

Not all relationships of this kind are straightforward, however. The Maures are becoming increasingly vocal in their demands to be allowed to dig wells around Dalonguébougou, but lack official clout since they are not tax-paying citizens of Mali. During the dry season of 1998, tempers shortened and there were two violent incidents that had their focus around water and wells. Water–exchange contracts can be fraught with difficulty. Early evening in the village is a time when elderly Bambara men can frequently be seen walking out to their village fields to check if herds are present, fulfilling the terms of the manuring contract. Box 2.4 illustrates the changing terms of a water contract within the context of a difficult relationship between partners.

Box 2.4   Changing terms of water contract – Saba Coumaré

One of the poorest households in the village, that of Saba Coumaré, dug a well in 1980 to attract visiting herds to manure their village field. The well-digging was funded by the migration remittance of the only young man in the household, causing a poor harvest in that season, which resulted in the family surviving from what they could beg or were given by neighbours. A manure–water exchange contract was established with one Maure household, which lasted for 10 years. In the early 1990s, owing to the loss of the household's single ox to disease and falling water levels in the well – coinciding with the death of the Saba's father (the household head) – the terms of the accord changed to exchange water for the use of a single ox. A second animal was regularly lent by relatives from another village.

Three years ago this agreement broke down when the Maure asked to use the well to collect drinking water for his family as well as to water his animals. When Saba Coumaré refused this, the Maure retaliated by polluting the well with *Acacia* leaves, which turn the water black, withdrawing his herd in the middle of the season and refusing to provide an ox at the start of the following season. For the following three years, the household relied on the goodwill of neighbours who lent one of their own oxen at ploughing time. This year, an agreement was reached with a visiting Maure, who watered 80 cattle, 100 smallstock and a camel at the well for part of the dry season, in exchange for the use of a single ox for the ploughing season.

Manure

Differences in access to manure and contracts for exchanging manure and water have already been touched on above. Further means of household-level access to manure are related to smallstock ownership and the dynamics of cattle entrustment. Although most households across all actor groups own at least some smallstock, the use of smallstock manure varies according to the 'manure wealth' of a household. If few animals are owned, or if smallstock are the only source of manure, the manure will be used on the household fields. Among the village Bambara, where cattle are also owned or where there is a well around which manure is concentrated, some smallstock manure will be available for use on individual fields. Some village

Bambara households that are manure-rich give smallstock manure to kin who own fewer animals or have no well.

Among the village Bambara, ownership of cattle does not always guarantee access to manure because of the way that the animals of several households are often mixed together to be managed by a single (Fulani) herder. The owner of the largest proportion of this mixed herd will usually benefit from the manure, as well as dry season watering labour provided by the other households that have animals in the herd. Households that have a holding of only one or two head of cattle pay heavily for this, not having access to the manure of their animals and expending a dispropor-tionately large amount of scarce labour during the dry season on daily watering. There are thus substantial economies of scale involved in the ownership of cattle. All households having animals in the herd are entitled to manure from the rainy season cattle *parc*, but few if any households take advantage of this. Wealthier households often feel they already have adequate manure to guarantee a crop, while poorer ones usually lack the labour necessary for the transport of manure from a site 7 km from the centre of the village.

Draught power

The importance of donkeys and oxen to the everyday functioning of the agro-ecosystem cannot be over-emphasised. For example, the introduction of donkey carts in the 1970s allowed the village Bambara to extend their bush fields far away from the centre of the village and begin the process of labour intensification that some are now practising there. Non-ownership of oxen, ploughs and donkeys is an indicator of poverty. Box 2.5 shows the way that one village Bambara household equipped itself, demonstrating several means of gaining access to draught power other than purchase.

Box 2.5   Means of access to oxen – Dotoun Tangara

Dotoun Tangara's household consists of a widow and her young family. They split off from a large household when the widow's husband was still alive, following a dispute between the husband and his brother. At this time the oldest child was 14 and the youngest had just been born. Soon after the split, the husband died. His brother offered to take the family back into the larger household but the widow refused this. The split was acrimonious and left them without equipment, animals or wells.

In the first year after the split, they began to cultivate a bush field by hand, having no alter-native. A neighbouring wealthy household, although not closely related, saw their plight and lent a pair of oxen and a plough. The profits from the first year's harvest were used to buy a plough and donkey cart. In the second year, the widow and her children again struggled to cultivate without the labour of an adult man, renting an ox from a Maure household for cash, and pairing it with a second animal borrowed from a sister in a neigh-bouring village, in exchange for ploughing her individual field. In the third year, an ox was rented with the same Maure, and a second animal was borrowed from a neighbour in exchange for providing dry-season watering labour. By the fourth year, the millet harvest was adequate to buy an ox from the profits, and in the fifth year a second animal was purchased from the *namadé* earnings of a daughter.

Local institutions are very important in enabling households that do not own adequate oxen to gain access to the necessary draught power. In 1980/1, 9 per cent of households gained access to oxen through exchanges for labour with other village Bambara households, free loans from neighbours, and, in one case, a Fulani herder (Toulmin 1992: 162). In more recent times, accessing the animals and equipment of others has become much more common, as is demonstrated by Table 2.26.

Table 2.26 Means of access to oxen, all village Bambara households, 1997/8.

Method of access to oxen	% of households
Own animals only	49
Hiring	40
Borrowing	9
Hiring and borrowing	2

The table shows that 51 per cent of households are not able to rely solely on their own animals. Only 20 per cent of households own no oxen and are forced to rely solely on hiring or borrowing, so 31 per cent of households are currently finding that they do not get adequate draught power from their own animals. The predominance of hiring as a method of obtaining extra draught power is in contrast to 1980/1. A local market for the hire of oxen has developed, and transactions in that market have replaced informal arrangements as the most frequent means of accessing draught power apart from ownership. In this context 'hiring' does not only refer to exchange of draught power for cash, but also includes exchange for goods, labour or – as outlined above – water.

Fodder
Crop residues were not extensively stored in 1980/1, and this activity was largely restricted to a few individuals with large holdings of smallstock. In more recent times, there is a huge variation both in the amount of crop residues gathered and stored, and in who does the work of growing, collecting and storing them (Box 2.6).

Storage and use of crop residues for fodder are largely determined by available labour. Several farmers observed that cowpea hay must be cut, baled, transported and stored at one of the busiest moments of the agricultural season, during the millet harvest. Thus retired people, who have few demands on their labour, are able to produce large amounts of cowpea hay, while several households were able to produce relatively little owing to other demands on their time. Other factors constraining the production of cowpea hay included lack of rainfall during a particular moment in the season, lack of money to buy adequate seed and livestock damage. However, no households produce adequate fodder in this way to supplement the diets of their domestic animals for a whole year.

Sales of cowpea hay are small-scale compared to millet, but the Maures and Fulani (as well as individual village Bambara smallstock owners) provide a captive market, as they do not intercrop cowpea with millet. There is also a growing market for cowpea hay in peri-urban areas (in Niono and Ségou the price of a bale of cowpea hay was

---

Box 2.6 Variations in access to and use of crop residues for fodder, several village Bambara households, 1997/8

- Ousmane Samaké's household produced 1,500 bales of cowpea hay from the household millet field, which are used to feed the domestic animals of the household. During the 1996/7 season they produced no cowpea hay due, they said, to lack of rainfall.
- Samba Dembelé's household use cowpea as a source of individually-managed income. Tacko Tounkara, an elderly widow, produced 470 bales of cowpea hay from her individual field, which she sold. Her two sons, Samba and his brother, both retired, produced 400 and 250 bales of hay from their individual fields for feeding their own animals. Her grandson, a young single man, harvested 465 bales of cowpea hay from the household field, which he was allowed to sell for his own profit.
- Nianzou Bah Tounkara is an elderly household head who has at least 50 smallstock of his own. He intercropped cowpeas with millet on his individual field and enlisted the assistance of his grandson in collecting and storing 200 bales of cowpea hay for the consumption of his own animals.
- Seriba Diarra and his wife and daughter harvested 20 bales of hay to feed their smallstock.
- Mougou Tounkara and his brothers harvested their cowpea hay but lost it all to an uncontrolled herd of cattle.

---

over five times that in the village), but villagers do not produce enough surplus hay to justify marketing it over such a large distance.

Differentiated strategies and multiple pathways

The discussion of crop–livestock integration practices, the history of agricultural change and the institutions mediating access to crucial resources in the two sites all combine to paint a picture of considerable diversity. Clearly, the opportunities for crop–livestock integration and agricultural intensification have varied for the different actor groups in each site. Opportunities depend on the resources owned by different groups in the locality, and the terms on which access to land, labour, water and manure can be secured. These terms will change over time as the negotiating strength of the different actors is affected by economic, environmental and institutional variables, resulting in multiple pathways of change. This section presents some of the axes of social and economic differentiation in the two sites, and relates them to the pathways of agricultural change introduced above.

Forms of social differentiation

Wealth and 'livelihood sustainability class'
Wealth is one of the most conspicuous factors of social differentiation. Many of the variables that villagers in both Zaradougou and Dalonguébougou identified as reflecting a household's 'livelihood sustainability' relate to concepts of wealth (see above). Livestock holdings, labour, cultivation equipment and other material goods were grouped together as '*moyens*' (literally, 'assets'). It seemed self-evident to the

villagers that greater assets provide greater security, and broaden the range of future options open to a household. Animal agriculture and draught power have become embedded in local perceptions of livelihood sustainability, such that in Zaradougou we can see a strong correlation between ox/plough ownership and 'livelihood sustainability class' (Table 2.27).

Table 2.27   Plough and oxen ownership by household livelihood sustainability class, Zaradougou, 1997/8.

Sustainability class	Mean oxen per household	Mean oxen per worker	Mean ploughs per household
Class I	6	0.50	2.2
Class II	3	0.39	1.6
Class III	0.75	0.06	0.5

In addition, the Ivorian plantations in Zaradougou have a crucial role in augmenting household 'livelihood sustainability'. Not surprisingly, there is a clear relationship between those households that invested early and successfully in the plantations and the size of cattle holdings. In 1997, 93 per cent of the cattle in the village were owned by the first six households to invest in Ivorian plantations. However, the villagers' classification goes beyond a simply material assessment of wealth by including both household structure variables and an evaluation of the household's management abilities.

Essentially, the most 'sustainable' households were inevitably large and complex, and have exploited mutually reinforcing attributes of well-organised, abundant labour and a long history of cultivating Ivorian plantations, the profits from which have been likely invested in livestock. These households were characterised by a higher level of choice about investment decisions than those identified as less sustainable. At the micro-level, they were more likely to exercise control over the investment of labour, and were likely to have access to a wider range of inputs: manure, compost or financial capital to invest in external inputs, technology and equipment.

The least 'sustainable' households were typically the fragments of once-large households with internal problems of social cohesion, indebtedness and insufficient labour, whose inherited equipment and livestock holdings were inadequate to maintain intensified production. Less sustainable households have a restricted range of investment strategies. Their access to flows of financial capital was often very limited and they were less able to repay the credit they took out. Their control over their investment of labour was often weak. The breaking-up of assets as a result of *éclatement* can leave such households without the labour or means to plough effectively, to engage in composting or to transport sufficient organic matter to replenish their fields.

Not surprisingly, household 'livelihood sustainability class' was a good predictor of the pathways of change that are available in Zaradougou. Greater 'livelihood sustainability', with its access to a diversity of labour or capital inputs, means that Class I households are the most likely to be pursuing a strategy of intensification. Such households are closest to the 'mixed farm' model of the CMDT, but pursuing a much more complicated assemblage of livelihood activities (see Box 2.7 for an example). Extensification has also been an extremely common means of increasing cotton production, and the most sustainable households have oscillated between (or simultaneously combined) both intensification and extensification pathways, attempting to balance labour versus capital inputs as prices of cotton or fertiliser rose and fell, or indeed when issues of tenure insecurity loomed on their village's border. Less sustainable households lack the labour or the management skills to execute such balances, and maintain cotton yields largely through extensification. Such households are also managing less secure Ivorian plantations, which often bring large financial and labour burdens. Crop–livestock integration in such households is more likely to be limited to investing in a core of draught oxen and donkeys, with occasional smallstock specialisation by a household member.

Box 2.7   Management of diversification activities – Aly Traoré

Aly Traoré's household comprises himself (the household head), his married son and his brothers, all of whom have families. The household is noted by its neighbours as one that functions well, with a high morale and a discernible atmosphere of teamwork.

Like most of the large Senoufo households in the village, in addition to the cultivation of cotton, the household also owns an orchard in the village and a plantation in Côte d'Ivoire. These three enterprises are managed at the level of the central household. One member of the household is the *caissier*, the person in charge of money. Some of the profits of the three major enterprises of the household are divided between the members of the household when costs have been met. Investments at the household level are decided by a council of male household members.

Smallstock and poultry rearing are carried out at the level of the nuclear sub-family (*ménage*) within the extended household. Although the *ménage* has no traditional social function within the complex household, it has an important contemporary economic function in allowing the disaggregation of certain income-generating activities. In this household, profits from these activities are kept by those who carry out the activity.

Finally, there are individual-level activities – off-season vegetable cultivation, sales of firewood, individual women's fields, shea-nut butter production, small commerce – from which the individual is allowed to keep the revenue generated.

The sustainability of this household is perceived as very high despite the fact that their per hectare production of cotton is considerably lower than that of other households in the same class, and it depends largely on the smooth functioning of this system of effective personnel management within the large household. There is no danger of household break-up, all members are compensated in cash for their labour and individual activities are sanctioned.

Ethnicity
Ethnic differentiation in Dalonguébougou formed the grounds for identifying its key 'actor groups', and, in concert with social differentiation along lines of wealth, age and gender, serves to predict patterns of crop–livestock integration and agricultural change. For generations the village Bambara have attempted to restrict access to the key resources of land and water: as more immigrants have settled in the village territory, and the Bambara's power was undermined by these growing numbers, ethnic identities and pathways have become intertwined with differential access to the various factors of production. Because of these differences, there has not been a

simple, linear path of agricultural intensification towards mixed farming, but rather a series of different routes.

At their crudest, the crop–livestock integration patterns in Dalonguébougou have followed three broad pathways. Firstly, the village Bambara have been increasing their grain production through the use of ploughs, increasing the cultivated area and the use of manure to maintain soil fertility on permanently cropped land. Secondly, herders like the Fulani and Maures have diversified into farming to increase the stability of their livelihoods, but may have to constantly renegotiate contracts for access to water to support their herds and households. Thirdly, groups like the visiting Bambara, who have the least secure tenure arrangements, have had to divorce their wet and dry season livelihoods (cropping in Dalonguébougou, herding elsewhere), which has limited their ability to intensify their now separated crop and livestock endeavours.

Within these broad pathways there are several different sub-paths, which arise because of groups' different levels of access to resources. For example, over the last twenty years, many village Bambara farmers have seen a shift in resource investment priorities away from manuring village fields towards expansion of bush fields. Those households with access to less human and financial capital cannot make this shift as easily as larger and richer households. Increasing bush field size requires labour and capital (to acquire the necessary draught power, whether through ownership or hiring), and larger households can achieve economies of scale. The increasing tension around water exchange contracts and the possibility of tenure changes in the near future have also made expansion of bush fields an attractive option. However, the loss of animals to disease and the development of an important cash market for draught has made extensification more costly: at 1997/8 prices, hiring a pair of oxen for two farming seasons costs the same as purchasing an ox. Households with no savings or regular source of income can afford the smaller annual amount, but find it hard to raise the money necessary for an outright purchase.

The other option, supplementing village field soil fertility, requires dry season labour to transport and apply manure, and in small households this may result in a trade-off between dry season labour migration and investment on the farm. Attracting a visiting herd requires the capital to dig or deepen a well, and is felt to be an increasingly insecure investment – the water table already shows signs of over-exploitation and Maures now are less open to water-manure contracts. These smaller, poorer households therefore face major constraints in either increasing the use of draught power to extensify bush fields or increasing manure use to intensify village fields. For herders, changing paths of crop–livestock integration have made their livelihoods more stable. They are now less likely to rely on a single activity, and cropping has made an increasingly important contribution to their household economies. Although the Fulani have benefited from access to more workable village soils, and the security of herding contracts with the village Bambara, this is particularly the case for the Maures, who now harvest substantial quantities of grain.

Generally, crop–livestock integration has increased the sustainability of livelihoods in the village through strengthening reciprocal relationships between groups, while still allowing people to gain a livelihood through their preferred expertise. The visiting Bambara, the one group who are not generally able to integrate crops and livestock, are also the group with the most vulnerable livelihoods. Their exclusion from secure access to cultivable land, pasture and water lends to their livelihoods an uncertainty that is far greater than the other groups in the village. If, however, they were to gain secure access, there would be losers elsewhere: it is hard to imagine, for example, what the impact of free access to well-digging would actually be.

Gender and individuals' pathways of change
Finally, although the discussion has been dominated by household strategies of crop–livestock integration, the strategies pursued by individual women and men also have important consequences for household viability. The diversity of these strategies (whether individual specialisation in agriculture/gardening, livestock, artisanal, business or migration activities) emphasises that pathways of change must be seen within a much broader context of livelihood diversification and intensification.

Some of the most important individual activities in Zaradougou that influenced crop–livestock integration centred on women's cultivation. Although women usually cultivate their plots by hand, some women's fields are ploughed by men. The only method of fertilisation to which women have consistent access is the use of shea nut residues remaining from the butter-making process. Women also use household waste and small ruminant and poultry droppings as fertiliser, but access to these depends on the structure and wealth of the household and the position of the woman within it.

In Dalonguébougou, access to manure for individual cultivation among the village Bambara is also characterised by a variety of different processes. For the village Bambara women, access to manure is related to age, position in the family and the relative wealth of the household. Women are given access to smallstock droppings as compensation for taking responsibility for bringing drinking water to livestock. Women's access to household waste is more or less universal, although several women will sometimes have shared access to the household waste pile. Quality of household waste is variable, depending on how close the pile might be to places animals would congregate (i.e. wells or shade trees) and the success of women's attempts to sweep smallstock manure towards it. Transport is clearly essential to manuring individual women's fields, and the amount of manure they have access to is partly a function of their ability to pay for transport, the availability of transport at a time of year when most households are also manuring their household fields, or their willingness to carry manure to the fields on their heads. Several women commented that transport had been hard to find in the previous season.

Finally, seasonal migration is an important means of generating income that can be invested in livestock, equipment, fertilisers or other income-generating activities like village shop-keeping. Yet this is an option only open to those households with suffi-cient male labour. For example, in Dalonguébougou men from small households must spend the dry season watering livestock – which precludes the possibility of migrating for work.

Conclusions: implications for policy

The contemporary models of crop–livestock integration promoted by the MDRE and by the CMDT are still greatly informed by the notion of the ideal 'mixed farm'. For example, in Mali Sud the models of crop–livestock integration (*intégration agri-culture-élevage*) acknowledge that livestock (read cattle) have an important role to play in the farming system as suppliers of draught power and manure, but implicitly one that is secondary to the ultimate goal of cotton production (CMDT 1995). The decentralisation process, which will promote local management of resources, and the implementation of the national Forest Code, have also renewed discussion of the ways in which livestock, and by association all livelihoods that do not subordinate livestock to agricultural production, can be made orderly and responsible members of local communities (Bosma *et al.* 1996).

Such approaches explicitly delegitimise practices that do not conform to the 'mixed farming' model. 'Failure' to specialise in cotton production, or to feed animals on crop residues instead of communally grazing rangelands, can be seen as an irresponsible deviation from the path to sustainability, and one that compromises the viability of the sylvo-pastoral bush (Tourte *et al.* 1971). From this perspective, social arrangements and institutions that mediate access to draught equipment, animals or to manure are considered as little more than interesting side notes to the process of agricultural intensification. The CMDT's classification system puts special emphasis on distinguishing the 'well-equipped' households of Class A and B from each other,[24] while lumping the vast majority of plough-using households into a single, inferior, 'incompletely equipped' Class C.

The dominance of the CMDT's 'mixed farming' approach in southern Mali also underestimates the viability of alternative farming systems. The study of Zaradougou showed that even cotton farmers themselves are diversifying into systems beyond livestock, with cash crop plantations in Côte d'Ivoire figuring prominently and orchard or *bas fonds* specialisation locally important. Macro policies have tended to focus on cotton as a vital source of foreign earnings for a severely indebted national economy. This has resulted in a policy bias that does not often address the possibility that a diversity of economic activities may increase the ability of the poorest to cope with the shocks and stresses inherent in a rainfed agricultural system. Outside the cash crop zones, the MDRE promotes a similar 'mixed farming' agenda. The reach of extension agents, however, is limited, and villages such as Dalonguébougou are too remote to receive regular visits. This village's complex, interwoven livelihoods dependent on land and water rights are effectively overlooked by MDRE altogether, and the principal sources of innovation are through migrants returning from other regions.

Given these policy failures and omissions, and the lack of evidence to suggest that all households will eventually converge on a 'mixed farm' model of crop–livestock integration, it is possible to make several suggestions based on both case study sites:

- **Agricultural change and crop–livestock integration follow multiple pathways.** These pathways are differentiated according to household access to key resources and are highly dynamic over time. Good policy should acknowledge the importance of the institutional arrangements that ensure flexible and secure access to the resources important to agricultural intensification in a given context. It should also promote technologies that enlarge rather than limit

---

[24]The ideal, Class A households represent the end point of crop–livestock integration and agricultural intensification, owning 10 or more cattle (sufficient to cull and to maintain a strong plough team).

decision-making opportunities for *all* actors' pathways of change, not just those of the most successful.

- **The 'mixed farm' model is not 'livelihood-neutral'.** Many technologies promoted as part of the mixed farm model (such as ox-powered traction or fodder crops) based on private ownership are inappropriate for many households that do not have secure enough access to key resources. Likewise, the mere ownership of equipment is not a sufficient indicator to suggest the potential successes of a given farming system: not all households will become rich and successful if they only acquire the right tools/animals. Policy needs to be set in a livelihood context, acknowledging issues of social power. Although Malian research and extension are becoming more 'poverty-focused', good policy must recognise that households facing poverty deal with entirely different constraints and risks than larger or wealthier households typically encounter.

- **The interactions of exogenous and endogenous factors have had important repercussions on pathways of change.** The overlapping effects of multiple policies have often had unintended consequences on the potential for agricultural intensification by altering relative factor prices, or making key resources suddenly unavailable. There are numerous examples of policy false starts (such as the various alterations of the maize market) and the interference of various, simultaneously enacted efforts (the devaluation of the CFA franc and the collapse of world cotton prices undermining CDMT credit programmes). While Malian institutions lack the power to alter global trends (such as continuing rhetoric favouring market liberalisation), more attuned domestic policy-making, in concert with the major foreign donors, could more effectively avoid future policy interference. In addition, policies that favoured increased flexibility, and minimised risks of catastrophic indebtedness, could help buffer village-level actors from future shocks.

If we compare existing official policy with the list of pathways of change given in Table 2.17 it is clear that, while intensification is a feasible option for only a few, they are the main beneficiaries of most of the research and extension efforts in Mali. Extensification is formally discouraged, although it has often resulted following the adoption of draught technologies. Minimal support is available to households pursuing the subsistence strategies, or indeed specialising in livestock or gardening and orchards (although in some locales extension is adapting to these local needs). There are therefore many that could yet benefit from official channels of research and extension.

Ultimately, policy will have to recognise that the debates about 'mixed farming' cannot be isolated from broader discussions about households' multiple livelihoods. The case studies here have shown that crop–livestock integration strategies are often on a par with other diversification efforts, supporting each other in good times, providing alternatives to each other in bad. It is impossible to ignore, for example, the role of the Ivorian plantations in the household economies of those villagers successfully moving towards agricultural intensification. Current policy focuses almost exclusively on agriculture and, in so doing, ignores the importance of external flows of capital in facilitating uptake of the technologies being extended.

The diversity of actor groups, and the multiple pathways of change that they have followed in these two very different sites, also suggests that effective policy can no longer afford to relegate the 'social issues' surrounding agricultural change to a separate domain, of interest only to academics. Very real issues of exclusion (of the visiting Bambara and the non-citizen Maures from Dalonguébougou, of the people of Zaradougou from their vital plantations in Côte d'Ivoire) threaten to undermine the successes of the present farming systems. Social power and the relative ability of households to negotiate access to key resources have also meant the difference between strategies that successfully intensify or rely on extensification to sustain production.

The case studies suggest that, despite difficult economic and ecological circumstances in Mali, there are opportunities for sustainable livelihoods based on viable crop–livestock systems. Offering further grounds for optimism, Mali's Institut d'Economie Rurale has been influential in advocating more meaningful interdisciplinary research to better situate crop–livestock integration and farming system changes in their livelihood contexts, while the CMDT is rightly credited as having positively influenced crop-livestock integration in Mali Sud (cf. Williams et al. 2000; Fok 1994). However, if policies improving crop–livestock systems for all actors are to succeed, policy-makers will need to acknowledge and promote the diversity of pathways of agricultural change that exist outside the present models.

3

Complexity, Change & Continuity in Southern Ethiopia:
The Case of Crop–Livestock Integration

GRACE CARSWELL[1]

Introduction

Ethiopia, with its long history of plough use, offers a unique opportunity to study the dynamics of agricultural change and, more specifically, changes in the interactions between cropping and livestock systems. Unlike many parts of Africa, 'the people of the plough' (McCann 1995) have pursued forms of integrated agricultural and live-stock production for centuries in the highland areas of the country. But such patterns are not uniform. The dominant image is that from the northern highlands and the richer grain–producing areas, where plough-based cereal farming is the major form of agricultural practice. This ignores the immense diversity of Ethiopian farming and pastoral systems, which range from transhumant pastoralism to dryland cropping to perennial and root crop-based systems to the various types of cereal cropping in highland areas. In many areas a variety of systems exist alongside each other, with differing degrees of integration of cropping and livestock elements.

However, support for a particular type of Ethiopian farmer has dominated research and extension attempts over the past decades. Since the late 1960s the focus of agri-cultural policy in Ethiopia has been on the expansion of food production by increasing yields through new and improved cereal varieties and inorganic fertiliser (Dejene and Mulat 1995; Keeley and Scoones 1999). This has prompted some high-quality research in plant breeding and agronomy, for instance, focused on efforts to boost production. A productionist emphasis threads through various extension

[1]This chapter has been compiled by Grace Carswell, with inputs from broader work on sustainable livelihoods carried out in Wolayta (see Carswell *et al.* 2000). The full team involved were Alemayehu Konde, Grace Carswell, Data Dea, Chris McDowell and Haleyesus Seba, with research assistance provided by Mestawot Taye and Meskerem Trango. Data entry, processing and analysis were assisted by Gemechu Degefa in Addis Ababa and Annette Sinclair at IDS, Sussex. Comments on earlier drafts of this chapter were provided by Ian Scoones and William Wolmer.

policies, under various guises, taking different names: integrated rural development programmes[2] were established from the late 1960s (Cohen 1987); the Minimum Package Programme from the early 1970s; and the Global Package[3] since 1993 (Takele 1996). All these approaches have meant that agricultural extension has, for many years, focused on promoting a package of technical improvements aimed predominantly at a cereal farmer making use of draught power, but with insufficient manure to supply fertility needs. Improved seed and fertiliser inputs have therefore been at the core of the packages, supported with a credit component.

Research stations throughout Ethiopia have advocated such solutions by demonstrating the potential yield improvements resulting from adopting such an approach. One strand of agricultural research has focused specifically on the use of improved crop varieties with chemical inputs (Croppenstedt and Mulat 1996; Mulat 1995; Mulat et al. 1997). A second strand of research is on improved traction and fodder, most notably through the research of International Livestock Research Institute (ILRI, formerly ILCA). From 1986 ILRI research has focused on increasing production on highland vertisols (Getachew Asamenew et al. 1993). A modified plough, called a broad bed maker, has been designed to facilitate drainage (Astake, Jutzi and Tedla 1989; El Wakeel and Astake 1996; Mohamed-Saleem (and Astake 1996). ILRI has also undertaken research into improved fodder sources (Nnadi and Haque 1988; Reed and Goe 1989), draught power (Gryseels et al. 1987) and improved traction (Gryseels et al. 1984; Jutzi et al. 1987; Astake and Mohammed-Saleem 1996; Mengistu Buta and Shapiro 1997).

The extent to which such research outputs have been adopted by farmers is extremely variable. For example, none of the improved ploughs (which would enable animals other than oxen to plough, or a single ox to plough) have been widely adopted, and the plough technology used by farmers today remains little changed. On the other hand, research around the use of improved seeds and inorganic fertiliser has been taken up by the Bureau of Agriculture and is promoted throughout most of Ethiopia through the Global-2000 extension package. However, the current extension package[4] may be helpful for some farmers but it is not necessarily suitable for all farmers in all areas, as many do not fit the assumed model of a cereal grower with sufficient labour and access to oxen and with particular technical needs and cash and credit requirements

Whether through national or international initiatives, most research has therefore focused on the technical challenges of increasing production in highland cereal-farming areas. As this chapter will show, this has had a number of fundamental limitations.

Firstly, the research and extension efforts, with their emphasis on relatively high-input technical solutions, have not addressed the needs of poorer people lacking

[2]Such as the Wollamo Agricultural Development Unit (WADU) undertaken in Wolayta from the early 1970s.

[3]This is a package of agricultural technologies initially promoted by the influential and well-funded international NGO Sasakawa Global 2000, and was subsequently taken up as a a the model for a national extension programme by the government.

[4]Recommendations for the so-called 'Global farmers' include: 4–6 ploughings (instead of 3–5); measuring out the fertiliser with a bottle top during sowing, instead of 'drizzling' fertiliser along the row; weeding twice with a hoe (makotkot). Many farmers prefer weeding at least once with a plough (shilshallo) if they have oxen, but labour is scarce.

the means to adopt such packages. Such efforts have also ignored the challenges of more marginal areas, where the majority of poor people live, choosing, instead, to focus on the higher-potential cereal-farming highland regions. Options for dryland sites, where links with more pastoral livestock-based production systems are evident, or the enset and root crop zones of the southern highlands have been largely unexplored.

Secondly, by focusing on a narrow range of technical options, research and extension efforts have failed to appreciate the wider livelihood context within which technical practices of agricultural and livestock management are set. The links between farm-based production and other sources of off-farm livelihood have thus been ignored, and the assumption, very often, has been that the lack of adoption of particular technologies has been for reasons of 'ignorance' or 'backwardness' of peasant farming, rather than incompatibilities with broader livelihood strategies.

Finally, such efforts have paid little or no attention to the range of social institutions that affect people's access to resources (such as oxen for ploughing), and have thus failed to understand the social and cultural contexts for technology use and adoption. As this chapter shows, there are a wide range of such institutional arrangements, which allow different people to gain access to resources that need to be taken into account if the nature and pathways of agricultural and livestock change are to be understood. This chapter demonstrates how these institutions are crucial; and in seeking technical solutions in isolation, an important area is being ignored.

This chapter reports on research carried out in Wolayta, southern Ethiopia, involving three sites stretching from the intensively farmed enset and root crop systems of the Wolayta highlands to more lowland settings, where dryland cereal and cotton cropping exist alongside extensive, pastoral production. This has provided an opportunity to look at agricultural and livestock practices, and broader livelihood contexts, in settings that do not conform to the standard highland cereal-farming model that has so dominated agricultural research and extension. Agricultural change in Wolayta is extremely complex. Rather than an evolutionary process of agricultural intensification with a set of stages through which a farming system inevitably progresses in a linear fashion, there are multiple pathways of change. These pathways depend on the nature of the cropping and livestock systems, the history of the area and the institutional arrangements that link people and their resources. In practice many pathways occur alongside each other and are followed by different people, in different spaces and at a range of scales.

There are three elements to the approach taken in this chapter that are worth highlighting. Firstly, our work focuses on key historical events that have led to changes in the integration and interaction between the cropping and livestock systems. These may be events that have had a direct influence (e.g. the introduction of the iron-tipped plough) or an indirect one (e.g. changes to the regulations for State Farm employees about private cultivation). Secondly, we have focused on how particular institutional arrangements mediate households' access to resources. Finally, the degree of difference within each site, between households, in the practices and strategies that are followed will be examined. 'Actor groups', differentiated by wealth, gender, ethnicity and so on, pursue different livelihood strategies, drawing on the cropping and livestock elements of the agricultural system to different extents depending on the resources that are available to them. These resources include land, livestock, labour, information and social networks. The chapter examines how the integration and interaction of the cropping and livestock system is differentiated within each site, and the final section draws the findings together, looking at the different pathways of change, and the implications of these for policy.

The study sites

Three sites in southern Ethiopia were selected across a range of agroecological zones, with differing population densities, rainfall and soil fertility, forming a notional transect from high to low resource endowment.[5] The selected sites also have differing lengths of settlement, agricultural histories and experiences of social change. Fig. 3.1 shows the location of the sites in Wolayta,[6] southern Ethiopia: Admencho, Mundena and Chokare. Admencho Peasant Association (PA)[7] is located in the highlands of Wolayta in Bolloso *woreda*, between the towns of Areka and Boditi. Mundena PA is close to the town of Bele in Kindo Koisha *woreda*. Chokare PA is in the lowlands of Wolayta bounded by Lake Abaya, the Abaya State Farm and the regional border with Sidama. The study site locations, and a transect illustrating each of the sites, are shown in Fig. 3.1.

A range of methodologies combining conventional survey tools and qualitative methodologies was used, including rapid rural appraisal methods, a questionnaire, key informant interviews, oral histories, group discussions and analysis of aerial photographs. The questionnaire was based on a sample of 100 households in each site. A household was defined as the group of people who live and sleep under the same roof, and eat the same evening meal. For sampling purposes lists of households in several *suchas* (villages) in each PA were drawn up using lists provided by the PA and interviews with key informants.[8] Participatory wealth-ranking exercises were carried out in each of the sites with a group of key informants.[9] In each site wealth-ranking criteria were drawn up, four wealth groups were defined and all households were allocated to a wealth group. Stratified random sampling was carried out from the household lists with a proportionate number drawn from each wealth rank.

Agroecological characteristics

Admencho is a densely populated highland area of high rainfall and fertile soils, while Mundena has lower and more variable rainfall and inherently less fertile soils. Chokare has fertile alluvial soils, although rainfall here is relatively low. The key ecological differences between the three sites are summarised in Table 3.1.

[5]The sites were also selected in part because of the existence of past survey data, such as two WADU surveys conducted in 1971: WADU (1976a) and WADU (1976b) for two of the sites.
[6]For further work on this area, see: Dessalegn Rahmato (1990 and 1992); Dagnew Eshete (1995); and Sandford (1992).
[7]The Peasant Association is the smallest administrative unit in Ethiopia.
[8]PAs in Ethiopia have lists of all households for purposes of land-tax and provision of relief, Food For Work, etc. These lists were checked for several *suchas* of each PA and in some cases expanded through interviews with key informants.
[9]The only exception being Chokare. Here 50 households were selected who reside in the PA, and 50 in the State Farm. People in the latter group were ranked according to their employment status (permanently employed, casually employed and not employed by the State Farm).

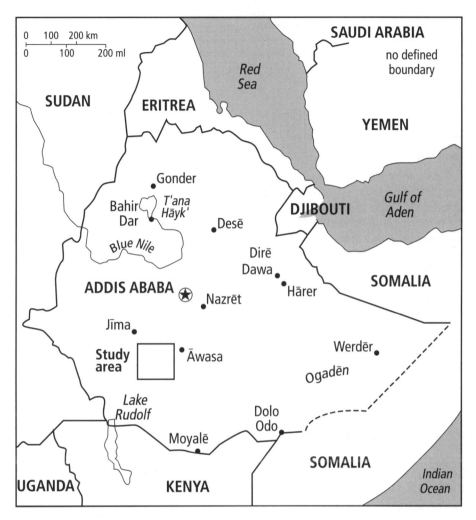

Figure 3.1 The southern Ethiopian study sites

Mundena
- Thinly populated resettlement area
- Erratic rainfall
- More extensive agricultural system
- High levels human and livestock disease

Admencho
- High rainfall
- Very densely populated
- Intensively cultivated, wide range of crops
- Long complex history of settlement, cultivation, land tenure and social relations

Chokare
- Fertile alluvial soils
- Irrigation
- Ethnically and linguistically mixed population; large State Farm population
- Recent increase in agricultural production by agropastoralists and State Farm employees

Table 3.1 Agroecological characteristics.

	Admencho	Mundena	Chokare
Rainfall	1350–2500 mm	900 mm	500 mm
Average annual temperature	19.4°C	25°C	27°C
Altitude	1800+ masl	1200–1300 masl	1000 masl
Soils	Fertile soils	Phosphorus-deficient soils	Fertile alluvial soils

There are a number of aspects of the environment that give rise to risk in the three sites. In Admencho loss of crops to disease and pests presents the highest source of risk. In Mundena loss of livestock to disease, in particular trypanosomiasis, presents the most serious risk, combined with the effect of drought. Periods of unusual rainfall are associated with drought and famine, although the occurrence of famines in 1984, 1988, 1991 and 1994 (Jenden 1995) suggests that rainfall patterns are not the only explanations for famine (see Fig. 3.2). A major drawback for cultivation in Chokare is the risk of flood, which occurred twice in three recent years, leading to temporary resettlement of households until the floods receded. The risk of flood damage to crops makes irrigation cultivation a relatively high-risk strategy for farmers.

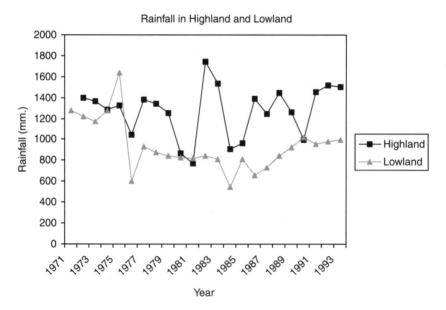

Figure 3.2 Rainfall data for highland and lowland Wolayta, 1971–93 (adapted from Eyasu (1997))

Socioeconomic patterns

Table 3.2 draws out some of the key socioeconomic factors in the three sites.

Table 3.2   Socioeconomic factors

	Admencho	Mundena	Chokare[10]
Size of PA	880 ha	5159 ha	PA = 24,985 ha State Farm (SF) = n.k.
Number of households in PA (tax-paying and non-tax-paying)	1360	800	PA = 905 SF = 868[11]
Population density of PA (km²)	927[12]	53	PA = 23 SF density = n.k[13]
Nearby concentration of population	Areka and Boditi towns	Bele town	Large State Farm population; and Humbo town
Infrastructure	Dense network of roads and markets	New road built to Bele	Poor communications; remote from markets and roads
Ethnicity and language	Ethnically and linguistically homogeneous	Ethnically and linguistically homogeneous	Ethnically and linguistically mixed
Settlement history	Long, complex history of settlement, cultivation, land tenure and labour relations	Settled in past 30 years	Transition away from pastoralism; increased cultivation and agro-pastoralism in past 25 years

In all sites the average size of households is approximately six, and everywhere there is a high proportion of children. The proportion of female-headed households[14] varies between 18 per cent in Mundena and 37 per cent in Chokare PA. Polygamous households are much more common in Chokare PA (23 per cent) than in the other sites. A high proportion of households in all sites belong to new Protestant churches: between 61 per cent in Chokare and 77 per cent in Mundena. Comparisons with past data show that this figure has significantly increased over the past 25 years. This change has many implications particularly through the influence on these new social networks on marriage patterns, working groups, burial societies, savings groups and other informal institutional arrangements.[15]

---

[10]Chokare Peasants Association and Abaya State Farm are administered completely separately. Their populations (and population densities) are therefore shown separately. Half our sample was taken from the PA and half from the State Farm.

[11]Figures from CSA (1996). It is unclear whether this includes temporary residents.

[12]The figure is exceptionally high. There are questions over the accuracy of the size of the PA, which would explain the density, but this could not be verified.

[13]The State Farm population lives in 'camps', which are densely populated villages the size of which is not known.

[14]This figure is calculated from the results of our survey. It includes households not listed by the PA as female-headed, but which are *de facto* female-headed households.

[15]See Carswell *et al.* (2000), for a discussion of change in religious composition over the past 25 years.

Admencho and Mundena are both relatively ethnically and culturally homogeneous, the population being predominantly ethnically Wolayta. Chokare has a much more ethnically mixed population of Sidama and Wolayta, as well as Oromo and Amhara. The State Farm population, although predominantly Wolayta, is also ethnically mixed. Admencho is characterised by high levels of social stratification, as the division between descendants of landlords and descendants of tenants and slaves is particularly marked. In the pre-Revolution period both Wolayta and Amhara landlords had numerous arrangements with tenants and slaves related to the use of land, labour and livestock, which still have repercussions today. In contrast Mundena, an area settled from 1972 as part of a voluntary resettlement programme organised by WADU[16], was largely settled by landless tenants and slaves from the highlands, resulting in a relatively homogeneous population. At the time of settlement each settler family was allocated 5 ha of land, and today the area remains fairly thinly populated. Since the official settlement began there have been periods of in-migration (particularly of relatives of settlers) and out-migration and return to homelands (particularly during times of stress, such as the 1984 famine).

Chokare PA is much more thinly populated than the other two sites. The PA is adjacent to a State Farm, which itself has a substantial population. The presence of the State Farm has a number of major influences: its population provides a large market for the area, and there are flows of information and technology between the State Farm and the surrounding farmers. For example, irrigation used by the State Farm has now been extended into private farms, while new seed varieties enter private use from the State Farm. Furthermore, there has been a notable trend of population settlement over the past two or three decades, and cultivation by recently settled agro-pastoralists and by State Farm workers has increased significantly during this period. State Farm workers also farm and manage livestock themselves. The Chokare sample is therefore divided into Chokare PA residents and State Farm (SF) workers.

Farming systems

Admencho is a highland area, with an agricultural system based on cultivation of enset (or false banana: *Ensete ventricosum*) and root crops such as taro and sweet potato. Small plots of land are intensively cultivated with a wide diversity of crops. Mundena is a more extensive system with larger plots but a similarly large array of crops is grown. Chokare is very different. Here a much narrower range of crops is grown and the history of cultivation is much shorter (see Table 3.3). Many Sidama agro-pastoralists have moved into agriculture in the past few decades. Some farmers in Chokare use irrigation on their private farms, which has extended from the State Farm that neighbours the PA.

Admencho is intensively cultivated, here households grow an average of nine different crops, higher than the average of seven grown in Mundena (see Table 3.4). In contrast, Chokare farmers grow an average of only two different crops, making it a less diverse agricultural system. Chokare has a wider range of activities besides farming, and 28 per cent of State Farm residents and 10 per cent of PA residents do not grow any crops at all.

---

[16]Wollamo Agricultural Development Unit, a World Bank-funded regional integrated development programme that included a resettlement programme from the highlands.

Table 3.3 Farming systems.

	Admencho	Mundena	Chokare
Cultivation	Intensively cultivated; small plots; rainfed	More extensive; larger plots; rainfed (irrigation under construction)	Mix of irrigated and non-irrigated
Main crops	Maize, enset, teff, sweet potato, coffee	Maize, sweet potato, taro, teff	Maize, sweet potato

Table 3.4 Crops grown.

	Admencho	Mundena	Chokare (All)	Chokare (PA)	Chokare (SF)
Average number of different crops grown by households	9	7	2	3	2
% of households not growing crops	0	2	19	10	28
% growing maize	100	97	79	88	70
% growing teff	86	72	0	0	0
% growing enset	95	65	0	0	0
% growing sweet potato	84	85	77	84	70

(SLP survey, February 1998)

Farms in Admencho have distinct plot types typical of highland Wolayta. A farm consists of a small *darkua* plot close to the house and a larger main plot (*shoqa*) further away. In addition, non-cultivated land is called *oota*. A plot of uncultivated grass in front of the house (*karea*) is used for social gatherings and for tethered grazing. These plots have different management strategies associated with them. In Mundena a similar division between the plots is found, although typically a larger proportion of the farm remains uncultivated (*oota*). This is in part because land was distributed to settlers and many farmers are not able to cultivate it all. Chokare is different from the other two sites, in that *darkua* plots (and the soil fertility management strategies associated with them) are less common. This is in part because *darkua* plots by their nature are next to the house, and State Farm workers live in villages away from their agricultural land. Furthermore, the application of manure, which is common on *darkua* plots in the other two sites, is less frequent in Chokare. The differences in size and proportion of plot types are illustrated in Fig. 3.3.

Mundena has the largest average area of land owned. It also has the largest area of land cultivated, and is the only site where a notably larger area of land is owned than is cultivated. Land availability is not a constraint to production in this site, and indeed households own large areas of *oota*. In comparison, uncultivated *oota* plots that exist in Admencho and Chokare are small. In Admencho this is because of the extremely high population density, while in Chokare a different picture emerges. Here, while households have in recent years claimed ownership rights over land for

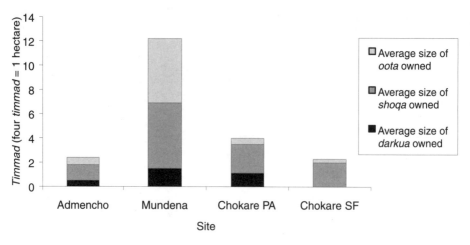

Figure 3.3 Size and proportion of plot types owned in three sites

cultivation, this is less common for uncultivated land. In Admencho and Mundena almost all households have a *darkua* plot, and in these two sites the crops associated with *darkua* plots are a central part of the agricultural system. The management strategies associated with *darkua* plots and the crops grown on them (often root crops) are based on nutrient recycling within the farm and so require fewer external inputs. *Shoqa* plots are much larger than *darkua* plots; the size of *darkua* plots is limited by the availability of manure while the size of *shoqa* is limited by availability of labour and oxen.

Livestock are key to the agricultural system of Wolayta for a number of reasons. The use of manure is critical in Admencho and Mundena, and the use of oxen for draught power is critical in all sites. In addition, livestock products make an important contribution to livelihoods. In all sites approximately the same proportion of households own livestock, for example between 78 and 80 per cent own cattle. However, the average number of livestock owned varies greatly (Fig. 3.4): most notably, the average number of cattle owned is much higher among the PA population in Chokare than elsewhere.

The distinction between the average number of animals owned and the average number kept is an important one. It highlights the importance of institutional arrangements that enable households to 'keep' livestock in their house that they do not fully own themselves. They may be shared ownership arrangements – whereby a household owns a half or a quarter of an animal, but keeps the animal in the house (*kotta* or *ulo-kotta*). Alternatively, they may be share-rearing arrangements whereby, for different reasons, a household keeps in their house an animal that belongs to someone else (*hara* or *tirf yegera*). In Admencho and Chokare more cattle are owned on average than are kept in the house, suggesting that some animals owned by people are kept outside those areas. The opposite pattern is seen in Mundena and the Chokare State Farm, suggesting that households in these two sites look after animals that belong to people from outside the area. The details of the institutional arrangements that give rise to these patterns, and that are essential in enabling access to livestock, are discussed below.

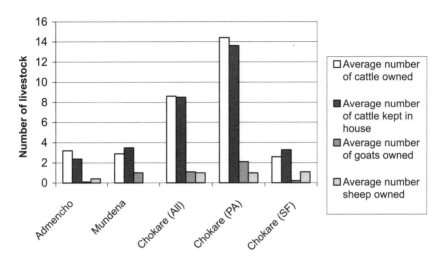

Figure 3.4   Livestock ownership and livestock access by site (February 1998)

In all sites wealthier households own more livestock than poorer households. Wealthier households also 'keep' more livestock than poorer groups, but in Admencho and Mundena the distribution is more even owing to the 'livestock-accessing' arrangements. In all sites wealthier households own more livestock than they keep, which implies that these households are involved in lending out livestock. Conversely, the poorer groups generally keep more animals than they own, implying that they gain access to these animals through long-term livestock-accessing arrange-ments. Women in Wolayta own livestock as *tabaa* (literally 'my own', which implies personal ownership) or as part of the households' assets. Women acquire livestock through gifts from parents on marriage (or birth of first born), following the death of a husband, or through purchase. They may own livestock both openly and in secret. The proliferation of shared ownership and share-rearing of livestock arrangements means that there are many ways for women to gain access to the products of an animal that they own secretly. Secret ownership of livestock is a strategy by which women can keep control of the income they earn (for example, from trading) and, particularly in polygamous households, provides an insurance policy in case of marriage breakdown.

Buzunech Lachebo recalls investing profits earned from trading in smallstock, and then buying a cow that she kept at her father's house. Her husband, who had two other wives, never knew about this arrangement. She explained:

> I kept it at my father's house, so I could get my parents to sell it, and buy me clothes and then I can say look what my father gave me. [Also] I did it because ... if he divorced us he'd never give us anything ... if I get divorced then I have something. ... For polygamy it is more common to do this secretly. ... I never told anyone. Not even my women friends! (Buzunech Lachebo, Mundena).

The covert nature of such arrangements means that it is extremely difficult to say anything concrete about the individual ownership of livestock by women, except that our survey figures are likely to be an underestimate. Ownership of smallstock is particularly important for women. For example in Admencho, a higher percentage of female-headed households own sheep compared to male-headed households, while in Mundena and Chokare a higher percentage of female-headed households own goats compared to male-headed households.

Components of crop–livestock integration

A diversity of farming systems, both within and across farms, is evident in the study sites. This results in a variety of forms of crop–livestock integration. This section will examine three key components of an integrated cropping and livestock system in each of the sites: manure application as a soil fertility management strategy; feeding of crop residues to livestock; and use of animal traction in the system of cultivation.

Soil fertility management and manure use

Different strategies for soil fertility management are used in the three sites and on different plot types (Table 3.5). Fertility inputs (manure or chemical fertiliser) are seen as an essential means of maintaining and/or increasing productivity in Admencho, where most land is intensively cropped for most of the year, and in Mundena, where the soils are inherently infertile. By contrast, Chokare, in an alluvial river valley, has extremely fertile soils and the application of fertility inputs is rare. In Admencho and Mundena livestock are kept inside people's houses, and the women and children of the household collect the dung each day. They deposit it in piles on their land, under instruction from the (usually) male household head, who later ploughs or digs it into the land.

Manure use in Admencho and Mundena is focused on the *darkua* plot and on areas where taro, a root crop, is to be grown. By growing heavily manured taro, farmers seek to build up the fertility of a piece of land and increase the size of *darkua*. The positioning of taro is thus of particular significance. The household head selects areas to be manured, and then negotiates with female household members who carry the manure from the house. Some men acknowledged that they had misjudged this on occasions and placed taro too far away, and so insufficient manure was placed on the selected area. Manure application decisions, in turn, influence decisions about the application of fertiliser on land that has not been manured. Extending the area of manured land is a central aim for all households (Data Dea 1998; Eyasu and Scoones 1999).

Table 3.5 Use of different inputs by site.

% of farmers with that plot type who use:	Admencho	Mundena	Chokare (All)
Manure as main input on *darkua*	87	91	11
Manure as main input on *shoqa*	10	4	4
Chemical fertiliser as main input on *darkua*	0	1	0
Chemical fertiliser as main input on *shoqa*	87	83	0

It is much less common for farmers to apply manure in Chokare. Only five households in our sample used manure, and no artificial fertilisers were used at all. Livestock are either kept inside the house or in kraals nearby, which may contain the livestock of one or more household. Dung from the houses and kraals is gathered into piles nearby so that large amounts of manure are available in the area, but these are generally burnt rather than applied to fields. There are a number of explanations given for this (see Box 3.1).

Box 3.1 Differing explanations of manure use in Chokare

A Wolay⁺ . woman, who used manure and had a manure ditch leading from the house to the garden, explained 'we follow our [Wolayta] culture'; while some Sidama informants stated that they did not use manure as it was 'not in our culture'.

'... lots of manure is thrown out or burnt here. We do not take a deliberate pain of spreading manure in our farms. Why should we? ... This doesn't mean that we lack strategy ... The current cropping lands were our former open barns and grazing lands. We ... change the sites of our barns at least once every two years. The former barns will then be ploughed to grow crops.'

'We don't [put manure on the land] because it burns [*tuges*] ... if you plant where there is manure that part will wilt unless there is continuous rainfall ... I saw that on my land – it was a place where animals were housed.

Farmers in Admencho and Mundena use chemical fertiliser to maintain or increase production. It may be used in addition to manure application, but is often applied to different plots and crops. For the majority of farmers in these two sites (87 per cent and 82 per cent, respectively) chemical fertiliser is the main input used on *shoqa* plots, and is used most frequently on cereals.[17] Farmers can either pay cash for fertiliser on the local market or get it on credit. In the past 'Regular' fertiliser was available on credit through the Bureau of Agriculture without a down-payment or follow-up by officials. This system is currently being phased out and replaced by the 'Global Package', the main soil fertility maintenance policy being promoted by the government through the Bureau of Agriculture.

The Global Package has been operating in the area since 1995 and has been incorporated into the national extension programme. A fixed package of chemical fertiliser and improved seed is bought on credit after a down-payment.[18] Unlike the Regular fertiliser, the Global Package involves very close supervision of

---

[17]One farmer in Admencho commented that 'The land needs a bribe to grow our crops' (i.e. it needs artificial inputs).

[18]The Global Package for maize is sold in Belg season (March to May), and that for teff in Meher season (June to October). Both contain 50 kg DAP and improved seed, and the maize package also includes 50 kg of urea. Each package is for half a hectare (2 *timmad*), and one package may be divided between more than one farmer. All farmers make a down-payment before they receive their fertiliser – for 'poor' farmers this is 10 per cent of the total cost and for non-poor farmers it is 25 per cent. An interest payment described as a 'service charge' is made as a percentage of the final payment. (In contrast, regular fertiliser involved no down-payment and interest was charged at a monthly rate for every month beyond a certain date.)

farmers, initially by the Development Agent,[19] and highly punitive measures. Failure to repay debts leads to threats to confiscate livestock, followed by forced sale of livestock. If the debtor has no livestock then part of his land may be taken by the PA and allocated to someone else to work on a sharecropping (*kotta*-land) basis. Under this arrangement half the harvest goes towards repaying the debt and the other half to the person working the land. There has been significant enthusiasm for this package among policy-makers and it has been promoted very heavily. However, there is evidence that adoption of the Global Package has not been entirely voluntary. This has significant implications for processes of agricultural intensification, as it implies farmers may be having to enter and follow a particular pathway of change that they have not chosen themselves. It also has implications for the integration of the cropping and livestock systems, as this package promotes two cereal crops (maize and teff), both of which require significant amounts of ploughing.

Tillage methods

The hoe is used for certain agricultural activities, or if the household cannot gain access to oxen. It is more commonly used for crops grown in the *darkua* and for root crops. The technology associated with the Ethiopian plough has changed little over many hundreds of years: it is made of wood and is attached to two oxen by means of a wooden bar. The only major change seen in Wolayta was the introduction of the metal tip (*marasha*, meaning 'that which ploughs') at the time of the Amhara invasion. Ploughing is used at various stages in the agricultural cycle, and in the land preparation stage land is ploughed repeatedly to ensure that weeds are cleared and the soil clods broken down sufficiently. The broad patterns of plough and hoe use are shown in Table 3.6.

Farmers prefer to weed maize by shallow ploughing (*shilshallo*) than use a hoe. This has the disadvantage of requiring the use of oxen and means that maize cannot be

Table 3.6 Broad patterns of hoe and plough use.

Activity	Maize	Teff	Sweet potato
Preparing land and sowing	Plough: 4–6 times	Plough: 6 times	Plough: 4–6 times
Shilshallo (weeding with plough) or *makotkot* (hand weeding with hoe)	*Shilshallo* with plough (once); *makotkot* with hoe (once)	*Makotkot* with hoe (once only)	*Makotkot* with hoe (once only)
Ushetes (gathering soil around base of plant with hoe)	Task can only be undertaken with hoe	Not done for teff	Not done for sweet potato

[19]A Development Agent (DA) works in each PA for the Bureau of Agriculture to promote the package. He (rarely is it a she) receives a 'bonus' of between 2 Birr and 3 Birr per package sold as an incentive to increase sales. The DA is also set a 'quota' of packages to sell each season, and any DA who exceeds the quota gets additional benefits such as invitations to workshops.

intercropped, but has the advantage of needing only low labour inputs and providing a fodder source. *Shilshallo,* being an activity that involves the plough, is the preserve of men as it is entirely unacceptable for women to use a plough in Wolayta culture. The official recommendation that farmers weed twice using a hoe (which is a female activity) is often rejected because of the additional pressure that this would add to female labour. In Mundena, for example, with water sources some distance away, women's labour is already over-stretched.

In Wolayta, only oxen are used for ploughing, and no cases of other cattle or donkeys being used for draught power were observed. It is widely believed that only fully-grown oxen are strong enough to be able to plough, and using other animals is taboo. Fig. 3.5 shows that in all sites a very high percentage of households surveyed used a plough. But a significant percentage of households own no oxen, and only a minority own the two oxen needed to form a span.

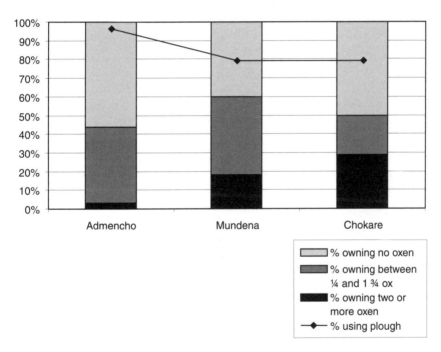

Figure 3.5   Plough use and oxen ownership (of those who cultivated)

Fodder management

A number of different sources of fodder are used in the three sites (see Table 3.7). In Admencho livestock are grazed on small areas of communal grazing land, tethered on the *karea* in front of houses and fed by 'cut-and-carry' with crop residues and cut grass. Cut grass is gathered from private plots: commonly part of the *karea* is fenced off to allow the grass to grow. Crop thinnings and teff plants on the borders of fields are also fed to animals. In Mundena there is ample grazing land (both common

Table 3.7 Fodder sources[20] in each site.

	Admencho	Mundena	Chokare	Chokare PA	Chokare SF
% using grazing only	0	1	3	5	0
% with intensive fodder management (no grazing)	3	1	16	2	29
% using both grazing and intensive fodder management	97	98	81	93	71

property and privately held). Here, the incidence of trypanosomiasis discourages farmers from allowing their animals out at times of the year and day when fly activity is highest. During these times animals are kept indoors and are fed cut-and-carry fodder. In Chokare there is ample grazing land in the PA as a whole (much of which is virtually unpopulated) and there is seasonal migration of livestock. However, in the State Farm livestock-owning residents use cut-and-carry, because of difficulties in accessing grazing land.[21]

Crop–livestock interactions: an overview

In both Admencho and Mundena the cropping and livestock systems are highly integrated, in many ways epitomising the idealised 'mixed farm' (see Chapter 1). A high percentage of households use ploughs and manure, and livestock are fed crop residues and cut-and-carry grass. Hay is made and animals are tethered on privately owned grazing land in Admencho. In Mundena greater use is made of common property resources for grazing, although intensive fodder management does exist, especially for milking cows and fattening oxen. In the Chokare site there is less obvious integration, and many livestock are taken away from the PA during the wet season. However, among the State Farm population intensive fodder management is important for many households with livestock owing to the difficulties in reaching grazing land. Table 3.8 provides an overview of the preva- lence of soil fertility management, tillage and fodder management practices in each of the three sites.

Yet, these broad patterns conceal very different historical experiences, different social settings and institutional dynamics. The emergence of the particular forms of 'mixed farming' seen across the sites, as will be shown below, has been a complex process, with periods of integration and dis–integration, involving both change, both sudden and gradual, and continuity. A simple pathway of change towards a single idealised model has not been evident, as will be made clear through an exploration of the histories of the multiple pathways of change in the study areas.

---

[20]Fodder sources are calculated for the wet season, for all animals in the household, for those households that own or keep animals.
[21]State Farm officials forbid residents from taking their animals across the bridge to the grazing land, as they believe this may cause damage to the bridge.

Table 3.8 Broad patterns in practices associated with crop–livestock integration by site.

	Practice	Admencho	Mundena	Chokare
Soil fertility management	Manure use	Common	Common	Rare
	% using manure as main input on *darkua*	87	91	11
Tillage	Use of draught power	Yes – oxen only	Yes – oxen only	Yes – oxen only
	% using plough (of those who cultivated this season)	96	79	79
Fodder management	Fodder crops grown	No	No	No
	Fencing of *karea*	Yes	No	No
	Feeding of crop residues to livestock	Yes	Yes	Yes
	Paddocking of livestock	No	No	No
	'Cut-and-carry'	Yes	Yes	Yes
	% using both grazing and intensive fodder management	97	98	81
	% with intensive fodder management (no grazing)	3	1	16

Histories of change: key events and the impact on farming practices in southern Ethiopia

Table 3.9 shows some of the key events that have directly or indirectly influenced the interactions between the cropping and livestock systems in each of the three research sites. A complex pattern is seen, with some key events – notably those involving significant shifts in political regime and so the form of intervention – being key in transforming systems substantially and relatively suddenly. Other processes of change have been more gradual and cumulative, including the impact of population growth and the changing agricultural and disease ecology of the area, which have had major impacts on the livelihood opportunities of different people. The following section, then, offers a brief sketch of some of the major shifts in the relationships between cropping and livestock systems over the last century since the invasion of the Amhara in 1897.

Before the defeat of Koa Tona by Menelik ploughs were used in Wolayta, but without the metal tip. This meant that *oota* (uncultivated) land had to be dug with a hoe or digging stick first. The metal tip increased the efficiency of the ploughing, and enabled people to plough up uncultivated land. This led to an extension in the area cultivated:

> The Amhara came and showed us the plough ... when Menelik came the Amharas came [with] the *marasha* (iron tip). Before the Amharas some people were ploughing existing cultivated land near to the enset – but not *oota* land – it was the Amharas who taught us to cultivate *oota* with the plough (Balacha Gogoto, Admencho).

Table 3.9 Key events and their links with changes in practices

Year	Site	Key event	Immediate impact	Implications for practices associated with cropping and livestock interactions
1897	A	Amhara takeover	Amhara *balabats* settled in Wolayta	Iron-tipped plough introduced
1897+	A	Amhara period	New crop varieties introduced	Increase in plough use
1897+	A	Amhara period	Taxation system (per land unit) to be paid to Amhara *balabats*	Encouraged landlords to attract tenants to their land
1897+	A	Amhara period	Tenants and slaves paid tribute (labour or produce) to Amhara landlords	Little change for tenants and slaves. They continued to negotiate with landlords (now Amhara, previously Wolayta) to gain access to land and livestock. Landlords had ample labour available to them
1936–41	A	Italian period	Amhara landlords removed and replaced by Wolayta landlords. Slavery officially abolished	Implications for labour: *siso* system formalised
1965	C	Abaya farm established	Loss of seasonal grazing land	Seasonal migration patterns altered slightly, pressure on grazing
1965+	C	Abaya farm established	Market for crops and livestock products developed in State Farm (SF) camps	Encouraged more production and greater use of plough
1965+	C	Abela settlement scheme began	Loss of seasonal grazing land	Seasonal migration patterns altered slightly, further pressure on grazing
1970+	A M	WADU period	Encouraged sowing in straight lines	*Shilshallo* weeding possible, more use of plough
1970+	A M	WADU period	Encouraged sowing in straight lines	Residue from *shilshallo* weeding a fodder source
1970+	A M	WADU period	Chemical fertiliser and cereals promoted	Shift away from manure and root crops
1974	A	Revolution	Changes to land tenure and previous power relations within society	All households able to make own cropping decisions.
1974	A	Revolution	Changes to land tenure	Privately owned grazing areas became public property.
1974	A	Revolution	Changes to previous power relations within society	Implications for labour. All households able to make own decisions over labour investment. Labour tribute no longer paid to landlords, decline in landlord-organised *dagos*
1974	A M	Revolution	Changes to previous power relations within society	Implications for livestock arrangements: in Admencho decline in *hara* arrangements

mid-1970s+	C	State Farm management poor	Previous ban on private cultivation and livestock ignored by SF workers.	Increase in livestock kept in SF camps. Associated with increase in cut-and-carry to camps
1978	C	Visit by Mengistu to SF	Renewed ban on private ownership and keeping livestock by SF workers.	Livestock banned from SF camps: increase in arrangements with PA residents
1982	A M	End of WADU	End of input subsidies.	Shift back to manure
1983	M	Villagisation	Households moved into clusters	Difficulties in manuring owing to distance between houses and fields
1983	M	Villagisation	Households moved into clusters	Loss of *darkua*
1983	M	Villagisation	Shrinkage in area cultivated	Bush encroachment led to increase in trypanosomiasis
1983+	M	Increase in trypanosomiasis	Livestock deaths	Reduction in availability of manure, and oxen for ploughing
1984	A M	Poor rainfall	Famine, livestock deaths and sales	Reduction in availability of manure, and oxen for ploughing
1984	C	Poor rainfall	Famine, livestock deaths and sales	Expansion of cultivation, first irrigation channel built
1984+	C	Increase in trypanosomiasis	Livestock deaths	Push towards cultivation
1987	C	Year of poor rain	Increase in irrigation	More labour-intensive cropping system
1995	A M	Global	Promotion of chemical fertiliser use	Possible implications for manure
1995	A M	Global	Advises two hand weedings of maize	Reduction in plough use for *shilshallo*
1995+	M	Increase in trypanosomiasis	Loss of livestock to disease	Reduction in manure available, and oxen for ploughing
1996	C	Neighbouring farm established	Further loss of seasonal grazing	Migration further hindered and cultivation further encouraged
1998	A M	End of input subsidies	Chemical fertiliser more costly	Possible return to manure and increased manure use

Prior to the 1974 Revolution Wolayta had a complex feudal system. The landlords were ethnically Wolayta until 1897, when an additional layer of administration in the form of Amhara *balabats* was superimposed. This persisted until the Italian period (1936–41) when the Amhara were removed, leaving Wolayta landlords once more in control. The arrangements between landlords and tenants and slaves varied: broadly tenants had no rights over their land, but some rights over their own labour, while slaves had no rights over their own labour, but some (unpredictable and minimal) rights over their land. In theory both groups could be evicted from the land that they cultivated at any time, but most remained for generations. In return, tenants paid a proportion of their harvest to the landlords. They either paid a flat rate or a half (*ikul*), third (*siso*) or a quarter (*irbo*) of the harvest. In addition, many also worked a labour tribute for their landlord. Slaves worked for the landlords on demand, although after the Italian period this was formalised into what became known as the *siso* system, where slaves were supposed to work two days a week only for the landlords. The landlords thus had ample labour at their disposal. Landlords also had control over grazing land in Admencho, and tenants had to pay to use this land.

Tenants and slaves (of all ages and sexes) worked for the landlords on many different activities. One of the most important was collecting dung from the landlord's household and depositing it on his land. Livestock belonging to landlords were often kept in the houses of tenants and slaves, and the manure from such live-stock was applied to the land used by those tenants and slaves. When allocating land to tenants the landlord would consider the efforts that those tenants would put into improving its fertility:

> When he gave land for tenants it would be on the edge – infertile and far from the main house – so their house would be on 'hard' land. They would also give a horse to look after – that was very good dung at making soil fertile (Dawit Degafu, Admencho).

Tenants and slaves also ploughed for their landlords using oxen owned by the landlord (whether kept by the landlord or the tenant). As the son of an ex-landlord explained:

> There were oxen of my father's in slave's [*chesenya*] houses. [For ploughing] the *chesenya* either used the animals in my father's house, or in their house. My father kept them there because even the *chesenya* himself is like an oxen *(boora malaka gedene)* [i.e. they were all his possessions] so we would give the *chesenya* oxen to look after. This was called *hara*. [That] ox [was used] … to plough my father's land, and also the *chesenya*'s land (none of the harvest of the latter went to my father). That ox belonged to my father… [and] when the ox was sold all the money went to my father (Balacha Gogoto, Admencho).

The existence of these institutional arrangements in the pre-Revolution period between landlords, tenants and slaves has legacies in highland Wolayta today. In particular the *hara* arrangement (see below) was common between a landlord and his tenants and slaves. The landlord could not keep all his animals in his house so he would farm them out to tenants and slaves. The tenants and slaves could use the products of these animals (manure, draught power and milk[22]), but they remained owned by the landlord.

Little is known about the early history of either Mundena or Chokare, but both were uncultivated until three to four decades ago. Mundena was settled in the early 1970s and prior to this was a *bazo* area (literally empty bush or grass land). It was used as seasonal grazing by households living in the neighbouring Kindo Koisha highlands, but was not cultivated until the time of settlement. Chokare was also a seasonal grazing area for Sidama agro-pastoralists who cultivated in the highlands to the east. It was only after the establishment of the Abaya Farm by a Belgian entrepreneur in the early 1960s that cultivation in the area began, and since then there has been a significant transition from pastoralism to agro-pastoralism. The establishment of the farm marked the beginning of pressure on grazing land for Sidama seasonal migrants, which was accentuated by the resettlement schemes at Abela (close to Chokare) that

[22]But the keeper of a cow was expected to give 'gifts' of butter to the landlord owner. Butter was given on two occasions: a small amount immediately after the birth (called *tera*) and then a larger amount some weeks later (called *nakuwa*). The keeper benefited from being able to keep the skimmed milk for own consumption.

began soon afterwards. The pressure on grazing land, the creation of a market in the form of State Farm employees, and increased loss of livestock to disease from the early 1980s conspired to encourage an increase in cultivation.

The resettlement schemes in Abela and Bele began under the governorship of Woldesemayet and were later taken over by the Wollamo Agricultural Development Unit (WADU). They involved the voluntary resettlement of landless tenants and slaves from the highlands to the lowlands, including Mundena. Assistance was given to settlers in the form of mechanised clearing and ploughing of land, subsidised inputs, supply of rations and marketing. WADU policies encouraged a shift in emphasis towards cereals (maize and cotton in lowland areas) grown with chemical fertiliser, away from root crops grown with manure. WADU also recommended that crops be grown in straight lines, which made weeding using a plough (*shilshallo*) easier. In addition, there were improvements to infrastructure (such as roads and bridges) and the provision of marketing (particularly for coffee in the highlands, and cotton in the lowlands). Initially the target farmers for these policies (such as the supply of credit) were landlords in the highlands, but after the Revolution the policy was extended to all farmers.

The Revolution and subsequent land reform obviously had major implications for farmers, particularly in Admencho.[23] The Revolution removed the ties of labour tribute, and ended the practice of payment of part of the harvest by tenants and slaves to landlords. All households were able to make their own cropping decisions about the land they cultivated and were able to decide freely how to invest their labour. Privately owned grazing areas became public property, and payments were no longer necessary to use these grazing areas. There were also changes to livestock exchange arrangements. Some of those who had been looking after animals for landlords simply kept them. Because of their feudal associations the shame associated with entering such arrangements meant that many former tenants and slaves and their descendants avoided entering any new arrangements. Furthermore, former landlords became increasingly reluctant to let their animals be kept by others. As the descendant of a landlord said: 'Should I give my animals to a hyena? They would never have given them back to me!' (Balacha Gogoto, Admencho). New arrangements to mediate access to livestock therefore developed in this new political and social context.

Following the Revolution the state took over Abaya Farm in Chokare, but there was no immediate impact on workers. A few years later, as management became increasingly chaotic and workers' salaries less reliable, some workers began to own livestock and cultivate privately in order to make ends meet. This coincided with increased settlement by Sidama agro-pastoralists in the area. By the early 1980s many agro-pastoralists were spending the whole year in Chokare, sending only shepherds with their herds for wet season grazing. Greater efforts were invested in cultivation, draught power was used increasingly, and in 1984 the first private irrigation channel was built. Initially the practice of irrigation spread slowly, but from 1987 (a year of poor rain) it spread more rapidly and, today, the majority of cultivators in Chokare use irrigation.[24]

---

[23]Settlers in Mundena were allocated land and did not have land and labour-accessing arrangements with landlords. Some of them did, however, have livestock-accessing (sharing or rearing) arrangements with their ex-landlords in the highlands.

[24]Currently approximately 75 per cent of those who cultivate in Chokare have some land that is irrigable. Irrigation is not necessarily used every year, but canals are opened up if rain is insufficient.

Meanwhile in the other two sites the use of inputs continued to be promoted throughout the 1970s, but the increasingly unreliable distribution system began to affect farmers' planting decisions. With fertiliser supply erratic the emphasis on cereals and chemical fertilisers was reduced, and there was a return to manure use. This was accentuated in 1982 when WADU pulled out, and farmers who had come to rely on marketing support from WADU (particularly for cotton) returned to those crops for which there was a more reliable market.

In 1983 the push for villagisation began, but this only really affected the lowland site, Mundena. Admencho was never villagised as the Derg regime fell before the plans were put into practice, while Chokare PA had a very small settled population at this time and was sufficiently peripheral to be ignored. Even in Mundena villagisation was rather half-hearted and short-lived. One effect of villagisation on farming was that it led to difficulties in applying manure to the *darkua*: livestock continued to reside in houses in the villages, but there was insufficient space to have *darkua* plots around the house. With permanent crops in their old *darkua* plots farmers continued to cultivate their *darkua* to the best of the ability without the application of manure. Villagisation in Mundena also coincided with an increase in the prevalence of trypanosomiasis. The increase in tsetse fly may have resulted from bush encroachment associated with a contraction in the area cultivated (Fig. 3.6).

This can become a vicious circle out of which it is difficult to break. Increased incidence of disease leads to a loss of oxen and other livestock, reduction in the availability of manure and draught power, a contraction in the area cultivated and further expansion of bush which encourages the fly, and so on. There is no doubt that in Mundena there has been, from the time of villagisation, a shrinkage in the area cultivated, which was in part related to the increase in trypanosomiasis,[25] and in part to the increasingly unreliable supply of inputs and marketing of cotton. This period was also one of high military recruitment of young men, which is believed to have led to labour constraints.

The major famine of 1984 led to further loss of livestock through sales as well as death, and in Admencho and Mundena the use of manure and draught power was inevitably affected. The shortage of manure was a particular constraint to production in the context of the partial breakdown of the input distribution system. The same event had a rather different impact in Chokare: the higher level of livestock dependency for livelihoods among the PA population meant that, when livestock were lost, there was a shift towards cultivation. Thus in this site the famine led to an increase in cultivation. Additionally, the poor rainfall led one farmer in Chokare to build the first private irrigation channel in the area, which was to play an enormously significant role in agriculture in the years to come.

In Chokare the recent establishment of a private farm adjoining the existing State Farm has reduced the availability of seasonal grazing land for agro-pastoralists. This is likely to further hinder migratory patterns and thus encourage a more settled existence with cultivation. The return of veterinary services to the area in the post-Derg period has had a positive impact on livestock disease in Chokare, although trypanosomiasis still remains a problem. In Mundena, however,

---

[25]The increase in trypanosomiasis prevalence is shown by BOA data from Bele: 8.8% in 1991, 15.8% in 1992, 18.5% in 1994, and 22.3% in 1996.

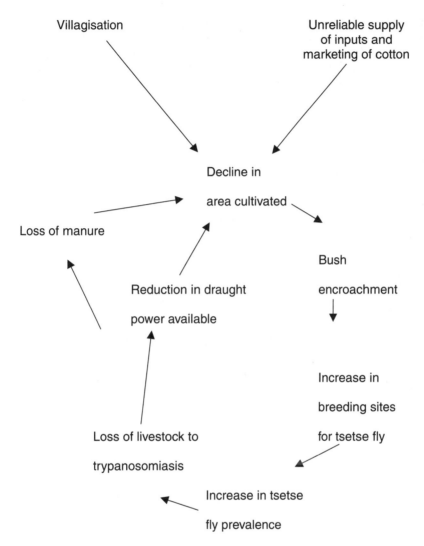

Figure 3.6   Trypanosomiasis and contraction in area cultivated

trypanosomiasis has been extremely severe over recent years. Our survey found that a staggering 22 per cent of the total cattle herd owned in Mundena died of trypanosomiasis in the 12 months prior to the survey.

In Admencho there is a widely held belief that population density increases have reduced the size of land available to individual households and led to a fall in grazing land available, with the result that there are fewer livestock in the area. The land tenure history suggests that the scenario has been much more complex. For ex-land-lords there was a significant worsening of fortunes at the time of the Revolution in terms of the amount of land, labour and livestock that they had access to and control over. Air photos of Admencho show some loss of grazing land,[26] but the massive declines referred to by many informants might be more around questions of private ownership of grazing land by landlords in the pre-Revolution period, which non-landlords had to pay to be able to use. It is unsurprising that ex-landlords and their descendants refer to a significant decline in both grazing land and in the numbers of livestock they owned. For the majority, who were tenants or slaves, the opposite was true, and they were generally freer to make decisions about how they invested their labour and used land.

The data that we have on livestock over time (see Table 3.10) is extremely patchy, but suggests that in the highlands the average number of cattle owned by all house-holds fell from 5.5 in the 1960s to 4.1 in 1971, to 3.2 in 1998.[27] Strikingly, if the average number of cattle owned by tenant households (1.75) is used as the baseline, the opposite is true, and there has actually been an increase in the average number owned. The same pattern holds true for the ownership of oxen, with an increase from 0.51 among tenant households in 1971 to 1.3 owned in 1998, suggesting that ownership is now more evenly distributed than before the Revolution. The same pattern is seen for cows, with average numbers falling for all groups, but rising for tenants. The proportion of households owning no cows (or heifers) has increased from 31 per cent of tenants in 1971 to 41 per cent of all households in 1990, before declining to 31 per cent in 1998. The same pattern is seen for oxen ownership, with 50 per cent of tenants owning no oxen in the 1960s, increasing to 66 per cent among tenants in 1971, before falling by 1990 to 56 per cent and to 42 per cent in 1998.

In the lowlands around Mundena the average number of cattle per household rose from 5.5 in 1967/8 to a peak of 7.4 in 1971, before falling gradually to a low of 2.9 in 1998. However, nearly two-thirds of cattle in the settlement areas were described as

Table 3.10   Changes to livestock numbers and density in the highlands (Admencho).[28]

	1960s	1971	1990	1990	1998
Average number of cattle	5.5	4.1 (all hhs) 1.75 (tenants)			3.23 owned (2.39 held)
Average number of oxen (for 1998, oxen + bullocks)	1.2	0.9 (all hhs) 0.51 (tenants)			1.3 (0.88 held)
% of farmers with no cattle	30				20
% owning no cows or heifers		31% tenants	41		31
% owning no oxen or bullocks	50% tenants	66% tenants	56	68	42
% owning one ox or bullock	30% tenants			28	19

[26]Analysis of air photos for all sites was carried out by Ben Warr.

[27]Our data distinguishes between livestock owned and livestock held in the household. In Admencho it is the case that on average households keep fewer animals in their house than they own. Unfortunately, none of the previous data makes this distinction.

[28]Data from 1960s, compiled by FAO 1979. Also WADU archives, WADU 1976a and 1976b (data collected 1971); Dessalegn Ramato 1990; IAR 1991 (data collected 1990); survey data, February 1998.

'hired' in 1971, which implies that they were kept in the house but not owned, probably under arrangements with people in the highlands. Most of the early settlers were indeed ex-tenants and slaves from the highlands, who, especially in the early years of settlement, continued the livestock-accessing arrangements with their landlords. Even so, the number kept in the house now (3.5) is significantly lower than earlier figures, confirming suggestions that average numbers of livestock held by households have fallen. This fall is likely to be in part a result of the impact of trypanosomiasis on cattle herds.

The density of cattle in Wolayta as a whole has increased steadily over time. In the highlands[29] the cattle population density has risen in line with human population increases. In the lowlands the picture is less clear. In the areas of Bele and Kindo Koisha cattle density appears to have increased, but in Mundena cattle density today is strikingly lower than earlier, owing to the impact of trypanosomiasis.

There are therefore a number of broad, site-wide, agricultural changes that can be identified over time which have had major impacts on crop–livestock interactions (Table 3.11). Triggers to these changes include the direct and indirect impact of policy combined with events such as famine and livestock disease. In Admencho and Mundena, externally driven policies and programmes (such as the establishment of WADU or the promulgation of land reform) have had a more direct impact than in Chokare, where the policy influences have been felt indirectly (e.g. poor management of the State Farm or restrictions on transhumant movement). Here, agroecological – notably through drought and changing livestock disease incidence – and social changes – notably in-migration of farmers from the highlands – have been more important Thus transformations in crop-livestock practice have not simply been the result of gradual shifts in factor proportions resulting from population pressure, as suggested by the Boserup hypothesis (see Chapter 1), but the result of a complex interaction of events and processes over time that has influenced pathways of change, often in unpredictable ways. The result is a wide diversity of practices evident today across the sites, which can only be understood in historical context.

These historical events and processes have been experienced by different social actors in different ways. Rich, poor, men, women, Wolayta, Sidama, old, young – all have had diverse experiences and responses that have affected cropping and livestock systems in the study sites. The way such diverse pathways emerge is intimately bound up with the social institutional arrangements that underpin and influence patterns of resource access. These are explored in the following section.

Institutional arrangements and crop–livestock integration

Both formal and informal institutional arrangements facilitate or constrain the ways actors (be they individuals, households or ethnic groups) access, use and derive well-being from resources. These institutions are the product of ongoing negotiations between actors with differing sources of power and social affiliation. This section focuses in detail on the institutions mediating access to the resources central to crop-livestock interactions, in particular draught power, livestock and fodder. As institutions

---

[29]Using highland, Bolloso *woreda,* and Admencho PA data.

Table 3.11   Changes to crop–livestock integration practices.

	Admencho	Mundena	Chokare
Tillage	**Amhara period:** iron-tipped plough and new crop varieties introduced. Greater use of plough **WADU period:** new varieties, Greater use of plough for *shilshallo* **Mid-1990s:** Global Package promoted, reduction in plough use for *shilshallo*	**Mid-Derg:** loss of livestock to trypanosomiasis; oxen access declines. May have led to decline in plough use **WADU period:** new varieties, sowing in lines. Greater use of plough for *shilshallo* weeding **Mid-1990s:** increase in livestock disease; reduction in oxen availability	**Mid-Derg onwards:** livestock-dependent livelihoods hit by famine and livestock disease; led to increase in cultivation and use of plough **Mid-Derg onwards:** poor SF management triggers more cultivation by SF workers and increased use of plough
Soil fertility management	**Pre-Revolution period:** manure use by landlords, tenants and slaves **WADU period:** promotion of chemical fertiliser use (at expense of manure) **End of WADU:** input subsidies end and shift back to manure **Mid-1990s:** Global Package: chemical fertilisers promoted at expense of manure	**Early 1970s:** chemical fertiliser use promoted from beginning of settlement **End of WADU:** input subsidies end and shift back to manure **Mid-Derg:** reduction in manure available owing to disease **Villagisation:** application of manure to *darkua* difficult as houses moved into clusters **Mid-1990s:** increase in livestock disease; reduction in availability of manure	Manure and chemical fertilisers rarely used
Fodder	**Pre-revolution:** grazing land privately owned by landlords **Pre-revolution:** landlords had ample labour for cut-and-carry of fodder sources **WADU period:** sowing in lines encouraged, enabled *shilshallo* weeding, producing weeds as fodder **Revolution:** grazing land publicly owned	**Mid-Derg, and mid-1990s:** increased disease enforces animals kept indoors during heat of day: increased use of cut-and-carry	**Mid-Derg onwards:** pressure on seasonal grazing land triggers increased settlement and cultivation. Seasonal migration for grazing declines **Mid-Derg onwards:** poor SF management triggered more ownership of livestock by SF workers; increase in use of cut-and-carry fodder
Land	**Revolution:** end of feudal system; tenants and slaves no longer dependent on landlord to access land	**Revolution and Derg period:** few changes to land tenure arrangements except at villagisation	**Mid-Derg onwards:** livestock disease and pressure on grazing land triggers settlement and cultivation
Livestock	**Revolution:** change to livestock-accessing arrangements with ending of feudal system	**Mid-Derg, and mid-1990s:** disease threatens highlanders' willingness to engage in livestock-loaning arrangements with lowlanders	**1978:** Livestock banned from SF camps – increase in institutional arrangements between SF and PA residents
Labour	**Revolution:** change to labour demands by landlords associated with changes to land-accessing arrangements	**End of WADU onwards:** general decline in frequency of working groups **Mid-Derg, and mid-1990s:** increased tsetse, animals kept indoors during heat of day; reduced use of *wudea* labour arrangement	**1978:** private cultivation officially banned for SF workers – increase in arrangements between SF and PA residents

Overall effects	Massive change to institutional arrangements following Revolution.	Contraction of land area cultivated, reduction in livestock arrangements with highlanders; changes to arrangements around access to and management of cattle associated with increase in livestock disease and reduced input supply.	Movement into agriculture by both SF and PA populations.

mediate access to such resources, understanding institutional arrangements, and their differentiation between and within sites, is a critical step in our exploration of pathways of change. As will be shown below, different institutional arrangements result in different pathways of change.

Typically, intra-household arrangements are the first step for accessing these resources, and those without sufficient resources within their own household will then look to institutions outside the household domain. These include inter-household arrangements, as well as larger and more formal institutions. Details of the institutional arrangements used to access different resources in the study sites are given in Table 3.12. The following sections explore different ways diverse social actors gain access to resources for agricultural and livestock production, and the importance of different institutions for different groups. Livestock, as we have seen, are key to all the farming systems in the study areas. For this reason, the first two sections focus on the social and institutional bases for long- and short-term livestock-accessing arrangements, before moving on to institutions governing access to fodder, and the way institutional arrangements are differentiated by gender and wealth status.

Long-term livestock-accessing arrangements

Long-term livestock-accessing arrangements include shared ownership (*kotta, ulo-kotta*), share-rearing arrangements (*hara*) and profit-sharing arrangements (*tirf yegera*). Through these arrangements individuals and households are able to gain access to animals that they do not fully own, build up a herd and gain access to animal products (draught power and milk). In addition, such arrangements enable households to acquire manure. These arrangements are highly complex, continuously under nego-tiation and subject to change in the face of changing power relations.

A *kotta* arrangement is one where the ownership of an animal is shared: in its simplest form two individuals contribute equal cash amounts to buy the animal. One of them is the part owner and manager; the other is part owner only. *Kotta* is commonly done with large stock and is a half-and-half arrangement. In the case of the *kotta* ownership of an ox both individuals have rights to the draught power of the animal, while in the case of a cow, use of milk will be agreed between the two parties. The two households will alternately milk the cow on a weekly or monthly basis, or after each calf.

Households enter into *kotta* arrangements for various reasons. A household undergoing a period of stress may sell off part of what was a fully owned animal in order to raise cash. By selling only half the animal they are able to maintain access to its products, and may plan to buy back the other half at a later date when their

Table 3.12 Institutions mediating access to crop and livestock resources.

	Land	Oxen	Manure	Labour	Fodder	Grazing	Credit	Information/ equipment
Intra-household practices	Inheritance	Inheritance	Inheritance; on marriage	Family	Household management	Tenure	–	–
Local inter-household practices and groups	*Kotta*	*Kotta; gatua; woosa; hara;* for labour	*Kotta; ulo-kotta; hara; tirf yegera*	*Dago, zayea, woosa*	–	*Wudea*	*Iddir, equb,* friends	Neighbours, migrants and relatives
Local inter-household practices and groups (with cash transactions)	Contract	Purchase (whole or part *kotta*); hire	–	Hiring labour	Purchase (hay for cut-and-carry)	–	Money lender	–
Formal organisations (including the state)	Peasant Association	–	NGO livestock purchase schemes – e.g. Redd Barna	–	–	PA; State Farm	BoA/Global; State Farm; NGOs, e.g. Redd Barna, SOS Sahel, World Vision	BoA, PA, NGOs, e.g. Redd Barna, SOS–Sahel, World Vision

fortunes improve. Alternatively, a household attempting to build up a herd may buy half an animal. The two owners will share-own equally any offspring produced by a *kotta* cow.

Box 3.2   *Kotta*-owned livestock

'I have some livestock with my brother ... There was an original *kotta* cow [and] offspring which are all part-owned by my brother. We use the oxen for ploughing and give my brother butter – twice after each birth' (Balta Dessalaa, Admencho).

As the brother lives outside the PA he does not use any of the products, but the gifts recognise and express gratitude for the shared ownership. The part-ownership of livestock by migrants living away from 'home' seems to be an important way for migrants to invest in their home area, and to maintain a 'presence' at home.

'All the livestock that I own are on *kotta* basis. I first started buying on a *kotta* basis about six years ago because things were difficult for me. ... Close friends gave me half the money and we bought the livestock together. ...The benefit of owning livestock on *kotta* ... is that if conditions become harsh then rather than making a quick decision to sell the animal I have to consider the interests of the other person – so I can't sell the animal immediately. It means the livestock stay in the home. Also if I own oxen on *kotta* basis it allows me to plough my land in a good way. If I have two halves of an ox then I have access to two oxen, but that money would only allow me to buy one full ox so I would only have access to one ox. I look after the animal, cut grass, pay for the medicine, etc. and although the other person has a right to share ... as I pay for these things he isn't confident enough to take the ox to plough and he only uses it one or two times a year.' (Chemiso Chelke, Mundena).

Institutions that involve part ownership are seen as particularly beneficial: it is better to own two halves than one whole, as this gives you rights of access over two animals (whether for ploughing or for milk). Owning two halves is a means of spreading risk, particularly in areas where livestock disease is a significant problem. Also in situations where fodder and grazing are in short supply someone else has to invest the labour and effort in feeding. This applies to Admencho where fodder is in short supply and there is a cash market in cut-and-carry grass. Where disease increases the cost of maintaining the health of an animal these arrangements are particularly favourable to the owner who does not manage the animal. Usually the owner-manager pays most medical costs of an animal in their care unless they get into serious difficulties and may seek help from the other owner. *Kotta* arrangements consequently may have increased in high trypanosomiasis incidence areas. There has, however, been a change in the spatial scale of these arrangements. It used to be common for richer households in the highlands to share-own animals with people in the lowlands, but the perceived threat of disease in the lowlands has become so bad that highland owners are increasingly reluctant to enter into these arrangements. As a result there are more arrangements conducted between people in the same area, largely as a means of spreading the risk of disease.

Ulo-kotta is a similar arrangement and is used for smallstock (goats, sheep and poultry). Under this arrangement the owner gives the manager an animal that remains the property of the owner, and any offspring are shared equally. If the offspring are sold, the owner may deduct the cost of the original animal from the sale of the offspring, share any remaining profit and then the original animal belongs to both of them equally. If they do not sell the offspring, then both the offspring and the original animal belong to both of them (minus the cost of the original animal, which belongs to the original buyer). *Ulo-kotta* is especially important for women who invest profits from petty trading in *ulo-kotta* animals and build up their herds.

A related arrangement is *tirf yegera,* which literally means to share for profit. In this arrangement one individual buys an animal and gives it to a manager who fattens it. When they sell the animal they split the profit, as explained by a young woman living in Chokare State Farm:

> I have a *tirf yegara* ox with a State Farm worker. It is common to keep animals for people, and after taking out the original money we share the profit. I look after it, feed it and use it for ploughing. He also uses it for ploughing. ... After selling he will buy another one, and again I'll fatten and sell (Berehanesh Warana, Chokare).

Households also gain access to livestock in the long-term through *hara,* a share-rearing arrangement. Under a *hara* arrangement one person owns an animal outright and gives it to someone else to look after. The manager has no ownership rights over the animal, or its offspring. Products (including draught power) will usually be shared, but this depends in part on geography as these arrangements are often between households who live some distance apart. Migrants to urban areas often use *hara* arrangements to invest in livestock in their home area. Animals belonging to migrants are kept by relatives who use the products of the animal, giving gifts (often butter) to the owner.

There are a number of reasons why an animal may be lent out: shortage of space in a house, shortage of fodder and as part of a patronage relationship. Arrangements similar to those of today's *hara* used to exist in Admencho between landlords and their tenants and slaves, and so *hara* arrangements between non-relatives are now stigmatised and are generally avoided:

> I have never done *hara* because when people give for *hara* they want to consider the family [who looks after the animal] as something inferior and they try to order them ... [and] they also want to own us so I have never done that and wouldn't want to (Tadessa Ganta, Admencho).

In contrast, *hara* is more common in Mundena where it is usually between poor individuals and richer relatives or friends in the highlands:

> I have one ox, two cows and two calves, which I am looking after for someone else. He is not a relative but is of the same clan (*zaray*) from the place where I came from. I asked him because I have no husband and only a small son ... I look after them and keep them healthy. He first gave me an ox about four years ago, and when it was old we sold it, and then bought another one which I look after. He kept the profit that remained. ... He is very kind. ... I give him butter after each birth, and the calves also belong to him. It is poor people who have nothing who do this (Buje Bundasa, Mundena).

Under *hara* arrangements the owner keeps all the profit when the animal is sold. Medical costs of an animal held under *hara* will normally fall on the manager rather than the owner, until the manager gets into difficulties. If the manager continues to have difficulties in keeping the animal in good condition the owner may take it back. The risk to the health of the animal and the cost of treatments (if the manager is unable to pay) means richer households are increasingly reluctant to lend animals to people in high trypanosomiasis areas. In Mundena a major implication of disease is therefore the loss of longer-term borrowing arrangements of highlanders' animals. Fig. 3.7 shows the frequency of participation in these long-term arrangements.

A high percentage of households in Admencho and Mundena share-own livestock through *kotta*, *ulo-kotta* and *missa-kotta* arrangements. In Mundena, about a third of households are involved in *hara* arrangements, far more than in the other two sites. In contrast to Admencho, the relative homogeneity of the settler population in Mundena means that there are no such historical reasons for households to avoid participating in *hara* within the area. Furthermore, the existence of ample grazing land and fodder sources in Mundena encourages households from outside the area to lend their animals to households in Mundena. In Chokare there is a lower rate of participation in such arrangements generally – perhaps because of the ethnically divided nature of the PA and State Farm.

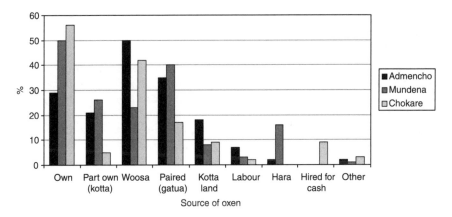

Figure 3.7 Participation in long-term livestock-sharing arrangements (for all livestock)

Short-term draught power and land-accessing arrangements

Short-term arrangements are commonly used to access oxen for ploughing, and are frequently linked with land-accessing arrangements. Most households do not own the necessary pair of oxen in full or part for their draught power needs.[30] The difference between the high rates of plough use and low rates of oxen ownership (among those that cultivated) was discussed above. In addition to the longer-term arrangements already discussed are short-term task-based accessing arrangements. These include pairing (*gatua*), borrowing for free (*woosa*), using in exchange for labour, hiring for cash and using as part of a land-sharing arrangement. Such

---

[30]Households were asked the number of livestock they owned (which could be a part of an animal) and the number of livestock kept in their house (which had to be a whole animal). This figure is for the number of animals owned by the household (including a part of an animal) irrespective of where the animal was kept.

arrangements are very common and are used by between 49 and 73 per cent of households in the three sites.

Gatua is a pairing arrangement whereby a household with access to one ox[31] pairs it with an animal of another household. The two households take it in turns to plough each other's field. No part of the harvest is exchanged as part of the arrangement. *Gatua* is reported to have increased as a result of the loss of animals to trypanosomiasis. Although it has the advantage of enabling a household with only one ox to plough its fields it means that the animal has to work on the fields of two households. This increases the work required of the animal, and is believed to further weaken it and increase its susceptibility to disease. The same is said of half-ownership (*kotta*) as animals have to work the land of two households.

A *woosa* arrangement is when one or two oxen are used for free. *Woosa* literally means to pray or beg, and is usually between friends and neighbours. No part of the harvest is exchanged as part of the arrangement. *Woosa* is common between relatives, in-laws and members of the same church, indicating that belonging to a strong social network can be key to gaining access to resources:

> I get oxen by begging from people in the Church or from others ... I ask one person today, and if they are busy I ask someone else until I get (Matewos Alola – Wolayta man living in Chokare PA).

Oxen may be used in return for labour. A household needing oxen borrows them from a friend or neighbour and in return agrees to work a certain number of days. The rates vary: in Admencho examples were given of one day of labour in return for one day of using a pair of oxen, while other examples were given of 2–3 days of labour for a day of using a pair of oxen. Oxen may be also hired for cash. Of our three sites this only occurs in Chokare, and at the time of our survey the rate was 10–12 Birr per pair per day.

A further short-term livestock-accessing arrangement is a sharecropping arrangement whereby access to oxen is linked to access to land and oxen are used in exchange for part of the harvest, also known as *kotta*. Oxen were accessed under this arrangement by 18 per cent of households in Admencho, and by nearly one in ten in Mundena and Chokare. Thus a landowner without access to oxen may ask someone else to come and plough his field, and will give half the harvest to the oxen owner. The case study below is of a woman who cultivates under a *kotta* arrangement with a town-dwelling oxen owner:

> I am a widow and I have no oxen ... there is a policeman who lives in Bele ... who comes here with two of his oxen, and uses my land. ... I arrange the labour – my neighbours come, and I give them coffee and food. The policeman and I share the harvest after paying our debts for fertiliser and seed (Buzenech Lachebo, Mundena).

The next case study illustrates the inter-linkages of land and livestock *kotta* arrangements:

> I own no oxen and only a small piece of land. Last season I made an arrangement with a person who owns some land neighbouring mine, and with another person who owns oxen. All three of

[31]The household does not necessarily have to fully own this animal, it may part-own it or hold it under a share-rearing arrangement. What is important is that under this arrangement the household is able to use the animal for draught power.

us contributed the seed and artificial fertiliser, and I did the ploughing, sowing and all the weeding. I will get a quarter of the harvest, the oxen owner gets a quarter, and the land owner gets a half (Abraham, Admencho).

Such *kotta* arrangements in Admencho need to be seen in the light of the land constraint. Here land owners can negotiate a good deal for themselves, and in the case above the land owner gets half of the harvest with no labour input. For others, such as widows, lending out land under a *kotta* arrangement is a vital means of maintaining a source of food in old age.

In Mundena there is a whole different set of constraints. Oxen, in particular, are a limiting factor, and individuals with a pair of oxen are able to get half the harvest for just a few days' work using those oxen. Here arrangements are entered into by households without oxen or by households wanting to gain access to different land or soil types, as illustrated by the following case studies:

> My friend lives near the forest where wild animals are – there he plants crops that are not affected by baboons (teff and boyna) and then comes here and does *kotta* [for the other crops]. We share the harvest (Maskale Japaray, Mundena).

> Usually I plant sweet potatoes on a *kotta* base on my neighbour's land ... because most of their land is *goba* [which is good for sweet potatoes]. Most of my land is ... not good for sweet potatoes (Jange Buche, Mundena).

Finding someone to enter such an arrangement with can be difficult in Mundena, particularly for those without access to male labour:

> When I ask [people to come and work my land] they say if you have someone who can plough then we'll give you oxen. No-one wants to come and work *kotta* here because they have a big enough area of their own to do – no-one has done *kotta* on my land since my husband died (Astero Anjulo – widow, Mundena).

Those most likely to cultivate other people's land under a *kotta* arrangement are young unmarried men. They do so in addition to working their family's land and do this in order to earn an income that they can keep for themselves:

> Before my father died I cultivated for two years under *kotta* with my neighbour ... and that money was for me (Dessalyn Bergene, Mundena).

These arrangements are affected by the availability of labour in the area. A new programme to construct irrigation works provides a cash income for some households, but to the detriment of other households:

> This year none of my land is done by *kotta*. I was looking for *kotta* but all people were working on the irrigation so no-one is available. ... I even said I'd cover the fertiliser and provide oxen, but no-one would do it (Astera Ako – female-headed household, Mundena).

In Mundena labour, in addition to oxen, is a major constraint. Policies that increase the demand for cash labourers have significant implications, as vulnerable households may lose access to labour through *kotta* arrangements. Female-headed households in Mundena are particularly vulnerable, as they do not have the network of relatives to call upon in times of extreme labour shortage.

In Chokare cultivating land on a *kotta* basis is particularly common among those without access to land, such as temporary State Farm workers:

> I don't have any private land, but for the last two years have worked other people's land on a *kotta* base. I do it because life became difficult here, and my salary was small (Mekonen Alo, State Farm worker).

> I ... have no land here ... I work on *kotta* base on other people's land. I work different land each year. The owner of the land provides land only – I arrange to get oxen by begging and I provide seed and labour, and then we divide the harvest equally. ... I work with Church members only. (Matewos Alola, Wolayta preacher living in Chokare).

The latter case illustrates again how membership of social networks, and church congregations in particular, can improve people's ability to enter into these kinds of arrangements.

The frequency with which long- and short-term arrangements to access oxen, in addition to ownership, were used (as a percentage of those households that used a plough) is shown in Fig. 3.8. This illustrates how each ox was accessed: some households used more than one method to gain access to oxen, and different methods are used in combination. While own and part-owned oxen are clearly critically important as a means for households to plough, other short-term arrangements are also significant. *Woosa* was the most important in Admencho, being used by 50 per cent of households, while 35 per cent and 40 per cent of households in Admencho and Mundena respectively paired animals, making *gatua* crucial. In Mundena animals being reared under *hara* arrangements were used by 16 per cent of households, while in Chokare 9 per cent of households hired oxen for cash. The following section will examine how institutional involvement is socially differentiated in the three sites.

Gaining access to fodder

Households also enter into arrangements with one another to gain access to fodder. One such arrangement is the *wudea,* which operates in Mundena and Chokare. This is a grazing management system that occurs seasonally: a number of households' live-stock are grouped together and taken out for grazing by each *wudea* member in turn.[32] There is also a cash market for fodder in Admencho: a one-off payment is made to the owner of a hay field, which allows the payer to cut grass whenever it is needed. In Chokare the State Farm allows herds to graze their fallow land and crop residues on payment of a cash fee. State Farm land is particularly sought after because of the location, ease of access and the quality of grazing, and households wanting to graze this land buy the right to do so by paying a fee to the Farm.

> After the cotton harvest all the *zelan* [Sidama] people come, and together [with SF workers] we contribute money to the State Farm and graze there. Last year I paid 2/50 Birr. ...We pay 1 Birr for one hectare and divide the money by the number of households who will graze the area. It is not related to the number of livestock. We pay the money to the State Farm – it is official and we even get a receipt. People are not allowed to graze their animals unless they have paid the money. ... Most of those who pay are State Farm workers ... but most of the livestock that graze are owned by PA people (Yaya Tigiru, State Farm resident).

---

[32]It is not used in Mundena during the hot season when animals are kept indoors to protect them from tsetse fly. In Chokare animals are taken further afield for grazing during the wet season.

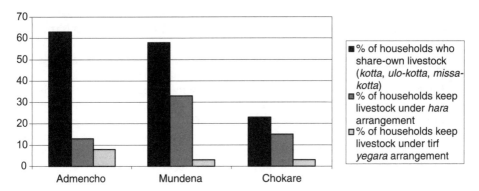

Figure 3.8 Access to oxen for ploughing (of those households that ploughed)

Differentiated livestock access by wealth and gender

In Admencho and Mundena a higher proportion of richer households are involved in lending animals out under both short- and long-term arrangements. In these sites animals are always kept inside the house, and so rich households, which own more animals, have to lend them out under long-term arrangements either because they do not have enough room to house them, or to ease pressure on fodder sources, or to spread risk from disease – particularly if animals are lent to households some distance away.

In all sites a higher proportion of poorer groups borrow animals over the long term. The only exception to this is in Admencho, where a lower proportion of the poorest wealth group borrow under long-term arrangements. The most likely explanation for this is that members of this group are so poor that their access to grazing land and labour (necessary for cut-and-carry work) in a site where fodder is a key constraint, is limited, and thus their ability to enter long-term livestock-accessing arrangements.

Involvement in short-term arrangements to access oxen for ploughing is also socially differentiated. In Admencho a higher proportion of poor households used oxen under *woosa* arrangements compared to richer households. In the other two sites a large proportion of poorer households used this method, but there is less of a clear difference between groups. Similarly, a higher proportion of poorer households in Admencho used oxen in return for labour than richer households, but there is no similar clear pattern elsewhere. Only in Chokare did anyone rent oxen for cash, and all were State Farm workers (who receive a cash income). Using oxen in return for part of the harvest was an arrangement entered into by a higher proportion of poorer households in Admencho, and richer households in Mundena. In Chokare this arrangement was used by a higher proportion of non-working State Farm residents and temporary workers, than permanent workers. Thus in each site there are broadly different constraints felt by richer and poorer households, and as a result different land and livestock-accessing arrangements are entered into.

In all sites male-headed households own slightly more livestock than female-headed households, but there is less of a difference in numbers of livestock kept in the house. This is an important distinction, for while ownership may be gender differentiated, access is less so, because of the institutional arrangements discussed. Both male- and female-headed households in Admencho own more livestock than they keep, but there is no difference between the two groups. In Mundena the opposite pattern is true, but again there is little difference in the pattern between male- and female-headed households. Thus, in Admencho and Mundena, the gender of household head does not apparently affect involvement in these long-term institutional arrangements.

However, some of these institutional arrangements are particularly important for women and female-headed households. In all sites a higher proportion of female- than male-headed households borrow livestock under long-term arrangements, and, conversely, a higher proportion of male- than female-headed households lend out livestock in the long term. Similarly, a higher proportion of male- than female-headed households are involved in short-term lending arrangements.[33]

Getting access to oxen for free does not resolve the problem of a shortage of adult male labour that many female-headed households suffer from. Ploughing is seen to be a purely male task, and female-headed households without adult male labour are effectively excluded from involvement in arrangements that provide oxen, but not the labour to plough with. In all sites of those households that use oxen for free under *woosa* arrangements, only 20 per cent were female-headed. One might expect vulnerable households such as widows to be more likely to enter *woosa* arrangements, but this is not the case as accessing oxen by *woosa* does not necessarily include labour. Similarly, no female-headed households gained access to oxen in exchange for labour or oxen for cash, as neither of these arrangements provide labour with the oxen.

In all sites there is a clear difference in involvement in sharecropping arrangements between male- and female-headed households. A higher percentage of female-headed households give out part of their harvest under a sharecropping arrangement, and a lower percentage receive harvest under a sharecropping arrangement. It does not follow from this that these households are in any way worse off for having to enter such arrangements: in most cases these households would not be able to cultivate their land at all if they did not enter these arrangements. It is through participation in such institutional arrangements that the livelihoods of these households are secured.

The institutions discussed in this section enable households or individuals who do not own resources to gain access to them. But this does not imply that everyone is equally able to access resources through these institutions. For reasons of history, power relations and social and cultural contexts some are better able to negotiate access to resources, resulting in different social actors following different paths of agricultural change. The following section will look further at the pathways of change that exist and some of the factors that influence these.

Pathways of change

Differences between the sites

As the previous two sections have shown, historical events and processes and institutional arrangements are central to any explanation of the observed multiple pathways of

---

[33]The only exception is in Chokare where a higher proportion of female-headed households are involved in short-term lending arrangements – perhaps because of the higher level of membership of polygamous households among these female-headed households in Chokare.

change. Table 3.13 summarises the range of pathways of change evident across the three sites, the practices involved and the resources required for such a pathway to be pursued.

Different pathways have different benefits. For example, one pathway may be better suited to households with labour constraints, while another might be suited to those with ample land. A different set of institutional arrangements will be critical for each. For example, to follow pathway D (intensification through increased labour inputs only, without associated increases in capital) the institutions that enable access to labour (working groups, etc.) are particularly critical. The enset and root crop gardening systems of the highland areas of Wolayta are good examples of this sort of intensification. This requires considerable labour for hand-hoeing, manuring and weeding. Policies obviously have an influence on options and choices. For example, the vigorous promotion of the Global Package (pathway C) may make it difficult to switch between intensification strategies, as labour and other inputs are diverted from other options. Trends (such as the increase in livestock disease) and events (e.g. famine) also influence the conditions for agricultural intensification, constraining some options and promoting others. The decline in livestock availability through, for example, trypanosomiasis mortalities has limited intensive ploughing and manuring options for many. Thus across the sites, depending on the prevailing conditions, a diversity of pathways is evident, influenced by the conjuncture of policy, historical events and trends and socioeconomic conditions.

Differences between and within households

The diversity of potential pathways of change is increased yet further when we look at differences between and within households, as the bundle of assets to which individuals and households have access determines which pathways of change they follow. Differences within sites are seen both between and within households based, for example, on wealth, gender, ethnicity and historical experience (Table 3.14).

Wealthier households are better able to follow pathways of agricultural change that require use of external inputs and credit. As Fig. 3.9 shows, there is higher usage of

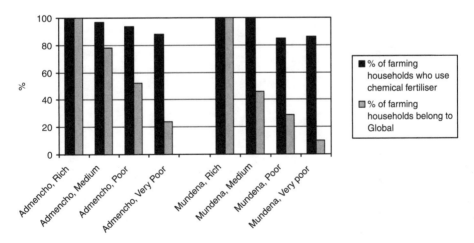

Figure 3.9 Indicators of following the capital-led pathway of change, by wealth group

Table 3.13 Pathways of change available in each site.

Pathway of agricultural change	Agricultural practices involved, resources needed	Crop-livestock integration practices involved	Available in Admencho?	Available in Mundena?	Available in Chokare?
A – Extensification	Expand area cultivated without increasing ratio of capital or labour to land	More ploughing; greater use of inputs (manure, chemical fertiliser)	No	Yes	Yes
B – Expansion of irrigated land (intensification with increased capital inputs)	Access to irrigable land, increased use of labour and/or other capital inputs	More ploughing	No	No (Yes, in future)	Yes
C – Expansion of production through increased (non-labour) inputs (Global model)	Focus on cereal cropping with external inputs. Access to credit, improved seed, more labour	More ploughing	Yes	Yes	No
D – Intensification through increased labour inputs only (based on gardening of enset, root crops, etc.)	Labour and manure	More ploughing, more manuring, more weeding, etc.	Yes	Yes	Yes
E – Towards a mixed farming model	Integrated cropping and livestock systems on one farm unit; use of chemical fertiliser	Private grazing; fodder market; oxen for ploughing; use of manure	Yes	Yes	Yes
F – Integration of communal rangelands and individual cropping	May be some external inputs for agriculture production	Ploughing, communal grazing; no fodder market	No	Yes	Yes
G – Specialisation of part of agriculture	For example: livestock production, fattening	For example: cut-and-carry fodder	Yes	Yes	Yes

H – Specialisation on livestock	Focus on livestock production, movement away from agricultural production	Ample access to grazing, fodder. May plough other people's land (*kotta*)	Yes	Yes	Yes	Yes
I – Separate intensification of cropping, and of livestock production	Based on external inputs	May require more ploughing	Yes	Yes	Yes	Yes
J – Abandonment of large livestock production	Focus on smallstock, may also be shift to livelihood diversification	Use of cut-and-carry for fodder, crop residues, household refuse	Yes	Yes	Yes	Yes
	Hoe-based cultivation; root crop; (away from cereals and ploughs); with livelihood diversification	Focus on garden production; decline in plough use	Yes	Yes	Yes	Yes
K – Abandonment of agriculture and livestock production	Opportunities for livelihood diversification	–	Yes	Yes	Yes	Yes
	Opportunities for migration	–	Yes	Yes	Yes	Yes

Table 3.14 Factors of difference influencing differences in pathways of change followed.

	Wealth	Gender	Ethnicity
Admencho	Wealthier households are better able to follow pathways that require external inputs, credit, etc. (influencing the ability to follow, for example, paths B & C)	Female-headed households may suffer from shortage of male labour, access to which is crucial for ploughing (influencing the ability to follow paths A, B, C, D, E, F, I)	Ethnically homogeneous, but clan system and history of landlordism, tenancy and slavery influential
Mundena	Wealthier households are better able to follow paths that require external inputs, credit, etc. (influencing ability to follow, for example, paths B & C)	Female-headed households may suffer from shortage of male labour, access to which is crucial for ploughing (influencing the ability to follow paths A, B, C, D, E, F, I)	Ethnically homogeneous
Chokare	Wealthier Sidama households are better able to specialise in livestock production (path H)	Female-headed households may suffer from shortage of male labour, access to which is crucial for ploughing (influencing the ability to follow paths A, B, C, D, E, F, I)	Cultural norms around agricultural practices: manure application by Wolayta; nomadism of Sidama (path H) Influence on networks with key individuals, crucial for access to land (esp. irrigable land) (paths A, B)

fertiliser and membership of the Global programme among richer wealth groups in Admencho and Mundena.

Male-headed households are more likely to follow pathways that involve increased capital inputs. Similarly, households with more adults, and households that participate in labour-accessing arrangements outside the household, are also more likely to be following these pathways of change (Table 3.15). Although more labour may be needed (with the increased capital inputs), an absence of labour resources may mean that a labour-led pathway is impossible, and therefore force a household to follow a capital-led pathway to the best of its abilities. Labour shortage within the household also influences pathways that necessitate increasing labour inputs alone.

The number of adults in the household may be a result of the position within the demographic cycle: young households, older households and widowed households have fewer active adult labourers in general. Many female-headed households suffer from labour constraints. This has major implications for decisions around which pathway is followed. In places where there is no land constraint, such as Mundena, there is no incentive for labour-rich households to cultivate land on a sharecropping (*kotta*) basis from labour-poor households who have access to land (as is the case in Admencho and Mundena) (see Box 3.3). Having plentiful adult labour enables a household to participate in other off-farm activities that provides other income that can be spent on agriculture (inputs, hiring labour, etc.). Thus ample labour not only

Table 3.15 Uptake of capital-led intensification by gender of household head and labour-related factors.

	% who use chemical fertiliser	% who belong to Global
Male household head	93	46
Female household head	88	30
Households with 3 or more adults	96	53
Households with 2 adults	89	38
Households with 1 adult	83	11
Participate in labour-accessing arrangements outside the household	94	47
Do not participate in labour-accessing arrangements outside household	83	29

Adult = aged 16 and over

enables a household to invest more labour on its farm (which, if this is the only activity, would lead to pathway D), but may enable the household to follow a more capital-led path (pathway C or E), as well as diversify its income (pathway K). Access to labour therefore gives households the widest range of options.

Box 3.3 illustrates how a household may use different practices within the farm for different plot and crop types, giving rise to different pathways simultaneously. There are few areas where an individual within a household has full control over cropping decisions, but broadly speaking men have more control over cereal crops grown on *shoqa* (which involve the use of the plough), while women have more control over root crops in the *darkua*. Labour demands for some agricultural tasks, and some spaces, are gendered. Labour demands in *darkua* are higher for women (through manure application, enset management and *makotkot* weeding with a hoe), while in *shoqa* the labour demands are higher for men (through ploughing, and *shilshallo* with oxen). Both male and female labour is critical to the agricultural system as a whole, and the lack of one labour type will encourage the household to follow a particular pathway of change. Thus a labour-led pathway of intensification, focused on the *darkua*, requires more female labour, while a more capital-led pathway in the *shoqa* requires more male labour.

The historical experiences of individuals and their land influences cropping decisions such as which crops are to be planted where and with what inputs. For example, in Admencho an area of Dasta Gadiso's farm is farmed in such a way that it would appear to be *darkua*, but it was neither close to the house, nor referred to as *darkua*. Only through plot histories were the reasons for this revealed: in the past the land had belonged to a tenant who died without sons, and this land was absorbed by Dasta, his ex-landlord.

Box 3.3   Labour availability, institutional involvement and pathways of change

Astera Ako is a widow with young children living in Mundena who suffers from a serious shortage of labour. She earns a cash income from selling livestock products (mainly butter). To get access to labour she uses either *woosa* or *asrat* arrangements[34] with Church members, or (when she can afford it) employs labourers. At the time of interview she was employing two young men to work on her *darkua*. She pays them cash, and provides them with food while they are working for her. She mainly employs people who dig in the *darkua*, and looks to *woosa* and *asrat* for other work such as ploughing and planting.

Astera wanted some of her *shoqa* land to be cultivated under a sharecropping (*kotta*) arrangement. This would have involved using a plough and buying inputs including fertiliser (a broadly capital-led pathway of change). However, her inability to find anyone prepared to sharecrop her land[35] meant that she was forced to focus on work that does not require oxen. This in turn means that she decided to purchase only a small amount of fertiliser (on the open market) and did not buy the Global Package, so did not use improved seed varieties. In the end she did, with the help of Church members, cultivate some *shoqa*. But the decisions that she made around fertiliser and seeds were made largely because she did not have secure and full access to draught power. Female-headed households in Mundena are particularly vulnerable as they do not have the network of relatives to call upon in times of extreme labour shortage.

Remnants of past soil conservation measures also explain spatial differences in pathways of change being followed at a micro level. In Mundena during the early settlement period WADU encouraged the construction of terraces as a soil conservation measure and to mark boundaries between plots. Where these still exist they may influence the pathways of change: for example, one poorly maintained terrace has partly broken down so that it acts as a funnel for rainwater. The severe soil erosion that has resulted led the farmer firstly to reduce the inputs he applied to that land, and eventually to abandon that part of his land.

Conclusions

Both across and within the sites a wide diversity of pathways of change is evident, conditioned by historical experiences, policy interventions, formal and informal institutional arrangements and patterns of social differentiation. A single, linear pathway of change is clearly not in evidence, nor a 'typical' farmer or farming system. Each pathway identified has responded to a range of conditioning factors,

---

[34] *Asrat* is a tithe arrangement with the Church. All Church members are expected to contribute part of their harvest to the Church, and to offer their labour for the Church on a regular (weekly or bi-weekly) basis. Church elders organise this labour, which is either used to work on Church land, or on the land of needy Church members, such as Astera Ako.

[35] Generally land is not a constraint in Mundena. Certain land types are more highly valued, and there is therefore some demand to cultivate these under sharecropping arrangements. Currently an irrigation construction works is providing a demand for cash labour, and many young men who might otherwise be doing some sharecropping work are instead working on the irrigation works. Young men often sharecrop some additional land before marrying, and the income that they earn from this is considered to be their own.

with outcomes often unpredictable. Different pathways of agricultural change and interactions between crops and livestock are followed at different times and scales and by different groups. Households may follow a number of strategies consecutively: they will do this taking into account the resources to which they have access, through the various institutional arrangements available, and the perceived risk of the different options. Which pathway is followed therefore depends on what resources are available and on the household's ability to access those resources, and this is far from uniform.

In all the sites a huge array of institutional arrangements exists through which households access resources. These institutions are flexible, dynamic and subject to change. The case of Admencho has revealed how the institutions of *kotta* (land – sharecropping) and *hara* (livestock rearing) have changed following the Revolution. In situations of extreme scarcity (e.g. following oxen death in Mundena as a result of trypanosomiasis) the institutional arrangements may come close to collapse (as illustrated by the decline in *hara* arrangements). Alternatively, other institutions may take their place, for example, the increased importance of work parties organised through the Church. Despite their immense importance for sustainable livelihoods, current research and extension pays little or no attention to these institutions, and they are virtually ignored by policy-makers.

So how does current research and extension policy respond to this variety of context and experience? As noted earlier, most research and extension efforts over the past decades have had a particular image of the mixed farmer in mind. But, as we have seen, this ignores many alternative practices and strategies. Table 3.16 lists the range of pathways identified for the study sites, how common they are for different actor groups, and the range of institutional and policy constraints that exist for those pursuing them. The table also assesses the degree to which current policy supports each pathway.

As previous sections of this chapter have shown, many policies potentially influence crop-livestock interactions – market reform, land tenure, credit, agricultural research and extension and veterinary services have all been seen to be significant. Yet few of the pathways identified are currently supported by such policies and interventions. For example, the research and extension system in Ethiopia today, with its hybrid seeds, chemical fertiliser and credit, as epitomised by the Global Package, has a particular model of an Ethiopian farmer in mind: a market-orientated, cereal producer who uses inorganic fertiliser inputs and has adequate access to draught power. The narrow focus on cereal crops (particularly maize), a particular geographical area (high potential), and particular groups (those with higher and diversified incomes who are able to make down-payments, etc.) leaves significant gaps. Other pathways are not really considered. The current extension package, for example, largely ignores those farmers who invest most of their effort in the more traditional root crop/enset, manure-based gardening system. In fact, almost all farmers in the study areas are involved in this on at least part of their land, and under this strategy the linkages between crops and livestock through manuring and residue recycling are critical.

In conclusion, our research has shown clearly the importance of institutional arrangements in facilitating access to resources that a household or individual does not itself own – resources that are essential for crop and livestock production and

Table 3.16 Pathways of change, additional constraints, actor groups and policy compatibility.

Pathway of agricultural change	How common overall?	Additional policy and institutional constraints	Actor groups likely to follow pathway	Support from current policy
A – Extensification	Rare, except for those with social network	Land availability	Those with key social networks to gain access to land	–
B – Expansion of irrigated land (intensification with increased capital inputs)	Now rare, little irrigable land left	Irrigability; water supply	Those with key social networks to gain access to land	–
C – Expansion of production through increased (non-labour) inputs (Global model)	Common for richer	Infrastructure, service provision	Richer groups	★★★
D – Intensification through increased labour inputs only	Common for poorer; common for all on part of farm	Other labour demands, labour market	Poorer (without access to additional inputs, but labour-rich)	–
E – Towards a mixed farming model	Average		Richer	★★★
F – Integration of communal rangelands and individual cropping	Common		All	★★
G – Specialisation of part of agriculture	Common	Markets	All	★
H – Specialisation on livestock	Rare, except for richer Sidama	Livestock disease, grazing/fodder availability	Ethnicity; richer Sidama	–
I – Separate intensification of cropping, and of livestock production	Average		Richer	★★
Ji – Abandonment of large livestock production – smallstock focus	Common, may be combined with K	Markets	Poorer	–
Jii – Abandonment of large livestock production – vegetable garden focus	Common, may be combined with K	Markets	Poorer	–
Ki – Abandonment of agriculture and livestock production: livelihood diversification activities	Common, may be combined with J	Markets, credit availability, opportunities to diversify	All (depends on type of livelihood diversification: coping/accumulating)	–
Kii – Abandonment of agriculture and livestock production: migration	Common, may be combined with J	Opportunities to migrate, regionalisation	All, especially young (depends on type of migration: crisis/ accumulating)	–

achieving sustainable livelihoods. Access to resources, and involvement in the institutions that mediate this access, is differentiated by site and actor group. The institutions may operate in a way that is more beneficial for one party than the other, but without the institutional arrangement both parties would be significantly worse-off. The result of these institutional processes over time is a variety of different pathways of change, associated with different socioeconomic groups and apparent in different agroecological settings.

In the Ethiopian context, there is an urgent need for a greater understanding of other pathways of change, beyond those conventionally supported by package programmes designed for relatively wealthy highland cereal farmers. This requires, critically, insights into the institutions that constrain or promote these, in order to ensure that a more comprehensive coverage of technology development options is achieved. Approaches better suited to poorer farmers, and those pursuing alternative strategies of agricultural and livestock production, which may be low-input and rely more on the efficient use of available resources, are particularly required. More flexible agricultural extension packages are needed, which are adaptable to the varying needs of different actor groups. Broadening research and extension so that it supports a wider range of pathways of change, particularly those being pursued by the poor and marginalised, is therefore a key policy challenge.

4

Crops, Livestock & Livelihoods in Zimbabwe

WILLIAM WOLMER, BEVLYNE SITHOLE
& BILLY MUKAMURI

Introduction

Zimbabwean smallholder farmers have long been mixed farmers in the sense that they have managed both crops and livestock rather than pursuing purely agricultural or pastoral livelihoods. However, a central tenet of agricultural research and extension in the country over the last 70 years has been the promotion of a particular technical package of land and animal husbandry whereby the two are tightly integrated on a 'mixed farm'. To this end efforts have been made to hasten the presumed 'natural' evolution of mixed farming by encouraging use of oxen for ploughing, the application of cattle manure to fields, and the feeding of crop residues and sown forages to cattle. Such a model has also informed much thinking about strategies for land reform and resettlement since Independence in 1980. It is our contention that this package owes as much to social and political as to technical aims and that it has neglected the diversity of other strategies pursued by smallholder farmers as they manage land and livestock and downplayed the importance of institutional arrangements to their livelihoods.

This chapter examines the dynamics of crop–livestock integration in Zimbabwe. It traces the history of crop and livestock management and explores the diverse strategies that underpin crop–livestock interaction or integration in four sites in order to unravel the pathways of change followed by different actors. We also attempt to uncover the institutional dynamics beneath superficially technical issues such as manure application and draught power use. This focus on social differentation and institutional arrangements challenges certain assumptions underpinning attempts to encourage the 'natural progression' to 'mixed farming' and thus has significant implications for research and extension policy.

The case study sites

The study took place in four areas in Zimbabwe. Chipuriro, Neshangwe, Ngundu and Chikombedzi were chosen to represent two notional transects between relatively higher and relatively lower resource endowment sites in the north and south of the country, respectively (see Fig. 4.1, Table 4.1). They differ markedly agroecologically and socioeconomically, and this has led to very different historical experiences of crop and livestock interactions in each.[1]

Chipuriro and Neshangwe are located in the northeast of the country in Guruve District, Mashonaland Central Province, which borders Zambia to the north and Mozambique to the northeast. The district is distinctly and strikingly divided into two areas by the vertiginous sweep of the Mavuradonha escarpment, which separates the highveld from the Zambezi valley. Chipuriro communal area is in Upper Guruve to the south, and above the escarpment, while Neshangwe is found 600 metres below in Lower Guruve in the valley. Ngundu and Chikombedzi, on the other hand, are located in the south of the country in Masvingo Province. Ngundu is in the granite *kopje*-studded Chivi District on the main Harare to South Africa road, and Chikombedzi is found in the extreme southeast of the country in Matibi II communal area, Chiredzi District, in the flat, dry lowveld bordering Gonarezhou National Park.

Table 4.1 Comparison of the ecological characteristics of the study sites.

	Higher resource endowment		Lower resource endowment	
	Chipuriro	**Ngundu**	**Neshangwe**	**Chikombedzi**
Average rainfall	750–1000 mm	550–800 mm	350–900 mm	330–660 mm
Average annual temperature	21°C	24°C	27°C	30°C
Soil type	Sand to sandy clay loams derived from granite	Mix of clay and sandy soils	Mostly sandy loams and clay, some red soils	Mostly black basalt clays, some red clays and sands
Vegetation type	Patches of *miombo* woodland: dystrophic savanna	Patches of *miombo* woodland: dystrophic savanna	Lowland *mopane*: eutrophic savanna	Lowland *mopane*: eutrophic savanna
Natural region classification	IIA	IV	IV	V

[1]This chapter draws on research carried out between 1997 and 1998 in Chivi, Guruve and Chiredzi Districts by the Institute of Environmental Studies, University of Zimbabwe and the Institute of Development Studies, University of Sussex. The methodology combined a questionnaire survey with qualitative methods including: rapid rural appraisal, key informant interviews, group discussions and oral histories; and use of archival materials. We thank Witness Kozanayi and Manyewu Mutamba from the Institute of Environmental Studies; Felix Murimbarimba from the Farming Systems Research Unit of the Department of Research and Specialist Services; Jacob Mahenehene; and our informants in Harare, Chivi and Chikombedzi. Ian Scoones, Gilles Kleitz and Bruce Campbell provided helpful comments on draughts of this chapter.

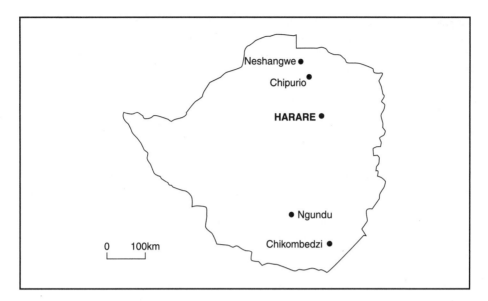

Figure 4.1   The Zimbabwe study sites

The key agroecological difference between the sites is that the areas with relatively higher resource endowments are characterised by higher, more reliable rainfall and lower temperatures, while the areas with lower resource endowments have lower, irregular rainfall and are consequently prone to drought – particularly Chikombedzi. This difference is reflected by the 'Natural Region' classifications.[2] It is important to note, however, that there are substantial differences between the two notionally higher resource endowment areas (designated as belonging to regions IIA and IV, respectively). In 1991–2 a particularly severe drought had devastating effects on livestock numbers in Ngundu and Chikombedzi; and in 2000 uncharacteristically heavy rainfall brought massive flooding to the Chikombedzi area.

The higher-altitude Chipuriro and Ngundu are characterised by patches of *miombo* woodland, while Chikombedzi and Neshangwe are dominated by swathes of *mopane* trees, characteristic of the lowveld. Soil types range from the heavy basalt clays around Chikombedzi to sodic and red soils. Yet, within any area, different landscape patches can be found resulting from variations in topography, micro-scale soil type variations and human action (such as old kraal and settlement sites) (Scoones 1997). Wildlife is more common in some sites than others. In the Zambezi valley site, Neshangwe, wildlife is plentiful, and elephants regularly damage crops and lions take livestock. More significantly, though, the dense bush harbours the tsetse fly which, until the success of recent eradication programmes, has historically prevented cattle

[2]The 'Natural Region' classification (Vincent and Thomas 1960) is based on rainfall amount and variability, with NR I having the highest, most regular, rainfall (over 1,000 mm a year) and NR V the lowest, most erratic rainfall. This classification has led to recommendations on the most productive and suitable land uses for the different regions. For example, areas designated as Natural Region V, such as Chikombedzi, have been characterised as only useful for extensive ranching.

ownership in the Neshangwe area. Crop damage by elephants to farms near Gonarezhou National Park is also common in Chikombedzi.

At 71/km² population density is markedly higher in Chipuriro than in Ngundu (44.5/km²), Neshangwe (c. 20/km²) and Chikombedzi (14/km²). However, the relatively low figure for the Chikombedzi area obscures the fact that, as is described below, land alienation and in-migration to the Chikombedzi area has led to a relatively high population density in the zone surrounding the township. In recent years the AIDS epidemic has had a drastic effect on Zimbabwe's demographic profile, and this impact is being felt in all four of the study sites.

Korekore are the majority ethnic group in Chipuriro and Neshangwe, while Karanga dominate in Ngundu and Shangaan in Chikombedzi. But all the sites are ethnically diverse as a result of ongoing migrations. At times different ethnic groups have pursued different farming strategies.

Differing infrastructural development means that the four sites have variable access to markets. Chipuriro is located near Harare, and Ngundu is located at a major junction on the main road to South Africa. Neshangwe is more remote, although a large cotton depot has been established nearby. Chikombedzi, on the other hand, remains relatively isolated from markets, as it is reached only after 90 km of badly corrugated 'dust' tracks after leaving the tarred road. The area and infrastructure were also badly damaged in the floods of 2000.

The farming systems

The main technical elements of the archetypal 'mixed farm', which have long been at the heart of Zimbabwean agricultural extension, are: application of cattle manure; the use of draught oxen; and the intensive feeding of livestock with crop residues and sown fodder. Indeed, in order to become a 'Master Farmer', trainees must broadly follow this model.[3] Yet farmers' current strategies with regard to these elements differ markedly across the four sites as crops and livestock are integrated to varying degrees and in different ways (Table 4.2). These differences are explored in the following sections.

Crops, fields and gardens

Farmers in Zimbabwe generally divide their crops between home fields near the homestead and more distant, generally larger, fields and, in some cases, gardens. In Chikombedzi, where population densities are lowest and land relatively available, the average away field size is largest (8 ha), putting a premium on draught power. In Chipuriro and Ngundu, where population densities are much higher, people cultivate more intensively on smaller plots (average away field sizes are 2.4 ha and 2.8 ha, respectively) and manure, for restoring soil fertility, as well as draught power, are valued inputs.[4]

---

[3]For example, the Master Farmer Trainee Record book used by Agritex in 1999 demonstrates the centrality of a mixed farming approach to the agricultural extension system.

[4]The quantitative data in this section is drawn from a questionnaire survey that sampled 200 households in each of the four sites.

Table 4.2   An overview of the farming systems in the study areas.

	Higher resource endowment		Lower resource endowment	
	Chipuriro	**Ngundu**	**Neshangwe**	**Chikombedzi**
Cropping system	Maize, cotton	Maize, cotton, intensive gardening	Cotton, maize on riverine terraces, river bank gardening	Sorghum, maize mainly for home consumption
Livestock breeds	Indigenous	Mostly Mashona crosses, increasing number of Brahman crosses evident	Indigenous, some trypano-tolerant breeds	Mixed breeds predominate – crosses of exotics with indigenous
Other elements of livelihood system	Wage labour	Wage labour, wood carving	Wildlife revenue	Livestock sales, remittances

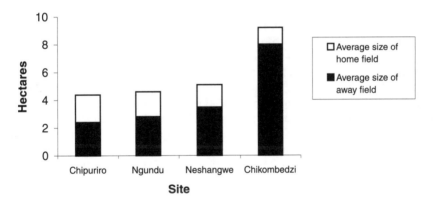

Figure 4.2   Average field sizes

A large variety of crops are grown in each area with marked variations in the particular mix. Maize is universally popular, both as a staple and a cash crop. Cotton is becoming increasingly important in all sites except Chikombedzi and is particularly central in Neshangwe. In Chipuriro, paprika has recently become favoured as a high-earning crop. A recent influential development has been the spread of contract farming, encouraged by the entry of new companies into crop marketing with deregulation and the privatisation of parastatals brought about by the Economic Structural Adjustment Programme (ESAP).

Farming is a particularly risky business in Chikombedzi where frequent drought means that yields of even drought-tolerant crops are often very low or non-existent. In three out of five years farmers in Chikombedzi experience food deficits. Recent development of irrigation schemes has improved production averages but has failed to cater fully for the deficit.

Gardens are a key element of people's cropping strategies and are becoming an increasingly important element of many people's livelihoods – especially so in Chipuriro and Ngundu (where 48 and 61 per cent, respectively, of households sampled had gardens). Vegetables are sold as far away as Beitbridge and Chiredzi. Gardens tend to be concentrated along rivers, or near dams or boreholes. Gardening is most common when the cropping season tails off (around April, with peak involvement in August and September) and ceases when cropping starts in November. Crops grown include tomatoes, leaf vegetables, okra and maize.

In Neshangwe there is a long history of gardening by the Korekore people on riverine plots. Vegetables are grown on river bank and river bed plots and maize on alluvial terraces (*dimbas*). Cultivation moves progressively towards the water as the dry season proceeds. Lack of water, and the large expense of digging wells or boreholes, discourages garden ownership in Chikombedzi (where only 12 per cent of households had gardens).

Soil fertility management

In the relatively higher resource endowment study sites use of soil fertility supplements including manure is markedly more common than in the lower resource endowment areas (see Fig. 4.3). In Chikombedzi large fields, fertile basalt soils and lack of rain mean that little or no soil fertility supplements are applied to the field. Manure, it is held, would scorch crops; and in Neshangwe low numbers of livestock and relatively fertile soils also militate against manure use.

Agritex (the Zimbabwean agricultural extension agency) has historically recommended that 37 tonnes of manure be applied to each hectare of cultivated land every four years. To fertilise a 3–4 ha field this would require a herd of 20–25 cattle to supply adequate manure. Unsurprisingly, such recommendations are rarely adopted in practice. In Ngundu, for example, where manure use is a particularly key component in maintaining soil fertility, both in outfields and in gardens, the general lack of livestock since the 1991–2 drought (see below) means manure is in short supply and tends to be applied on a rotational basis. Mr Komwedzai, for example, applies enough

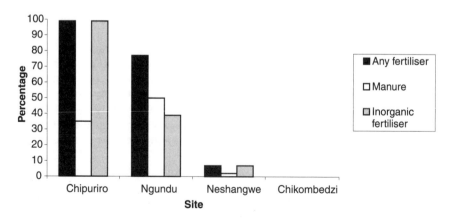

Figure 4.3 Percentage of households applying soil fertility supplements.

manure to his tomatoes to last two to three seasons. Since tomatoes do not use a lot of this fertility, when he subsequently rotates the field with maize it will use the residual fertility and both crops benefit from the application. Farmers also take advantage of micro-scale variations in topography and soil fertility and strategically apply manure to key niches in the landscape (Scoones 1997). A range of other strategies are entered into to manage scarce manure supplies or access manure. Box 4.1 describes two of these.

Box 4.1 Manure management strategies

Mr Komwedzai has an innovative strategy of manure use. To increase the volume of manure, as per Agritex recommendations he adds grass and crop residue to the kraal, which is mixed with the manure by the trampling of the cattle. Agritex recommend that the manure should be dug out of the kraal in July/August, left in a heap to decompose [and so seeds in the manure rot and do not germinate in the field] and applied to the fields in October. But Mr Komwedzai digs out the manure in May to apply to his irrigation scheme plot and early planted crops. He continues adding grass and crop residue to the kraal. This is also for fodder purposes as grazing land gets scarce in the dry season.
Then in September/October the manure is dug out of his kraal a second time – as with the addition of grass and crop residue its volume will have increased substantially. This manure is then applied to late-planted crops such as maize and tomatoes (which do well with well-decomposed manure). The advantage of this strategy is that manure is made available for early crops where previously there was a deficit. By emptying the kraal a second time before the rains Mr Komwedzai also avoids the problem of accumulating too much manure in the wet season, which gets boggy and potentially infectious to cattle.
Another farmer in Ngundu, who is without cattle, deliberately leaves his crop residue *in situ* and has trees in his fields. As most of the surrounding farmers gather their crop residue for fodder and many fields are winter-ploughed, wandering livestock in search of grazing are attracted to the crop residue and shade in his fields. This means that manure is deposited in large amounts there.

A closer examination of soil fertility management strategies in Chipuriro and Ngundu reveals important differences. Of the farmers sampled the amounts of manure (by the cart load) reported to have been used in the last agricultural season were fairly similar in the two sites. However, substantially more artificial fertilisers were used in Chipuriro, and substantially more local fertilisers (termitaria, leaf litter, compost and household waste) were used in Ngundu. This cannot be ascribed purely to wealth as this pattern is equally marked among the wealthiest in each sample. Yet for households lacking cattle or other livestock alternative sources of soil fertility are crucial. The value of these was exemplified by one widowed woman we interviewed with no cattle, who pointed to her compost heap and said 'that is my husband'. A variety of strategies are employed such as leaving crop residue near termite mounds as termite fodder, which reportedly assists in the production of nutrient-rich termite mounds.[5]

---

[5] Notwithstanding this the bulk of research on organic fertilisers in Zimbabwe has to date been on cattle manure – including work on the quality of kraal manures from different sites, manure preservation and storage and application rates (Murwira *et al.* 1995; Munguri *et al.* 1996; Mugwira and Murwira 1997).

Those households with gardens are particularly avid users of manure and other soil fertility supplements. Although also not officially recognised by agricultural extension advice and standard models of mixed farming, the manure of livestock other than cattle is valued very highly, particularly for spot application in combination with compost in gardens. Chicken and goat manure was ranked especially highly in Ngundu as a very powerful source of nutrients. Donkey manure is also sometimes used.

The manure management strategy, central to the mixed farming model that has informed agricultural extension since the colonial period, is only a possibility for a minority of the population (and given cattle losses in recent droughts this is a shrinking proportion). In the fields of Chipuriro and Ngundu and in the gardens of all four study sites a range of opportunisitic strategies that fall outside current official extension recommendations are being followed in order to secure soil fertility.

Livestock

Our survey provided initially very surprising figures on cattle ownership (see Fig. 4.4). The average number of cattle per household was highest in Chipuriro at 6.3. While a low average number of cattle per household is to be expected in Neshangwe (1.5), in the Zambezi valley, where non-trypano tolerant cattle have only recently been able to survive in the absence of tsetse fly, the extremely low figures for Ngundu (2.6) and Chikombedzi (2.1) were startling, especially given that Chikombedzi, in 'Natural Region V', is designated a 'ranching' area and the lowveld Shangaan population have a reputation for having massive herds of high-quality cattle. This is explained by the severe effect of the 1991–2 drought from which livestock numbers are still recovering. Of course, these average numbers of cattle per household conceal a wide range – livestock ownership is markedly skewed by wealth, age and gender.

Smallstock, especially goats, play an increasingly important role in people's livelihoods as a source of revenue, and donkeys are also becoming increasingly popular as draught animals in Ngundu and Chikombedzi. Here again is a departure from the ideal envisaged by the mixed farming model in which cattle are the major form of livestock

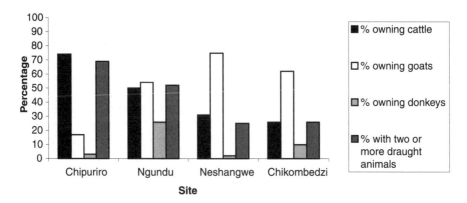

Figure 4.4   Livestock ownership

holding. This, as we have seen, has implications for soil fertility management strategies as well as for tillage and transport techniques.

Tillage

In all four sites livestock are valued extremely highly for their role as draught animals and in particular for ploughing fields. Agritex officially recommends that one span of oxen is needed to cultivate each 1.5 to 2 ha. In all sites there is a perceived shortage of draught, and a variety of important institutional arrangements are entered into by farmers to secure access to draught animals at the appropriate time of year. A further strategy used by farmers in Zimbabwe – less common in other parts of Africa – is to cobble together any number of animals to form a ploughing span. As well as oxen, donkeys and cows are used in various combinations, as Fig. 4.6 demonstrates.

Ngundu shows the largest variety in type and combinations of animal used for draught power. Rarely are oxen only used, but the use of donkeys, combinations of oxen and cows and oxen/cows and donkeys is common. Farmers have adapted to changing circumstances using the resources available to them rather than sticking to rigid extension advice derived from the mixed farming model that holds that only oxen are appropriate draught animals.[6] Agritex's position is to discourage ploughing with cows because it is thought to reduce their reproductive performance. But as one extension worker admitted: 'farmers are rational, and subsistence generally means grain not meat, so the input to grain production is valued more than calves. Cow fertility is more "abstract" than a draught power shortage.'[7]

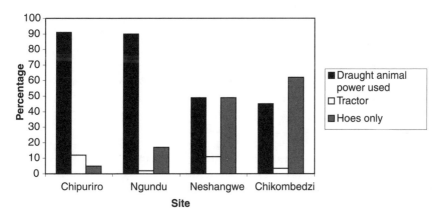

Figure 4.5 Percentage of households using draught animal power, tractors or hoes for tillage in 1997/8[8]

---

[6]Some research has been started on donkey and cow traction (e.g. Nengomasha and Jele 1995), but much research and extension continues to ignore the reality of farmers' practices.

[7]Interview: Agritex, Livestock Production Department, 22/6/1998.

[8]A household might have used more than one combination if ploughing with multiple spans.

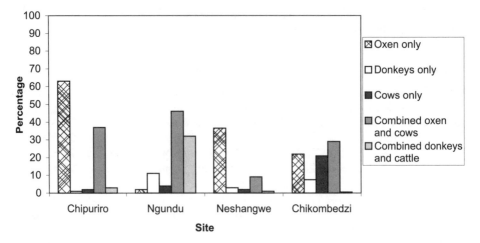

Figure 4.6 Percentage of households using different types of draught animal power in 1997/8

However, the most striking fact is the high percentage of farmers who do not plough with animals or tractors at all but simply hoe their fields. In Chikombedzi this constituted the majority of households in our sample (62 per cent) in the 1997/8 season. In the face of severe livestock deaths many farmers, at least temporarily, have had to abandon animal draught. This is borne out by the large areas of previously cultivated land left fallow for lack of draught power.

Zimbabwe is unusual in the African context because of the relatively large number of tractors employed in smallholder farming. However, the percentage of households owning or hiring tractors for tillage was low in all four sites (see Fig. 4.5). Tractor use is more common in Chipuriro where the population is relatively wealthy and Neshangwe where the Lower Guruve Development Association, private operators and the District Development Fund all hire out tractors for tillage.

Fodder

Use of *in situ* and cut-and-carried crop residue as livestock fodder is another indicator of crop–livestock integration. Fig. 4.7 shows the percentage of cattle owners using different fodder sources other than open grazing for their animals in the dry season across the sites.

Open grazing of cattle and smallstock is universally the most common source of fodder. However, in many areas this is increasingly insufficient. Land alienation, population growth and expansion of arable land and reported unofficial sales of 'communal' land by kraalheads to outsiders have caused encroachment on grazing land. Grazing areas increasingly consist of pockets of uncultivated land such as hillsides, roadsides, riverbanks and *dambos* (valley wetlands) and post-harvest on fields. Again opportunistic, flexible strategies, in this case based on mobility and tracking of key resources, are employed rather than the standardised technical packages such as

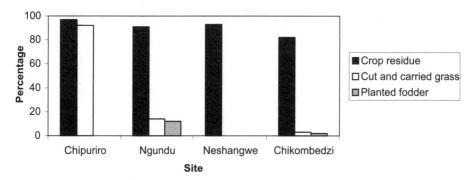

Figure 4.7   Percentage of cattle owners using different sources of fodder in the dry season

paddocking, stall-feeding and silageing advocated by extensionists and researchers.[9] In Ngundu, Chikombedzi and Chipuriro farmers have begun to negotiate grazing arrangements with adjacent commercial farms and resettlement areas, and engage in livestock-loaning arrangements to track available fodder (see below). In Neshangwe some grazing areas are now being designated as settlement areas or arable land under the Mid-Zambezi resettlement programme or occupied by spontaneous settlers, but grazing land remains relatively abundant.

In the dry season cattle graze *in situ* on the crop residue/stubble in harvested fields. Maize residue left in the fields is only accessible to cattle up to August–September when farmers plough in or burn the crop residue before the planting season. There were various explanations given for burning crop residue: some non-cattle owners want to deny the cattle owners access to their fodder because the cattle owners charge exorbitant prices to those without livestock for hiring draught power (see below); and burning crop residue also rids farmers of termites and the maize stalk borer pest and makes for easier ploughing.

In all four of the study sites crop residue is used as fodder for cattle and smallstock in the dry season. Soon after harvest crop residue (particularly maize) is often collected for storage on platforms built near, or above, kraals. This is as predicted by the mixed farming model in intensive farming systems, with shortages of grazing land, supporting relatively high population densities (as in Chipuriro and Ngundu) where 'cutting' grass and other types of fodder and 'carrying' it to the livestock kraals is also practised.[10] In supposedly more extensive rangeland grazing systems such as Chikombedzi, it is surprising, and not in accordance with standard linear crop–livestock integration models, to find 'intensive' fodder management strategies such as

---

[9]Recently research has been carried out in Zimbabwe on such themes as: harvesting and storage of crop residues and impact on nutritive value (Wood unpublished); crop residue treatment (Manyuchi and Smith 1992); browse utilisation and management strategies (Illius and Ncube unpublished); mixed crop silages; intercropping with forage legumes and grass species enrichment (Ndlovu and Francis 1997) but there has been very limited uptake of such fodder improvement technologies.

[10]This has the second desired effect of bulking up manure supplies when it is trampled into kraal floors.

feeding crop residue to livestock.[11] The reason for this is that farmers are adopting this specific element of the 'mixed farming package' as a drought-coping strategy when faced by severe shortages of dry season grazing. Even when crops fail to mature in drought years they can be gathered and used as fodder. In Chikombedzi there is also a burgeoning trade in maize residue from a nearby irrigation scheme, and many farmers are now building crop residue storage platforms for the first time.

Another less common source of fodder for cattle and goats is commercial feed (including hay, maize husks, sugar cane tops, agro-industrial by-products and feed supplements), which some farmers in Chipuriro buy to pen-fatten stock for sale, or in the case of Chikombedzi, to keep their animals alive in times of severe drought. As well as the purchase of feed supplements a range of tree and plant products are utilised to provide livestock feed during drought periods, including: lopped branches, tubers, pods and fruits. Only in Ngundu has the planting of fodder trees and crops taken off. This can be attributed to the presence of an active farmer participatory research group who have been experimenting with planted fodder.

Although Chipuriro most closely fits the archetypal mixed farm model, different elements of the mixed farming package are employed to varying extents and in varying combinations in all the sites (Table 4.3).

This overview of the current situation has pointed to the importance of social institutions in mediating access to resources such as draught power. It is also important to remember that rural livelihoods in Zimbabwe are also characterised by a heavy dependence on non-agricultural income streams. Wage labour, remittance income and local trade play an important role and influence cropping and livestock

Table 4.3 Summary of the indicators of crop–livestock integration by site.

	Higher resource endowment		Lower resource endowment	
	Chipuriro	**Ngundu**	**Neshangwe**	**Chikombedzi**
Manure	Used intensively on away fields in combination with inorganic fertilisers	Scarce cattle manure used carefully on key niches – with smallstock and poultry manure	Not used except on gardens	Not used except on gardens. No fertility improvements required on good soils of fields
Draught power	Mainly oxen teams and tractors	Mixed spans of oxen, cows and donkeys	Half using hoes, of the rest a majority using oxen only	A majority hoeing by hand
Fodder	Cut-and-carried fodder in the dry season	Cut-and-carried fodder common	No cut-and-carried fodder	Cut-and-carried fodder common in the dry season

[11]The conventional wisdom is exemplified by a consultancy report on cattle in Sengwe (the communal area adjoining Chikombedzi): 'Supplementary feeding from crop residues cannot reliably be incorporated into a livestock management programme, due to the unsuitable climate for crop production' (Stanning 1985: 81).

management through their impact on capital and labour availability. Remittance income is particularly crucial in Chikombedzi, where there is a long history of both legal and illicit labour migration to South Africa, and at any given moment a majority of young men will be working south of the border. Some households in Neshangwe and Chikombedzi also receive small dividends from the Campfire scheme for disbursement of game hunting revenue. Household livelihood strategies in all of the study areas are dynamic, with much daily, month-to-month and year-to-year variation as people react to such contingencies as the timing and amount of rainfall, labour migration opportunities, inflation, remittance incomes and transport costs. A high degree of differentiation in the livelihood strategies pursued occurs both between and within households. The site-level household data presented above therefore does not reveal the differences between and within households according to age, gender and wealth. These issues will form the themes of later sections but first, having outlined snapshots of the current pattern of crop–livestock interactions, it is necessary to delve into the history of each site in more detail and explore how particular events have triggered or constrained interactions between crops and livestock over time. An historical analysis will reveal the broad pathways of change followed in each site.

Agricultural history: key events influencing crop–livestock interactions

The history of crops and livestock and their interactions in Zimbabwe is obviously a rich and detailed one, which it is not possible to enter into in great detail here (see Wolmer and Scoones 2000). However, this section will briefly discuss the history of settlement, farming and livestock husbandry in each of our four study sites and draw out particular episodes that have been important in influencing the pathways of crop–livestock integration. Rather than following a uniform, linear path of agricultural intensification, characterised by a progressively more integrated articulation of crops and livestock in response to increasing population densities, the sites have experienced different pathways of change. These have been driven by conjunctures of events – ecological, social, political and economic (Table 4.4).

Pre/early colonial period

In the nineteenth century most settlements in the Ngundu area of Chivi were sheltered from Ndebele raiding parties on secure hilltop sites. Farmers in Chivi and Chipuriro cultivated rice, small grains and root crops by hand with hoes in *dambos* (valley wetlands) among the hills (Wilson 1986). Much of the wetlands were under the control of a male lineage head who directed work parties to hoe, ridge and mound the land. Households without access to *dambo* land pursued, instead, opportunistic dryland cropping strategies involving a form of shifting cultivation (*citimere*) over wide areas – the vegetation was partially cleared and burnt, and a small grain, usually millet or sorghum, grown for about three years, before the farmers moved on. The rinderpest pandemic of 1896 and heavy tribute raiding by the Ndebele meant that livestock holdings were low.

A similar shifting agriculture was practised in Neshangwe where people settled in dispersed clusters near rivers. Initially wild animals' bones were used as hoes (*hwete*),

Table 4.4 Summary of key events.

Date	Key event	Location	Impact on cropping and livestock management
1896	Rinderpest pandemic	All	Livestock and wildlife decimated; tsetse fly frontier rolled back owing to lack of hosts
1890s	Arrival of British colonialists	All	Alienation of best-quality agricultural land for use by colonialists begins
1926	Appointment of 'Agriculturalist for the instruction of Natives'	All	Agricultural extension begins in reserves. Manure application and ploughing advocated
1930	Land Apportionment Act	All	Further alienation of most productive land for European settlement and farming
1942	Natural Resources Act	All	Riverbank cultivation banned
1951	The Native Land Husbandry Act (NLHA)	All	Destocking of livestock implemented and actively resisted
1961	NLHA abandoned	All	
1970s	Liberation War	All	Agriculture disrupted, freedom farming, livestock deaths
1980	Independence	All	
1980s	Tsetse clearance	Neshangwe	Introduction of draught oxen encourages cotton cultivation
1991	Structural adjustment	All	Removal of subsidies on agricultural inputs
1990s	AIDS epidemic escalates	All	Labour shortages
1992	Severe drought	Ngundu Chikombedzi Neshangwe	Large-scale death of livestock leading to shortage of draught power and cattle manure followed by more rapid recovery in smallstock populations
2000	Severe flooding	Chikombedzi	Death of livestock

which had a life span of only one season. Each household had several small fields surrounding the homestead, which would be used in rotations of three years. These were widely scattered as a precaution against Ndebele raiding parties. Fertile river valleys were also intensively cultivated. Tsetse fly infestation prevented livestock ownership, although there are rumours that the ancestors of the Korekore had medicines that could cure their livestock and people of tsetse-related diseases.

Early travellers' accounts and colonial reports from the Chikombedzi area generally describe the Shangaans as uninterested in farming, especially arable farming, with a focus instead on hunting, gathering and fishing and trading meat from hunting with Shona people. However, dryland agriculture has long been a very important branch of production, even if it was restricted by drought. Bannerman (1980) points out that the

Shangaan cultivated seven varieties of sorghum in pre-colonial times, as well as finger millet, groundnuts and bambara nuts. Maize was grown for green consumption; and pumpkins, water melons and sweet potatoes were grown along river banks. Although the Shangaan may not have had cattle when they entered Zimbabwe, they were certainly familiar with them (Bannerman 1980). The rinderpest pandemic wiped out much of the wildlife in the lowveld, and with it most of the tsetse fly. This enabled farmers to hold stock in the region, and cattle became very important assets in the 20th century (see Fig. 4.8 and 4.9).[12]

During the pre- and early colonial period, then, livestock production was not integrated much with arable production, with no use of manure and no ploughing across all four sites. Agriculture was divided between opportunistic shifting cultivation of drylands and permanent cultivation of wetlands and riverbanks, and livestock holdings – particularly of cattle – were limited.

Colonial era

The colonial era ushered in a period of radical intervention in smallholder agriculture. Most dramatically the Land Apportionment Act of 1930 led to the establishment of 'reserves' for African farmers and their eviction from land designated as

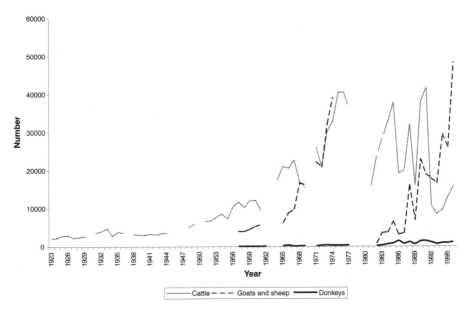

Figure 4.8 Matibi II Communal Area livestock populations

[12]Detailed records of livestock numbers for communal areas have been kept since the 1920s. Although these should not be taken to be totally accurate and boundary changes have altered the sizes of both areas, Figs 4.8 and 4.9 give a good indication of the changing livestock populations over the last 80 years in Matibi II and Chivi communal areas – in which Chikombedzi and Ngundu are respectively located.

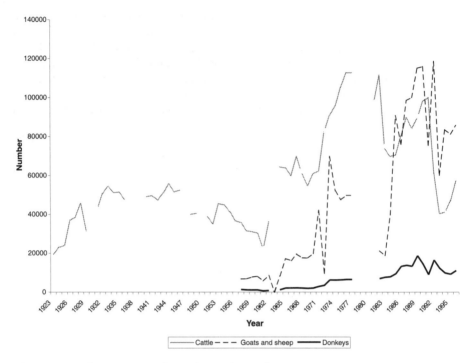

Figure 4.9 Chivi Communal Area livestock populations

'European', when large tracts of land were allocated to European settlers and companies. This led to rising human and livestock populations in the reserves and encouraged migrant labour to the European farms and mines. The subsequent need to intensify smallholder farming on smaller areas of land provided part of the impetus for the establishment of an agricultural extension system, In the words of Emory Alvord, the 'Agriculturalist for the Instruction of Natives':

> To give Natives now on Reserves more land at present would be most unwise. They would only ruin it and destroy its fertility in the same manner as they have already done on the land which they already have. For them the solution is not to be had in more land but in better farming the existing land (Alvord 1948: 18).

A succession of legislation underpinned an increasingly interventionist colonial approach to smallholder agriculture, culminating in the Native Land Husbandry Act of 1951. The recommended method for agricultural intensification was in large part to integrate crops and livestock on mixed farms as 'the foundation of permanent agriculture for the African is based on "mixed farming" i.e. cattle and tillage' (Alvord 1943). To this end extension efforts centred on the promotion of draught animal power, manure use, improved fodder management and the establishment of consolidated landholdings (alongside crop rotation, destumping and contouring of fields). Mixed farming would thus help to stave off land demands by Africans and release labour for commercial farming, mining and industry (Palmer 1977;

Drinkwater 1991). The introduction of these 'improved methods' of mixed farming are investigated in more detail below.

The plough
A number of factors were to change the face of smallholder agriculture in Zimbabwe at the beginning of the 20th century. The cessation of raiding by the Ndebele and gradual recovery from the rinderpest pandemic, together with favourable rainfall conditions, access to large grazing areas and a reduction in disease incidence meant that cattle populations grew rapidly. The introduction of the plough also meant that cattle became an increasingly important agricultural production input through the expansion of draught.[13]

The irony, given the dismissive colonial attitudes to agriculture in Chikombedzi,[14] is that – as the Native Commissioner for Ndanga District notes – the Shangaans were much quicker at adopting 'modern' agricultural practices than their highveld neighbours. In 1910/11 out of 51 ploughs the Shangaan owned 41, and were even ploughing the fields of the Duma, and in 1916 the Shangaan owned the only scotch-carts in the district (Mtetwa 1976). Native Commissioner Forestall in Chivi District similarly admits that the Shangaan were quicker to adopt the plough than many of the Shona to the north of them:

> In agriculture natives are commencing to use ploughs ... Hitherto ploughs have only been used by the Shangaans and natives of Matibi who have been continually in contact with the Northern Transvaal natives, but of late the Muklanga of the upper portion of the district have brought seven ploughs, and the other headmen are showing a keen interest in the matter.[15]

Bannerman (1980) ascribes this, in part, to the fact that, through migrant labour, the Shangaan came into contact with the market economy and technologies of South Africa much earlier than others. Also in the heavy soils of the lowveld the plough had a greater advantage over the hoe than on the lighter soils of the plateau, and in a dry climate the adoption of new implements was possibly far more critical than it was to people in the better-watered highlands.

Ploughs were probably first bought in Messina by men working in the South African mines. However, it was not until transport links improved that people were able to bring them to the area in numbers. Mr Macheke, a school teacher who grew up in northern Transvaal, before moving to Chikombedzi when his father married, remembers his father telling him that in the 1920s he taught his cousin, who had plenty of oxen but was still using hoes, how to team oxen to plough from his experience in South Africa.

---

[13]Colonial accounts of African agricultural practice inevitably lapse into pejorative terms. In particular the 'primitive' use of the hoe was singled out. In 1941, for example, the ANC for Sipolilo (Lower Guruve) wrote: 'In the Zambezi valley the Hoe is the Plough and some 16,000 folk scratch a bare living; nothing except labour is ever exported from the valley' (ANC Sipolilo 1952). Yet, as Derman (1995) points out, these same District Commissioners noted that it was possible to obtain three crops a year from alluvial riverine areas in the valley where the lands were planted to maize, rapoko, sorghum, beans, ground peas, sweet potatoes, etc. but they nonetheless concluded that because a hand hoe was used, the agriculture was primitive.
[14]Wright (1972: 201) typifies colonial attitudes to Shangaan farming: 'Shanganes [*sic*] are skilled in bushcraft, highly observant naturalists, and fearless and effective hunters. They are lackadaisical agriculturalists, untidy hut-builders and not even particularly good stockmen.'
[15]National Archives of Zimbabwe, NVC 1/1/8, NC Forestall to SON, 15/12/1909.

Ploughs soon spread from the white-owned commercial farms and mission stations to the other reserves. As Scoones *et al.* (1996) point out:

> the arrival of the plough was probably the single technology change with the most dramatic impact on agricultural production in the twentieth century. Across the communal areas only one in 333 people owned a plough in 1910, by 1920 one in 45 people did and by 1940 nearly every family owned one (CNC Annual Reports). This pattern was repeated in Chivi, where the Native Commisioner reports the presence of only 18 ploughs in the district in 1902, 1,300 a decade later and over 5,000 by 1959.

Similarly, in Sipolilo Reserve (Guruve) there were no ploughs reported to be in use in 1910, by 1927 there were 47, by 1933 there were approximately 300, and by 1941 'where there are cattle the use of the plough is almost universal' (NCs' Annual Reports). Native Commissioners were constantly citing increased numbers of ploughs in the district as evidence of agricultural progress and celebrating its use:

> The teachers and some of their relatives, on the mission farm 'Chibi', use ploughs and cultivate in European style, and in this way set a good example and teach the natives living in the vicinity (NC Chivi 1910).

> The drought during the season (1915/16) has shown natives that with their poor methods of cultivation those who used ploughs reaped much better crops than those who only cultivated with the hoe (NC Chivi 1916).

> It is difficult to estimate the number of ploughs brought into the District, as they come in from all sides. It is a not uncommon sight, however, to see natives wheeling them along the road, when out on patrol. This District, with others, shares the custom for a bride to refuse a suitor until he has purchased a plough (NC Chivi 1928).

In all sites studied, barring Neshangwe, where the tsetse fly proscribed plough cultivation, the use of the plough precipitated a shift in cultivation system from one concentrated on labour-intensive cultivation of wetland patches, combined with some shifting cultivation, to land-extensive cultivation of dryland areas. Low population densities meant that large areas were available for agricultural expansion. Dryland cultivation offered the potential for high overall output if large areas were cultivated with millets and sorghum. Individuals and families could now plant large areas with relatively little labour; the constraining factor increasingly became livestock for draught, instead of human labour for intensive hoe cultivation (Scoones *et al.* 1996; Scoones 1997).[16]

'Plough entrepreneurs' (Ranger 1985) were able to expand their areas of cultivation significantly, clearing large areas and cultivating extensively. Some were extremely successful, creating large surpluses and trading stored grain in drought periods (see Wolmer and Scoones 1998). A new, successful social grouping of entrepreneurial frontier farmers had been created in the reserves with the arrival of the plough – often relatively young, independent and sharp about business and dealings. However, in large part because of this success, much colonial commentary and extension advice became more ambivalent about the use of the plough:

---

[16]Wilson (1986) makes the additional point that the introduction of the plough facilitated a marked increase in production, and a greater economic independence of households (and particularly of women and juniors) because of the decline in the necessity of large work parties.

Approximately 1300 ploughs are in use in the district, but it is questionnable if there is any distinct advantage – except from a labour saving point of view. Ploughing is carried out in such an indifferent manner, that only a depth of a few inches is obtained. A large acreage is certainly cultivated, but usually more than the natives can cultivate properly with the result that the yield per acre is less than they obtained from the soil which was hand tilled (NC Chibi 1923).

Manure
The application of kraal manure to fields has been another central tenet of agricultural extension messages in Zimbabwe since the 1920s. Alvord's vision is revealed by his portrayal of his ideal African farmer – the intensive 'Master Farmer' applying large amounts of manure to a small amount of land – and his parables on the dangers and evils of the old methods (Drinkwater 1991). Yet officials were often frustrated by the lack of adoption of this technique. Farmers complained about the labour need to carry manure to the fields, the lack of transport, and the weed growth it encouraged. The Native Commisioner for Chivi, for example, regularly complained about the lack of adoption of manuring practices in his reports:

> Nothing is done to improve the light sandy soil predominating in this district although hundreds of tons of kraal manure are available and continual advice is given on this subject (NC Chibi 1922).

> I made every endeavour to get the natives to manure their lands this season, and at some kraals I have superintended the manuring of half an acre to an acre of land and hope to be able to demonstrate the advantage to be gained. My efforts have not, I must admit, been attended with much enthusiasm on the part of the natives, the complaints being that it entails considerable labour in carrying manure in small baskets from the cattle kraal and that it will mean a lot of extra work in weeding (NC Chibi 1924).

However, a combination of increased population pressure and changes in technology began to transform the farming system from the 1940s. Land scarcity necessitated an intensification of dryland farming, and the greater availability of animal-powered transport meant that manuring was increasingly practised (Scoones *et al.* 1996: 28).

> Manuring of lands is increasing and would be more general were transport vehicles more numerous … in order to increase the weight of the attack on bad farming methods several more demonstrators could be usefully employed (NC Chivi 1941).

In Chipuriro inorganic fertiliser started to be used in the 1960s after the introduction of cotton. In addition to the demonstrators, some local people who had graduated from Domboshava agricultural training college with certificates in farming helped the demonstrators to teach farmers on the use of manure. In the 1970s the use of inorganic fertiliser and organic manure continued and intensified with an increase in cotton production and a decrease in soil fertility.

Land holdings and fodder
Colonial authorities in Zimbabwe assumed that intensively managed mixed farms with individualised rights to land would gradually evolve and that this 'natural' development should be actively encouraged. As one writer put it in 1923:

> As time goes on the native will gradually drift from kraal life to individualistic life. The process has begun and will continue more rapidly every year … Individual tenure appeals to the

progressive native, because it enables him to adopt advanced methods, such as sinking, irrigation etc., which are impossible when living the kraal life (Wilson 1923: 83).

The concept of mixed farming, with its systematic crop rotations on individualised arable holdings to which livestock holdings are closely tied, was one of the main reasons and subsequent justifications for the 'centralisation' programme for land reorganisation of the 1930s and 1940s. This involved the division of land into separate consolidated blocks of arable and grazing, with a line of resettled homesteads dividing the two. This programme was subsequently made law with the Native Land Husbandry Act of 1951, and attempts to enforce mixed farming on a planned basis became more coercive. Continued land alienation and growing populations in the reserves also put pressure on land, with an increasing proportion being used for farming. This meant that livestock had to increasingly rely on key grazing resources within the landscape (such as hillsides, river banks and roadsides) and crop residues became increasingly key to dry season nutrition.

Livestock interventions
Interventions in livestock husbandry in the colonial era were focused on cattle. Initially initiatives concentrated on developing a disease control programme in the reserves, the building of dip tanks and the imposition of cattle movement restrictions (in particular to control Foot and Mouth disease). Reductions in cattle populations through disease were in some cases aggravated by colonial control policies. In 1934, for example, the Assistant NC for Nuanetsi reported that Foot and Mouth disease broke out on Nuanetsi Ranch and that 'drastic and rather severe' restrictions and quarantine methods were adopted by the Veterinary Department.

> In many cases natives had to drive their cattle 100 and 200 miles to the quarantine areas where the cattle, 5000 head, were closely herded in small areas; as a result of these methods the mortality from poverty was considerably greater than in past years. ... These restrictions, combined with increased sales to dealers at the outbreak of Foot and Mouth, and the slaughter of calves during the innoculation period under Vet Dept regulations led to a reduction of cattle stock of 4161 over the previous year's total.[17]

Tsetse fly clearance programmes allowed cattle to thrive in the southeast lowveld early in the 20th century (but not until post-Independence in the Zambezi valley). Tsetse fly reappeared in the Chikombedzi area in the 1950s, and the rise in cattle populations in the late 1950s coincides with efforts by the Department of Veterinary Services to eradicate tsetse again (see Fig. 4.8 and Wright 1972).

These explicitly technical interventions in cropping and livestock during the colonial period disguised an implicit set of institutional and social commitments. The transformation of agriculture required both a physical reordering of landscapes and a reconfiguration of the social order. The reorganisations of village residential, arable and grazing patterns owed much to attempts to render citizens visible to surveillance and thus more amenable to segregation, subjugation and administrative control (Phimister 1986; Robins 1994; McGregor 1995). Imposing 'the rectangular grid of civilisation' on the landscape was an antidote to its perceived disorder and unruliness (Comaroff and Comaroff 1992) and made the collection of taxes and

---

[17]National Archives of Zimbabwe, S 235/511, ANC Nuanetsi, 1933 Annual Report.

monitoring of people easy.[18] The creation and maintenance of a class of successful small-scale farmers who had modernised their agriculture along the recommended lines was central to 'agricultural demonstration' (see Sumberg 1998). The creation of an elite clique of early adopters of new technologies known as 'Master Farmers' was seen to be an important way of encouraging the spread of 'civilising' ideals, while diffusing dissent and unrest (Ranger 1985).

Post-Independence

The massive decline in both goat and cattle populations in the mid to late 1970s (see Figs 4.8 and 4.9) is directly due to the Liberation War. Notwithstanding the fact that livestock population data for this period is often not very reliable, or simply was never collected, there is clearly a marked reduction in numbers. In Chikombedzi, for example, most of the population were moved into 'protected villages' and dipping of livestock ceased. Cattle were left to wander free when people were relocated into the keeps, and many were lost. They were killed for food by families living out in the bush and by the guerrillas who also forced families to kill cattle for them. The Rhodesian army also shot cattle to stop them getting to the guerrillas. Dip tanks were regularly targets for guerrilla attack, and livestock also died from diseases owing to the lack of dipping. Also during the Liberation War 'freedom farming' (*madiro*) became a means of protest, and people ploughed up areas previously reserved for grazing. After the war dipping of cattle was resumed and there was another influx of new arrivals to the region from other parts of Zimbabwe. Many of these people brought cattle with them. These factors contributed to the recovery in cattle numbers.

In Neshangwe tsetse clearance, the arrival of immigrants, the introduction of cotton, the drilling of boreholes and construction of roads and clinics in the 1980s had particularly dramatic effects on agricultural practice. Up to 37 per cent of households surveyed had moved into the area since Independence. Migrants, lured by the cotton revenue and the ambitious Mid-Zambezi Project, brought cattle, which provided draught power,[19] and goats and tractors were introduced. This draught power allowed field sizes to increase dramatically. Agricultural extensification took place with large areas put into cotton. Money from the cotton cash crops was reinvested in cattle. There was thus a shift from a farming system rooted in a combination of shifting cultivation and riverine plots to extensive cotton growing alongside the riverine plots.

The use of pesticides, the plough and drought-resistant cultivation of cotton resulted in high crop yields from 1987. Similarly, the arrival of hybrid maize varieties transformed the agricultural landscape in all of the study sites. Yield increases meant that maize became a viable competitor with small grains on dryland fields. Since

---

[18]The need to maintain soil fertility and increase productivity through scientific farming methods was not the only way in which 'science' was employed to justify spatial and social reorganisation. Beinart (1984), Ranger (1985) and McGregor (1995), for example, highlight the role of ecologists and soil scientists in implementing coercive soil conservation programmes, and Robins (1994) describes how medicine was invoked in the cause of replacing the 'disease-infested huts' with rows of modern housing. McGregor also shows how Alvord was not averse to using the language of conservationists rather than agricultural scientists to justify his programme for mixed farming to audiences sceptical of the whole idea of 'native development' (1995).

[19]Most cattle were acquired during the period 1992–7 (58%), followed by 1986–91 (19%), then 1980–5 (6%), and finally the 1970s (17%).

Independence the use of hybrid maize has steadily increased and, initially, credit packages stimulated the use of inorganic fertiliser, although, with the removal of subsidies in the 1990s, fertiliser use has since fallen to a low level (Scoones *et al.* 1996).

Drought and livestock

The drought years of 1982–4, 1987 and 1991–2 are all marked by significant reductions in livestock populations. Particularly in the south of the country (Chikombedzi and Ngundu), drought appears to be having increasingly severe impacts on livestock populations. Yet it has had a differential impact on different types of livestock, with cattle being worst hit and smallstock populations recovering more quickly. This is particularly evident after the 1991–2 drought, where the slow recovery of the cattle population can be contrasted with a very rapid increase in smallstock numbers (see Figs 4.8 and 4.9). This has inverted the previous pattern of most livestock consisting of cattle, and has resulted in a severe shortage of draught power for many farmers. This is also reflected in changing patterns of livestock ownership (such as shifts in the gender dynamics of goat ownership – see below). Investment in goats by both men and women is a strategy for seeking security in a context of reduced cattle holdings.

Cattle populations have been rising again in recent years (see Figs 4.8 and 4.9), but in the face of another potentially serious drought farmers in Chikombedzi were selling stock in 1998. Another development is that the composition of cattle holdings is changing, with an increasingly large proportion being cows and heifers and relatively fewer oxen and steers, as the example of Matibi II shows (see Fig. 4.10).

Donkey populations have also expanded fairly steadily in Ngundu and Chikombedzi. This is in part a consequence of their increased use for draught power with the growing vulnerability of cattle to drought. Donkeys were first imported from South Africa around 1905, and they have become increasingly important over time. In 1907 only 18 donkeys were reported in the whole of Chivi District, but by the early 1920s there were several hundred. Since then the donkey population has

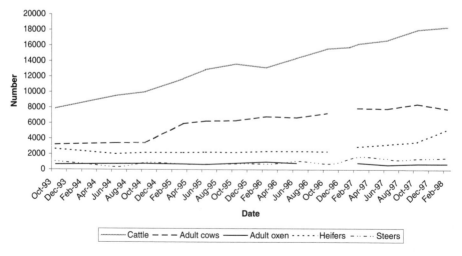

Figure 4.10   Changing composition of cattle holdings in Matibi II, 1993–8

expanded enormously, and by 1996 over 10,000 were recorded for Chivi. By 1996 the livestock census recorded over 1,000 donkeys in Matibi II communal area alone. However, the severe floods in early 2000 had a drastic affect on livestock populations in Matibi II – once again exacerbating draught power shortages.

Two further ongoing events that cannot be ignored in any analysis of rural dynamics in Zimbabwe are the Economic Structural Adjustment Programme (ESAP) and the HIV/AIDS epidemic. Market and fiscal reforms and the privatisation of parastatals have had a range of conflicting consequences. The deregulation and introduction of new private players into the marketing of cash crops has encouraged cotton growing, particularly in Neshangwe, Chipuriro and Ngundu. Agricultural inputs and the cost of living generally have become much more expensive, and extension and veterinary services scaled down. The long-term effects of the HIV/AIDS epidemic in Zimbabwe remain to be seen, but it is already having dramatic impacts on household labour availability and remittance income, as well as placing heavy demands on women's time, in particular for home-care of out-patients.

Despite the contemporary rhetoric on land reform in Zimbabwe, the post-colonial era did not herald the abandonment of all the colonial policies on land use, cropping and livestock management. Indeed, some land use planning exercises directly continued colonial ones, and agricultural extension has continued to be informed by the mixed farming model of the Rhodesian years. Bans on river bank gardening were again enforced, and the villagisation and land reorganisation schemes of the 1980s directly echoed the centralisation programme and the Native Land Husbandry Act, even using the same air photographs and maps as their basis (Scoones *et al.* 1996; Drinkwater 1991). Even the resettlement programme (including the current 'Fast Track' process), aimed at rectifying the land inequalities of the colonial era, has adopted many of the basic technical elements of Alvord's mixed farming model. Chapters 1 and 5 explore the reasons for the remarkable persistence of a set of technical recommendations that have little relevance to a great many Zimbabwean farmers.

Pathways of change

The pathways of change evident in the case study sites cannot be described simply as agricultural intensification, with the progressive integration of crops and livestock in response to changing population densities. Rather, a variety of pathways have been brought about by a conjunction of agroecological factors and specific key events.

The broad pathway that emerges from the historical account of Chikombedzi, for example, is one of linking and delinking of various elements of the cropping and livestock system – the plough, manure and fodder – over time. This history of integration and dis-integration of crops and livestock cannot be ascribed only to changing population densities, although these have played a part. Increased population density (through natural increase, land alienation and the immigration of displaced people) has not led directly to increased manure use, use of gathered crop residue as fodder or more use of draught power. In fact, manure use is confined to gardens; increasing use of gathered crop residue is related to perceptions of drought risk, and livestock deaths have led to an abandonment of animal traction by many households. Rather, events such as the eradication of tsetse fly; increasing migrant labour; changes in the nature of migrant labour; colonial agricultural extension; the Land Apportionment Act; the Liberation War; ESAP; and drought have come together to alter the livelihood strategies of different actors at different moments. It is not so much a case of crops and livestock becoming more or less integrated in these different areas, rather that the interactions are being, and constantly have been, reconstituted as farmers adapt to changing circumstances and new institutional configurations emerge, with steps taken at one point defining future possibilities.

Table 4.5 summarises the broad pathways for each site, although it must be remembered that these are very broad brush trends and as such mask a great deal of diversity, as will become evident below. The next section will go on to describe how particular institutional configurations have affected these pathways of crop–livestock integration for different people in different places.

Table 4.5   Broad pathways of cropping and livestock management by site.

Site	Broad pathway
Ngundu	From wetland cultivation and shifting cultivation to a low-input, land-extensive, opportunistic form of agriculture to a reduction in cattle holdings and an increased focus on smallstock and hoe-based garden agriculture and off-farm income
Chipuriro	From shifting cultivation to intensive mixed farming based on the integration of communal rangelands and individualised arable production with increased use of inorganic fertiliser, manure, draught power and improved fodder management
Neshangwe	From hoe-based river bank cultivation and shifting cultivation towards extensive cash cropping of cotton with draught animal power and tractors
Chikombedzi	From pastoralism/river bank cultivation to hoe-based agriculture complemented by smallstock focus and off-farm income

Institutions mediating access to resources central to crop–livestock systems

Technical studies of crop and livestock management often ignore the fact that crop and livestock management practices are a product of social context. Understanding these practices thus requires insights into the histories of social as well as technical change. This in turn requires an understanding of the institutions that mediate this change. The point of departure for this section is that particular institutions, located within different 'domains' – from intra-household practices to formal national and international organisations – often acting in combination, shape the ways in which people access and use the resources central to crop–livestock inter-action (see Chapter 1). Institutions, in this context, incorporate both 'formal' and 'informal' groupings and practices. The resources to which they mediate access include land, labour, draught power, livestock, manure, capital equipment and information (Table 4.6). This table is only a schematic illustration of the many and complex institutional arrangements at play across four 'domains'. This section will focus in detail on the institutions mediating access to draught power, labour, live-stock and manure.

Table 4.6 Institutions mediating access to key resources necessary for cropping and livestock management.

Institutional domain	Land	Labour	Draught power	Livestock	Manure	Feed	Credit	Capital equip't	Info.
Intra-household practices	Inheritance; Subdivison	Family labour	Sharing/teaming; Borrowing/loaning	Livestock loaning (*ronzera, kufiyisa*)	Gifts	Borrowing		Remittances; Plough sharing	
Inter-household groups and practices	Land for draught power; Customary access	Work parties (*dhava, humwe, hoka*); Labour exchange; Church groups	Livestock loaning; Work parties; Labour for draught power	Livestock loaning; Brideprice (*lobola*); Bartered for goods; Exchanges with communal farmers	Kraal sharing	Communal grazing	Savings clubs	Plough-sharing; Barter arrangements	Farmer groups
Inter-household cash transactions	Land leasing	Hiring labour	Hiring draught power; Hiring tractors	Local marketing	Sales	Crop residue sales	Informal loans	Hiring	
Formal organisations	Kraalhead (*sabhuku*) councillor		District Development Fund	Exchanges; Auction; Commercial buyers; Cold Storage Commisson		Commercial feed manufacturers	AFC; CotCo; Cargill; CotPro	Ex-Combatants' fund; NGOs	Agritex; Vet. Dept., ZFU

Draught power and labour access arrangements

A total of 70 per cent of households sampled in all sites used animal draught power to plough in the 1997/8 season. However, only 44 per cent of the households sampled own two or more draught animals. The situation in Ngundu is particularly striking – 83 per cent of the households with less than two draught animals were able to plough using animal draught power in the 1997/8 season (see Fig. 4.11 below). This discrepancy points to the key importance of negotiating access to draught power and the existence of institutions for non-owners of draught animals to gain this access. Cliffe (1986: 34), in the context of describing policy options for land reform in Zimbabwe, notes:

> Discovering the varied patterns of draught and labour exchange and the ways the stockless have of coping in the different parts of the country is of more than anthropological interest. More information on the topic would provide government with a more accurate picture of the plight of the disadvantaged section of the peasantry, indicate the social constraints within which land reform policy has to be formulated so as to benefit them, and also reveal what basis there is for promoting various forms of co-operation and sharing as a partial solution. This is a vital imperative precisely because some such co-operation, so that the community can make more effective use of a restricted number of livestock and reduced grazing area, is an essential long-term objective.

Yet there have been few previous studies of the complexities of draught access arrangements in Zimbabwe. Notable exceptions, however, are Bratton (1984) and Muchena (1989), and some of their findings are summarised in Box 4.2.

Box 4.2   Draught access arrangements

Bratton (1984) describes the extent of draught exchange,[20] its institutional forms and its social and economic consequences. He analyses the effect of differing levels of social capital (in the form of group membership) on draught exchange arrangements. He concludes that draught exchange is a contextual social practice common to a wide assortment of farmers rather than having been fully institutionalised as a formal procedure of organised farmer groups (but where non-cash exchange occurs with non-kin it is usally within such groups).

Muchena (1989) conducted an investigation in Buhera. She concludes that the nature of draught contracts may well maintain inequality while spreading access to draught power. For example, the cost to the household without cattle, which pays for draught with labour, could be the reduction in output as a result of having less labour available for its own production – thus widening existing disparities in favour of draught owners

> 'A potential for draught sharing arrangements exists ... However the evolution of the market economy has slowly eroded the spirit of community ownership and use of resources on a communal basis. But once a viable market for draught power is created and enough compensation is offered in return, more draught owners will be willing to release their animals for use by other farmers. Payments can be in the form of crop residues which can then be fed to the animals and ensure stong draught teams that perform well' (272–3).

---

[20]Defined as borrowing or lending of draught.

Across all the study sites there is a serious shortage of draught power. This is most keenly felt in the southern study sites – Ngundu and Chikombedzi. The Liberation War had a devastating effect on livestock populations, as did the droughts of the mid-1980s (see above). Just as people were beginning to restock successfully the 1991–2 drought wiped out the cattle population again. The most serious implication of this shortage of cattle, emphasised again and again, is the resulting difficulties in ploughing fields with animal draught power. This is explicitly recognised in a government report:

> ... over 50% of smallholder farmers have no draught animals, and generally no access to mech-anised alternatives. Farms in this predicament achieve less than half the yields and incomes of their counterparts who own draught animals. The problem is getting worse primarily due to drought. Efforts to mechanise these areas have so far not had much success. Government assis-tance through DDF [the District Development Fund] have had some impact but this has adversely affected the development of private sector tillage units in the smallholder sector (Government of Zimbabwe n.d.).

In this context a multiplicity of arrangements exist for accessing draught power. These arrangements are flexible and complex, continually changing between and within seasons. As Bratton (1984: 6) points out:

> A variety of [draught exchange] arrangements are negotiated, some *ad hoc*, others regular, repet-itive and institutionalised. The form that these arrangements take depends on the social and organisational relations among participating households and the permutations of draught exchange arrangements are limited only by the need and inventiveness of the farmers concerned.

A variety of strategies can be combined. These include:

- Draught pairing or teaming animals with family or close friend to form a span.
- Hiring for cash or grain.
- Borrowing – although such an arrangement is rarely without the expectation or hope of some help (e.g. with ploughing) at some stage from the recipient.
- Working in kind – a farmer who owns more than one span of cattle but has a shortage of labour can lend out spans to others in return for help with his own ploughing in the form of labour.
- Exchanging ploughing services for a portion of land for one season.
- Work parties *(hoka, humwe, nhimbe, dhava)*.
- Long-term loaning arrangements *(kufuyisa/ronzera)* – cattle are borrowed long-term (lent out by those with many cattle of their own – but can be called back at any time).
- Hiring tractors from fellow farmers, from 'small-scale' commercial farms or from the DDF or NGOs.

Our survey data gives some indication of the importance of these types of institutional arrangements across the four sites (see Fig. 4.11). The category 'hired/exchanged' draught animal power encompasses the range of arrangements outlined above. These are discussed in more detail below.

'Hiring/exchanging' arrangements for draught animal power are common in all sites, and particularly so in Ngundu. In every site except Chipuriro it was more common for those who used draught animal power to enter into these arrangements than to use their own animals (as ownership of more than two draught animals is rela-tively uncommon). However, the survey data also illustrates that many people,

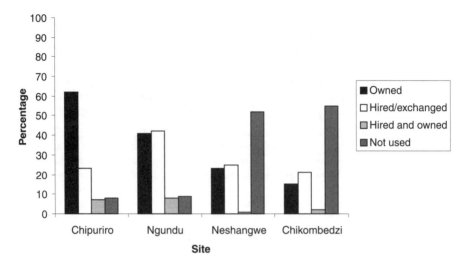

Figure 4.11 Source of animal draught power in 1997/8 season

particularly in Chikombedzi, are still unable to access draught and have to resort to hoeing their fields by hand instead (62 per cent in Chikombedzi). Not illustrated in this figure are the percentages using tractors for tillage, which are largest in Chipuriro and Neshangwe at 10 and 12 per cent respectively. The vast majority of these hire, rather than own, tractors for tillage.

Intra-household and inter-household sharing/teaming and borrowing of draught power
Bratton (1984: 10–11) observes that:

> Shona society imposes an extensive and demanding network of familial duties which must be honoured. Close relatives are permitted to call upon one another for help whenever resources like draught are short. Fathers are expected to share with their sons and sons' families; brothers and cousins are expected to share with their 'brothers' and families. Where the farmer is a woman the exchange is usually with relatives by marriage since she lives with her husband's kin. … The high level of draught exchange among kin does not occur at group behest but is nego-tiated among family members as social obligation traditionally dictates.

Thus 'borrowing' of draught power rarely means 'free' in an absolute sense. The implicit assumption is that the borrower will be available for assistance at a later date – although this depends on the particular family, and in some families kin draught sharing is becoming commercialised (see below). Those 'freely lending' cattle rarely acknowledge that there is any payment in kind, and the 'recipients' rarely say they receive help for which they do not pay in some way, yet this masks complex negotiations.

'Closeness' in both the spatial sense and in terms of family links and friendship is one of the key determinants of whether or not people enter into draught sharing arrange-ments, and who they do so with. These arrangements are not restricted to patrilineal kin groupings, but can encompass wives' families and non-relatives. The importance of friendship, 'trust' and a good reputation were continually emphasised when probing reasons for choosing who to enter into livestock loaning or draught sharing relationships

Box 4.3   Flexible arrangements

Newton and Robson Zivhu
In the early 1970s before Newton had draught animals of his own his brother would come and plough his fields with his animals. Newton then acquired animals and formed a 'part-nership' with his sister-in-law, Mai Collen, starting in 1975. Initially each had one beast and they teamed up to make a span. Originally only she had a plough; three years later Newton also acquired one. They continue to plough and manage their oxen together – keeping them in the same kraal. The cattle are tended together by children from each family and manure from the kraal is shared equally. They currently have 9 animals, 4 belonging to Mai Collen and 3 to Newton. He would also intermittently team up with Robson, his brother, to plough -- an arrangement that suited both because of the different natures of their fields. However in the 1991–2 drought all of Robson's animals died and Newton started providing free assistance in ploughing his fields. By 1995 Robson had managed to build up his own herd of draught animals again (he currently has 1 donkey and 2 cattle) and has a teaming arrangement with Mr Munyengterwa (a local storeowner). He no longer asks for assistance from, or teams with, Newton because 'his workload is already too much' as the cattle owned by Newton and Mai Collen also plough Newton and Robson's mother's fields and also for other relatives and a widowed neighbour.

Mai Farai Zhivi (born 1952; 3 children; widowed)

Pre-1991/2:	Before the drought Mai Farai had 10 cattle. There were enough to have 4 large animals used just for pulling ploughs and another 2 for pulling the cultivator. She would assist some relatives with ploughing for free and sometimes hire out her spans.
1993:	9 of her animals died in the drought, leaving one 9-month-old cow. Her family had to hoe the land.
1994:	Her brother entrusted a donkey to her. This was spanned to the young cow and used to open up furrows for planting (rather than ploughing the whole field).
1995/6:	Mai Farai teamed her animals with another young cow belonging to Mr Matuka, a friend and neighbour (and borrowed Mai Collen and Newton's span). This was not a very powerful span and could only be used to plough the contours with easily workable soils. For the contours with heavier soils that required more serious traction she hired Mr Chipudzi and his son to plough with their 4-donkey span.
1997:	Her cow and Mr Matuka's had calved the previous year and so their respective cows and calves were again teamed to plough each other's fields. Mai Farai's donkey (entrusted to her by her brother) was still available to replace the calves when they were tired.
1998:	Her cow produced two further calves in June 1997 and she planned to introduce them to ploughing this year. Mr Matuka now has 3 cattle in total. They still intend to pair up to plough with each other. The donkey, however, will be used only for transportation. Mr Matuka and she now hire out their teamed span to plough other people's fields.

with: 'Some people use cattle very roughly'; 'If you treat other people badly, tomorrow you will do that to cattle. Such a person should not be trusted'; 'A rough-rider is always blamed'. Sharing relationships based on trust operate across lineages and even ethnic groups. Investment in social networks by cultivating allegiances, 'drinking beer together' (cf. Berry 1989) and building up a good reputation is crucial. As well as friendship links, sharing relations with in-laws are common, emphasising the importance of marriage as an institution providing channels of access to livestock and labour. But trust and reputation seem to be as important as kinship. Although as Mapfumele (a kraalhead in Chikombedzi) observed: 'if we are sitting around the fire and the sparks cause two children to catch fire – you help your child first!'

Box 4.3 illustrates cases in Ngundu where relatives have shared draught power by teaming their draught animals. It also illustrates how these arrangements are embedded in wider social networks and affiliations with complex reciprocal obligations. These arrangements are not 'breaking down', as is sometimes blithely commented, but are constantly being renegotiated and restructured. Pairing/teaming suits both parties, particularly when their fields are on soils that require cultivation at different times. It is also useful even when both partners already own a span as it enables one span to plough a furrow and another to follow after the planter covering the land.

Exchange arrangements
Households also regularly enter into more formalised barter/exchange arrangements when negotiating access to draught power. Examples of arrangements observed include: exchanging labour for draught power, land for draught, and grain for draught (see Box 4.4).

As Jacob Mahenehene's case illustrates, the respective draught and non-draught owners enter into deals with very different bargaining positions – and the terms of a deal are often much better for the draught owner. Some informants perceive it to be difficult to persuade people to enter into draught sharing arrangements. Babi Siwawa comments: 'people don't understand these arrangements – they think they will be tricked. Their education is low and they are jealous. They think it is better to carry on suffering on their own than to help someone else get rich.' Draught exchange arrangements can actually maintain inequality and exacerbate social stratification while spreading access to draught power.[21]

Work parties
Work parties, where someone invites people to assist with work and in return brews beer or *maheu* (a non-alcoholic sorghum-based drink) and provides food for them, are another means by which people are able to access draught power for ploughing. They are also a means of attracting labour for such activities as weeding, brick-making, carrying manure harvesting and building. It is implicitly recognised that attendance at a work party will be reciprocated. These are variously known in our study sites as *humwe, nhimbe, hoka* and *dhava*.

---

[21]Also despite the large investment of time, effort, friendship and money in negotiating access to draught power it by no means guarantees a good harvest. Indeed, most of the case studies from Chikombedzi refer to the 1997/8 season when almost no-one managed to harvest anything at all because of drought.

Box 4.4   Exchange arrangements: labour and land for draught

Jacob Mahenehene [Chikombedzi] (born 1968, married)
In the 1995/6 season Jacob made an arrangement with Langton Siwawa to plough his fields in return for the use of his span on his own field. However, Langton subsequently hired a boy to do the ploughing and renegotiated the deal with Jacob. Instead Jacob and his wife were to weed Langton's fields for four days. In return they had the use of one of his spans for one 'day'. However, Jacob had ploughed from 6.00am to 11.00am when Langton turned up saying he was overworking his animals and should stop. Jacob found this unfair – for four days' work by himself and his wife he thinks he should at least have been able to use the span in the afternoon as well.
In 1996/7 Jacob hired Samuel and his 3 donkeys to plough a quarter of his field for 5 buckets of maize. He paid a further $200 to hire draught power for another quarter, used hoes to cultivate another quarter and left the final quarter fallow.
In 1997/8 Jacob negotiated with his sister-in-law (the wife of a brother working in South Africa who owns 5 oxen and 3 cows). In return for spending seven days ploughing her fields he was allowed to take a span for two and a half days to plough his own fields. However, by this time, owing to the sparse rains, the soil was no longer moist.

Frank Sekenya [Ngundu] (born 1960; settled in Ngundu 1987, married)
Frank and his wife have one cow of their own. However, since 1993 they also keep 4 animals belonging to Frank's mother-in-law, one belonging to a cousin (Mr Mago) and one belonging to a nephew in their kraal, making a total of 7 head of cattle – all suitable for draught power purposes. This puts them in a situation of being relatively 'rich' in terms of draught power, which they take advantage of to the full. As well as ploughing his own fields Frank enters into a variety of draught arrangements:
● He ploughs his relatives' fields (those owning the animals entrusted to his care).
● He hires out his spans to plough other people's fields. As well as by other farmers he is hired by DRSS to plough two research trial sites where the farmers lack draught power.
● He sometimes ploughs the fields of his neighbours and close friends – Albert Kwangore and George Dube – for 'free', and in return they help with the ploughing labour when he ploughs commercially (they also receive a small fee).
● He ploughs a furrow through the fields he has to pass through on the way to and from his own fields (Mai Namo and Morgan Pambare's fields).
● He ploughs the fields of two (currently) neighbours in return for a 'contour' on which he can plant and harvest his own crops (Mrs Jimson Chibooza and Mrs Gede).
● He occasionally attends *humwes* for ploughing – most recently for George Dube.
The land and money gained in this way belongs to his immediate family alone (not to the relatives who own the animals he is entrusted with). But he does provide maize grain for his relatives should they need it.

Across all the study sites, there are oft-repeated claims made about the decline of these recriprocal labour and mutual help institutions: 'people only want money now', 'they are jealous of other people's success', 'there is no communal spirit of helping each other these days', 'I want money not beer.' This trend of increasing monetisation and individualisation of production at the expense of mutual help is borne out most in the Chipuriro and Neshangwe cases.

Yet in Chikombedzi, where people still do perceive a decline in these arrangements, drought and poverty (rather than a notion of reduced communal spirit or monetisation) are most commonly cited as the reason. Babi Siwawa, for example says:

> now there are fewer *dhavas* than in the past because we are short of food with the drought. If you have a *dhava* you must be sure that the people who come enjoy themselves. If you treat them badly [by not providing enough food and drink] they will not come again.

Recurrent drought and harvest failure means there is often insufficient sorghum needed to brew beer or *maheu*. Also, with lack of rains the period in which the soil is moist and ready for planting is very short – 'if you run around following other people [to *dhavas*] you will find the soil is dry by the time you plant your own crops' (see Box 4.5).

Box 4.5   Work parties

Amos Chimenya (Ngundu)
Amos has had no draught animals since 1978. At various times he has received 'free' assistance from family and neighbours who loan their spans for ploughing, sometimes in return for labour. He also sometimes hires spans. But his main strategy for gaining draught power has been to hold *humwes*, which he does every year. In recent years this strategy was most successful in 1993 when seven spans turned up to plough. Amos attributed this to the fact that he was still working (selling meat) at the time and 'people thought they would be well fed'. More recently he has had difficulty in attracting many people to plough at his *humwes*. The problem as he sees it is that at the onset of rains everyone wants to plough at the same time and they do not have enough spans to plough for other people as well. In the 1997 season, expecting six spans, Amos had bought $20 worth of fish, a chicken (costing $45), six pots of beer (at $60 each) and $20 worth of mealie meal. But only two people attended his *humwe* (Mr Makonde and Mr Matinere) and they ploughed from 7 to 10 in the morning. This meant that only a small portion of his fields were ploughed and the rest was left fallow.

On the other hand, limited rainfall and soil moisture can encourage even those with draught power to call work parties for ploughing to take maximum advantage of it. For example, Mr Mavenge, in Chikombedzi, organises *dhava* for ploughing nearly every year. This is despite the fact that he already has three spans of oxen of his own. In a recent year approximately 30 people attended – some with spans, some with hoes and some empty-handed and 'in search of beer!' With the coming of the rains he wanted to make maximum use of the soil moisture and plough and plant as large an area as soon as possible. In this respect those with draught power are better situated to hold *dhava* at the 'peak' period. Those without draught power are more likely to have to hold ploughing *dhava* before or some time after the rains if they want to attract those with spans – thereby missing the optimal period.[22] The timing of *dhavas* is announced and discussed within communities to ensure that they do not clash.

---

[22]Although, as Worby (1995) points out, there is a certain amount of staggering in peak periods owing to micro variations in soil type and rainfall.

Religious affiliation has a large impact on *dhava* attendance, with many members of churches avoiding *dhavas* where beer is brewed and more likely to attend 'maheu' *dhavas* for members of their own congregation.[23] New Church work groups (such as Vapostori and the Zionist Church) are a rapidly growing phenomenon. These have long been in existence but their use seems to be escalating. Members of the congregation gather together to form a commercial work party who are hired out for labour-intensive tasks such as weeding and brick-making. The money is used to pay for Church gatherings. They are perceived as being very efficient and cost-effective ('no need to provide food and beer and they are diligent workers unlike some lazy people who turn up to *humwes* just for the beer') and, in some areas, such as Chipuriro, they are increasingly replacing work parties. Church members also assist each other in times of crisis. With the numbers of people belonging to 'new churches' growing, membership of religious groups is increasingly a means through which relationships are forged between households.

In Chikombedzi, as elsewhere, it is common to hear people say that there are fewer *dhava* now than in the past. However this is not a universal trend – rather, some families are avoiding *dhava* for various reasons while others continue to rely on them. The trend seems to be for such reciprocal work parties to become more tightly kin-based with mainly close relatives or friendly neighbours attending each other's.

Similarly in Ngundu, while many people no longer attend beer work parties, *humwes* have not disappeared. They have, though, become more focused on tighter clusters of like-minded family and friends, with others no longer participating owing to religious dislike of beer gatherings or a more commericialised/individualised outlook.

Many farmers talk of holding or attending *humwes* for ploughing in the seasons after the drought – but it is not possible to say categorically that the drought led to a breakdown in such group work practices (cf. Bratton 1984) or, on the other hand, to a reinforcement of such mutual aid (cf. Scoones *et al.* 1996). Rather both trends can be observed side by side – depending on the specific social networks and kin relations within which each household is embedded.

Hiring of draught power
Alongside this proliferation of mutual help arrangements there has undoubtedly been a trend towards increased commercialisation of draught access. Markets for draught power are found in all four sites, but hiring draught for cash is particularly, and increasingly, common in Chipuriro and Neshangwe.

Chipuriro is the most individualised and 'marketised' of the four sites. Close to Harare, with high agricultural potential and high population density, its situation best fits the scenario outlined above, with 'traditional' mutual help practices being eroded and usurped by cash transactions. In Neshangwe the rollback of the tsetse fly zone has only recently permitted livestock to be held in the area. This means that livestock holdings are still relatively low and cotton provides relatively high revenues. These two factors contribute to a large demand for the hire of draught animals and tractors.

---

[23]Commonly people distinguish between *humwes* where 'seven day' beer is provided and those where *maheu* (unfermented sweet malt drink) is provided. Generally it seems that 'beer *humwes*' are less common and less well attended than in the past. In part this is a result of the fact that many converts to churches such as Apostolic Faith do not drink alcohol or even malted grain and thus view *humwes* as 'for beer drinkers only' and do not attend them.

Hiring draught power is not a new phenomenon, though. Hiring of draught oxen and tractors was reported to have occurred in Ngundu in the early 1960s.[24] Yet, with the spread of the market economy, it has been a growing trend. Hiring draught power has certain advantages over borrowing. It usually enables speedier access than complex negotiations with kin or friends, enabling farmers to plough at the optimum time soon after the first rains and take advantage of available moisture.

Donkeys and scotchcarts are also hired out for transporting materials, and increasingly there is a market for hiring tractors. In 1998 some farmers were the beneficiaries of one-off payments made to ex-combatants from the Liberation War. In Chikombedzi, where draught animals are in short supply and considered an increasingly bad risk, some of these ex-combatants invested in tractors and trailers that they hire out for ploughing and transport.

There are also formal organisations providing draught power. The District Development Fund (DDF) provides tractors, but is overstretched and relatively expensive.[25] With a large demand it is rarely able to plough farmers' fields at the most appropriate time. In Neshangwe the Lower Guruve Development Association (LGDA) also provides tractors, and in Chikombedzi one can be hired from a cooperative irrigation scheme. In Chipuriro there were also reports of a commercial farmer from neighbouring commercial farming areas who ploughs rural farmers' fields using his tractors. A variety of institutions for draught access therefore enable non-draught animal-owning farmers to integrate crops and livestock through the use of the plough. Given the high percentage of farmers owning less than a span these institutions are vital to rural livelihoods in Zimbabwe.

Two apparently contradictory patterns are unfolding simultaneously – one is for draught access arrangements to become increasingly commercialised, and the other is for people to draw on kinship links and social networks more heavily to negotiate a variety of draught sharing, borrowing and exchanging arrangements. These different patterns are exhibited to varying extents in our four study sites. In Ngundu and Chikombedzi, where severe drought has recently brought about draught shortage, farmers are combating uncertainty by entering into a range of constantly renegotiated exchange and sharing arrangements. Yet hiring for cash is also increasingly common – one in a range of possible institutional strategies. A particular portion of field might even be ploughed early with hired draught and planted with maize, and the remainder left until a 'free' arrangement can be negotiated. In Chipuriro, where fewer households are without draught power and equipment, draught access has become more commercialised. Similarly, in Neshangwe, where draught animals have only been relatively recently introduced, and subsidised tractors are readily available, draught hiring for cash predominates. Bratton (1984: 21) described draught exchange as 'a transitional phenomenon ... not destined for any long-run or permanent place in raising general standards of productivity in communal lands. In time, the practice may even dwindle to little more than an historical curiosity.' This does not appear to

---

[24]Worby (1995: 24, n.4) notes the presence of young men hiring themselves out to plough for others without sufficient oxen or labour in the 'Reserves' after the First World War.

[25]Although in the context of rampant inflation DDF's price increases have sometimes lagged behind those of private operators.

be the case. These arrangements look set to remain vital if a large number of Zimbabwean farmers are to continue gaining access to draught power.

Livestock loaning

Livestock loaning arrangements (*kufiyisa* in Shangaan; *kuronzera* in Shona) have played, and continue to perform, a crucial role in many of the study areas. These constitute another means of accessing draught power, but are also employed as a means of accessing manure, a drought-coping strategy and a means of spreading herding labour. In the colonial era livestock loaning arrangements were also employed as a means of 'hiding' livestock from official view to evade destocking requirements. Again there is, at first glance, a story of breakdown and gradual disappearance of these arrangements – but this is not borne out in practice in Chikombedzi in the way that perhaps it is in Chipuriro and Ngundu.

Under such arrangements, the livestock borrower gets to use the draught power and milk and rarely, although more frequently in the past, a heifer every few years. The advantages to the lender include: cattle in smaller groups tend to be looked after better; the reduced cost of herding and veterinary care; a decreased risk of losing the whole herd in a disease outbreak – as they are spread around; it avoids overstocking in their own kraal; and it avoids the necessity of building a larger kraal.

Before the Liberation War, when some farmers had extremely large herds, *kufiyisa* arrangements were particularly widespread in Chikombedzi. Makuso Siwawa, for example, moved to Chikombedzi from Mberengwa in 1952. He built up a herd of 800 cattle most of which were held in *kufiyisa* arrangements by a large number of people. The general decline in livestock holdings with the 1991/2 drought means that fewer animals in total are loaned or borrowed, but more people than in the past are entering into these arrangements. *Kufiyisa* is thus becoming smaller in scale – sometimes involving only a single beast. It is particularly common for people to keep part of their herds with relatives or friends in Sengwe (the adjoining Communal Area) where grazing land is relatively much more abundant and where many people lost all their stock in the drought and want draught animals, although in some cases cattle will be brought back to Chikombedzi for the ploughing season. The reason for the resurgence in this institution is that it is, in part, a means of spreading the risk to livestock of drought – which is perceived as more of a threat in recent years.

Kufiyisa arrangements also exist between Communal Area farmers and farmers in the nearby 'small-scale' commercial farms.[26] These operate on the same basis with the borrower having access to the draught power. Some 12–16 animals – mainly cows – are involved. This benefits the small-scale farm, as the owner is able to keep more animals than his official stocking rate and allow grass to regrow in certain areas. Mr Rukanda, for example, loaned 5–7 cattle to 10 families after the 1991/2 drought who had approached him asking for help. He 'graded' them on the basis of need. He maintains it was done out of charity. However, when another drought threatened, he called almost all of these animals back as he was destocking all his older animals. Four

---

[26]Small-Scale Commercial Farms, formerly termed 'African Purchase Areas', are black-owned farms with freehold, as opposed to communal tenure.

of the small-scale farmers also borrow cattle from communal farmers, as they can ensure that the cattle will get good grazing.

These flexible institutions are today somewhat constrained by veterinary controls demanded by the European Community to combat the spread of Foot and Mouth disease. The movement of livestock out of the so-called 'Red Zone', or vaccinated zone, (into which Chikombedzi falls) is prohibited unless it is directly to a slaughterhouse; and movements within the red zone require veterinary permits. These restrictions therefore inhibit drought-coping mechanisms.

Box 4.6 Livestock loaning arrangements in Chikombedzi

Hanwan Makondo
As a young man he was lent two oxen under a *kufiyisa* arrangement by his father-in-law. With the relatively large harvests he gained with the draught power he was able to exchange grain for two heifers (at 10 bags a beast). He was then able to plough with his own span. By the 1991/2 drought he had 12 animals of which 6 died and 6 survived. In 1993 Hanwan began lending an animal to a friend – Thomas Makajan. Now Hanwan has 19 head, 5 of which are looked after by Thomas (the offspring of the original loaned animal). Hanwan is able to ask for the animals back at any time if he wants to sell them – however, he trusts Thomas sufficiently to look after them responsibly even in drought years.

Mr Moyo
Before the war he had 49 cattle loaned out – to Mr Machende (11), Mr Zuland (18) and Mr Alomela (20) – all in Masukwe. They were all paid with heifers. This arrangement lasted approximately six years until the coming of the war when all these animals died. After the war Moyo exchanged the few oxen that had survived (at Chikombedzi) for cows, and these gradually multiplied, such that by 1991 he again had 21 head on loan to Mr Mazondo in Masukwe. All these bar one died in the 1991/2 drought. He has subsequently bought an animal and, with breeding, currently has 6. However, this is seen by Moyo as too few to loan out, and he is holding on to them – relying on crop residue from his plot at the irrigation scheme rather than loaning to the relatively more abundant grazing areas to keep his cattle fed throughout the dry period.

Manure sharing arrangements

Institutional arrangements for the exchange, sharing or sale of manure are uncommon in Zimbabwe. Manure sharing arrangements, where two farmers with few livestock kraal their animals together and alternately use the manure, were reported to occasionally take place in Ngundu. There is also a market for poultry manure for application to gardens. Manure access is something that must be negotiated for within households also. Sons with no livestock of their own must arrange with their fathers, for example, how much manure they can take for use on their own fields.

The pattern that emerges across the range of institutional configurations is one of diversity and differentiation. Statements claiming the 'breakdown of traditional mutual help institutions' are certainly true for some people in some places, but disguise the fact that in the face of marketisation and trends towards individualisation of production by many, others are relying on social networks. Drought and economic structural adjustment have contributed to increasing vulnerability that has led people to invest in these social networks as a means of gaining access to resources (cf. Berry 1993). We must be wary both of assuming that, as market forces permeate Zimbabwe's Communal Areas, non-wage kin and community-based relations give way, and of portraying reciprocal help institutions as emblematic of a 'traditional' egalitarian ideal (Worby 1995).

A generalisation regarding changes in institutional arrangements that is justified by our findings is that the arrangements people are entering into are less stable and more opportunisitic than before. In the face of increasing uncertainty, people are running 'portfolios' of constantly renegotiated institutional arrangements – from livestock loans to work parties – with a range of actors and networks, new and old. Another trend is for the emergence of new social support networks. Particularly striking is the emergence of new churches with close-knit congregations who share labour and draught power and hire themselves out as work parties. However, there is not only a wide diversity of experience between our study sites, but also across and within households. Differences in wealth, gender and age influence the social networks people can draw on and their power in negotiating arrangements, a theme dealt with in depth in the following section.

Institutional arrangements are historically dynamic. Key events, such as drought and the introduction of new technologies, have shaped the arrangements people enter into. The introduction of the plough in the early 20th century, for example, led to a decline in the necessity of large kin-based hoeing work parties and allowed many women and young men out from the patronage of 'big men' (Wilson 1986). More recently reduced livestock holdings have encouraged a proliferation of draught access arrangements among vulnerable households, and livestock-loaning institutions have been adapted as a means for safeguarding livestock in uncertain climatic conditions. Notwithstanding this, we must treat with caution Cliffe's (1986) notion that such forms of cooperation and sharing can be actively promoted by policy (see above). As Bratton (1984: 20) puts it:

> Because draught exchange is primarily a social practice, it is not easily susceptible to engineering by outside agencies. Farmers choose their own collaborators – usually close relatives (or neighbours – draught exchange is of necessity localised since cattle cannot be driven very far). Ties of cooperation of this sort cannot be legislated from above and may even be damaged by hasty or clumsy intervention.

Social differentiation

Studies of agricultural systems in Zimbabwe have increasingly taken on board the self-evident fact that communal area farmers constitute a very diverse group. Inevitably people are socially and economically differentiated by gender, age, wealth, class and ethnicity. Equally unsurprisingly, these different people pursue different livelihood strategies, drawing on crops and livestock to different extents depending on their resources (natural, economic and social capital), experience and expertise. Yet, as we have seen, agricultural extension in Zimbabwe remains wedded in many respects to a model for crop and livestock management – the mixed farming model – that is a realistic option for only a minority of farmers. This section maps out some of the axes of social and economic differentiation in rural Zimbabwe and relates these to the differing strategies for crop and livestock management discussed earlier. In the next section, we go on to identify a range of pathways of change experienced by different groups across the study sites and make suggestions as to how policy could more productively engage with those pathways not envisaged by the unitary mixed farming model.

Draught power ownership

It is particularly instructive to compare the assets and strategies of draught power owners and non-owners, categories that also provide a good proxy for wealth. As we have seen, for those who do not own enough draught animals or who lack labour, negotiation of access to these inputs is of key importance. Notwithstanding the institutional arrangements people enter into to gain access to draught power, ownership of draught power is highly correlated with other forms of asset ownership and with particular farming strategies relevant to crop–livestock integration. Fig. 4.12 represents the amount of times the average values of three particular categories for non-draught owners in our sample must be multiplied to equal the values of draught owners.[27] For instance, the average size of away fields is eight times larger for draught owners than non-draught owners in Chipuriro, twice as large in Ngundu and Neshangwe and 1.5 times larger in Chikombedzi. Strikingly, in Ngundu draught power owners are 11 times more likely to apply manure to their fields than non-draught owners.

Ownership of draught animals is also positively correlated with greater numbers of all types of livestock owned. Similarly, those with draught animals are more likely to have a garden, use inorganic fertiliser, receive remittances, and own a borehole or well. Yet draught animal ownership has more of an impact on manure use than draught use since, although there are institutional mechanisms for accessing draught power, there are few for manure access. Farmers without their own draught animals are therefore more likely to hoe, or plough late, and use less cattle manure more carefully on particular field niches and gardens.

Gender

Conventionally men and women in Zimbabwe have grown different crops in different spaces using different techniques. They have also owned different types of livestock. Extensive, plough-based agriculture, where grain crops are planted on dryland fields, is a male-dominated activity in Zimbabwe. By contrast hoe cultivation, vegetable gardening and smallstock husbandry have tended to be more the preserve of women. However, these gendered roles are not static and, in the light of some of the events described above (such as drought, ESAP, etc.), some of our study sites have exhibited changing associations of farming/animal husbandry activities and gender. In particular, men are increasingly colonising women's spaces (gardens) and activities (smallstock husbandry) in Ngundu, Chipuriro and Chikombedzi, as draught power shortages discourage extensive outfield cultivation and vegetables command premium

---

[27]Draught ownership here refers to the ownership of two or more draught animals.

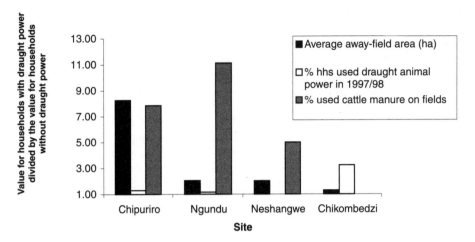

Figure 4.12 Factor comparisons between draught owners and non-draught owners

prices for urban and local markets. This has implications for the ways in which crops and livestock are integrated, as smallstock manure assumes increasing importance in soil fertility maintenance strategies.

Ethnicity

In all of the study areas a variety of ethnic groups are represented. Chipuriro is dominated by Korekore (76 per cent), with Zezeru constituting the next largest group (12 per cent). The largest ethnic group in Neshangwe is also Korekore, with a significant number of our survey (26 per cent) claiming non-Zimbabwean nationality – Mozambican or Zambian. Ngundu is mainly Karanga, with small numbers of Ndau, Ndebele and others. The Chikombedzi sample is mainly Shangaan (80 per cent), with a significant minority of Karanga (12 per cent) and some Ndebele. There are differences in strategies followed by ethnic groups and, equally important, different perceptions of these strategies.

Different ethnic groups tend to be characterised locally according to their involvement in agriculture. Ethnic groups are still popularly stereotyped in terms of how 'backward' or 'modern' they are – with an implicit notion of progress away from the most backward state of minimum cultivation and livestock rearing. Since Alvord's day this view has been propagated by extension officials. A system where agriculture or livestock dominates is also considered 'unbalanced' and relatively backward. Systems characterised by both cropping and livestock but focused on 'traditional' crops, as is the case with sorghum cultivation in Chikombedzi, or 'traditional' techniques, such as floodplain cultivation in Neshangwe, are considered 'backward'.

In Neshangwe, the VaDoma (who live north of Neshangwe) are regarded as the most 'backward' as they still pursue nomadic lifestyles based on foraging and hunting with little agricultural activity. In the same communal area the Korekore are also sometimes perceived as a backward group who practise traditional agriculture along the floodplains and are essentially goat owners who have yet to make a success of cropping on lowlands. They are seen as late adopters of new technologies and practices, which is still often ascribed to suspicion and superstition – much as it was in the colonial era. However, studies in the Zambezi valley by Derman (1995) and Spierenburg (1995) show wealth, education and wage employment to be the predictors of agricultural practices and cattle ownership, rather than ethnicity.

In Chikombedzi, similar characterisations can be drawn between the Shangaan and the Shona (and other immigrant groups). The colonial authorities were fond of using pejorative accounts of Shangaan agricultural acumen, preferring to caricature them as good hunters and miners (in the face of evidence that they adopted the plough earlier than their highveld neighbours). These perceptions have carried over to the present day when Shona and Ndebele immigrants are the main cattle owners and are perceived as better farmers and more 'modern' than the 'backward and traditional' Shangaan.

In Chipuriro and Ngundu the associations by ethnic group are less obvious. Though there is an acknowledged variety of ethnic groups in these communal areas, the distinctions between them are no longer obvious. Differentiation is now related more to the status of the household and membership of that household to particular projects. Thus, for example, in Ngundu cotton and maize farmers who belong to a conservation tillage project are held in high regard. Similarly, in Chipuriro, the tobacco and paprika farmers associated with the commercial farmers are also thought to be successful. And in Neshangwe the farmers that were brought by the Mid-Zambezi project have a certain kudos. Although ethnic differences are not so obvious, kinship and group ties are important in Ngundu and Chipuriro. Various arrangements have been forged between relations. A new type of relationship is also becoming more evident where kinship is defined within the context of religious affiliation.

Age

Cropping and livestock management strategies are also differentiated according to peoples' stage in their life cycle. As people grow older, marry, have children, and enter into and break out of social networks they are able to call on different complements of resources. Over time 'traditional' life cycle stages change. For example, in Chikombedzi young labour migrants are no longer able to invest in cattle in the way that their fathers were. Changes in the status of migrant labourers (they are now mainly illegal 'border jumpers'), changes in the type of work being undertaken (farm work and urban odd-jobs replacing mining) and increased competition for work have all contributed to the diminishing buying power of returned migrants. Now it is more common for young men to return with consumer durables, such as radios and mountain bikes, than with enough money to invest in cattle.

Multiple pathways of change

Zimbabwean communal area farmers turn out to be a highly heterogeneous group, employing different agricultural and livestock husbandry strategies depending on the economic, natural, human and social capital they are able to marshal. Over the long term these day-to-day strategies map out particular pathways of agricultural change.

Over time the pathways of change in each of the four sites studied have been driven by conjunctures of events and mediated by particular institutions. Taken together these insights lead to an important conclusion about crop–livestock dynamics in Zimbabwe: it is a nonsense to speak in terms of one linear evolution towards integrated mixed farming systems over time as the 'natural' pattern from which others deviate. There are, rather, multiple pathways of change with different elements of crop–livestock integration being adopted or discarded by different people in different places. Even the four differing 'broad pathways' of each site described earlier disguise a great deal of diversity. Obviously in some respects there are as many pathways as farmers, as everyone's day-to-day strategies and thus longer-term pathways of change are bound subtly to differ. However, looking across the four sites we have identified a range of pathways that many people are pursuing in common. These are depicted in Table 4.7, and five are described in more detail below. Of these 11 pathways only three are explicitly recognised and engaged with by agricultural extension and research. This means that the complexity and diversity of other potential pathways, so crucial to many Zimbabweans' livelihoods, are being largely ignored and, consequently, inadequately supported.

Pathway from land-extensive agriculture to intensive mixed farming by 'Master Farmers'

The increasing integration of crops and livestock along the lines of the mixed farming model has definitely been an identifiable pathway of change across Zimbabwe. As we have seen, manure and draught power use and improved fodder management have been central tenets of agricultural extension since the 1920s and have been adopted by many, in large part owing to land shortage encouraging intensification. Those closest to this pathway in our study areas were the relatively wealthy livestock owners in Chipuriro and Ngundu. They use cattle manure in the recommended fashion; have at least one oxen span; and store crop residue for dry season fodder. What has not emerged, though, are individual farm homesteads with private grazing and arable in the farm boundary. Instead communal rangelands are integrated with individualised arable production. Across all four sites probably only 10 to 20 percent of households are following this pathway, although it is implicitly assumed to be universal by much agricultural research and extension. However, this broad pathway conceals a certain amount of variation. As we have described, farmers may have been adopting only specific elements of this package of technologies owing to resource constraints or simply because their goals differ from those built into the mixed farming model (e.g. they are collecting crop residues as a drought-coping mechanism, rather than to intensify livestock management).

Pathway from subsistence cropping of maize and small grains to cash cropping of cotton and contract farming

A second pathway of change – particularly evident in Neshangwe – is for shifting cultivation and riverine cultivation to give way to extensive cropping of cotton (driven by, and in turn encouraging, the uptake of draught animal power) alongside riverine cultivation. Manure has been less important than inorganic fertilisers, and stall feeding of crop residues has not played a part in the transformation of the farming

Table 4.7 Pathways of agricultural change.

	Pathways of agricultural change	Groups	Complies with current policy?	Context and conditions
Extensification pathways	Extensification of maize, sorghum or cotton production with animal draught power	Richer households (Neshangwe; Chikombedzi)	–	Land availability; social networks to gain access to land; capital to buy or hire oxen; high crop prices; tsetse fly eradication
	Extensification of maize, sorghum or cotton production with tractor power	Richer households (Neshangwe; Chikombedzi)	*	Land availability; social networks to gain access to land; capital to buy or hire tractors (e.g. ex-combatants); high crop prices
Intensification pathways	Intensification of maize and cotton production following the mixed farming model (oxen draught, manure application)	'Master Farmers' Richer households (Chipuriro, Ngundu, Neshangwe)	***	Labour; capital to buy or hire oxen; extension advice
	Intensification of maize and cotton production with application of inorganic fertilisers and/or irrigated plots	'Master Farmers'; Richer households (Chipuriro, Ngundu, Neshangwe)	***	Contract farming; irrigation schemes; labour; capital to buy inputs and buy/hire draught power
	Intensification through use of mixed spans of oxen, cows and/or donkeys for tillage	Medium and poorer households (Ngundu, Chikombedzi)	–	Labour; draught power shortage; capital to hire draught power

	Intensification of vegetable gardens, wetlands and key niches	All, especially women	—	Labour; growing markets for garden produce
Livestock-focused pathways	Towards small ruminant production	Poorer households, women (Chipuriro, Ngundu, Chikembezdi)	—	Perceived increase in drought risk; growing local and external markets for goats and sheep; tsetse fly incidence
	Intensification of cattle production based on pen-fattening with crop residue and commercial feed and/or dairying	Rich households (Chipuriro)	**	Labour; capital to buy inputs
Diversification pathways	'Subsistence' production supported by off-farm income, trade, and/or wildlife revenue	Poorer households (Neshangwe, Chikombezdi)	*	Wards within Campfire schemes; opportunities to diversify; access to common property resources
	Abandonment of crop and livestock production for off-farm income	Poorer households, young men and women (Ngundu, Neshangwe, Chikombezdi)	—	Opportunities to diversify; access to common property resources
	Abandonment of crop and livestock production for labour migration	Poorer households, young men (Neshangwe, Chikombezdi)	—	Migration opportunities

system. This type of intensification diverges from that envisaged by Alvord and others of the homestead mixed farm in that it is explicitly cash crop production-orientated, and inorganic fertilisers and, in some cases, tractors have played a more important role than manure and animal draught power. In recent years this type of farming has owed much to contracts entered into by farmers with cotton companies (and now sorghum and paprika buyers) to provide inputs in return for sales.

Pathway from extensive outfield cultivation to intensive gardening and 'niche farming'

A further pattern that has emerged in recent years is for farmers to shift the spatial target of their investments of labour and manure from relatively large outfields to gardens closer to the home and particular field niches. This is particularly marked in Ngundu where there is a good market for garden-grown vegetables. Men have become increasingly involved in gardening (previously a 'women's job'). This has also been stimulated by draught power shortages, as gardens can be cultivated by hand. Smallstock and poultry manure is applied when cattle are not owned.

Pathways from a focus on cattle as a key agricultural input to a focus on smallstock and donkeys

In the context of recent severe droughts in Zimbabwe, particularly in the south, another clear trend with respect to crop and livestock management has emerged. Livestock deaths and draught shortages have led more farmers to hand-hoe or use cows and donkeys instead of oxen for tillage purposes. Similarly, smallstock manure is playing a larger role in soil fertility management. Also smallstock production in its own right is assuming a greater importance for household livelihood strategies (particularly in Chikombedzi and Ngundu). It is difficult to say at this stage whether these are permanent trends and whether we will continue to see a reconfiguring of crop–livestock integration to involve non-cattle livestock. This will depend on the extent to which cattle populations in the south of Zimbabwe bounce back from the devastating impact of recent droughts and flooding.

Pathway from cropping and livestock management towards a diversification into off-farm activities

A further dynamic increasingly found in all four of the study areas is for farmers to spend an increasing amount of time on a widening portfolio of off-farm activities. This diversification tends to be in addition to cropping and livestock management rather than abandoning it. Legal or illegal cross-border labour migration (to South Africa) and trade (with South Africa and Mozambique), of which there is a long history in Chikombedzi, are becoming an increasingly important livelihood strategy for people, particularly young men. Similarly, recipients of Campfire receipts in Neshangwe and Chikombedzi,[28] or sculptors selling wood-carvings on the road to South Africa in

[28]Receipts from Campfire, however, have been negligible when divided among communities in these two sites, and there is a certain amount of disillusionment with Campfire – a feeling that the costs of crop and livestock depredation by wildlife and the coercive controls on resource use outweigh the meagre financial gains to households.

Ngundu, are broadening their 'livelihood portfolios' by diversifying into off-farm activities. This pathway, by choice or by default, is increasingly popular with those who do not possess the necessary complement of land, labour and draught power to pursue agricultural intensification on the mixed farming model.

Conclusions

The package of technologies associated with the mixed farming model has driven policy on crop and livestock integration in Zimbabwe. The mixed farming model also is the basis for many technical planning assumptions for land reform and resettlement. As land reform and resettlement are again high on the political agenda an awareness of these assumptions becomes imperative. This model has led to the diversity of other potential experiences, and the non-technical institutional arrangements so central to farming in particular and to livelihoods generally, being ignored in the design of resettlement schemes and the formulation of policies for the improvement of land and animal husbandry.

Extension recommendations informed by the mixed farming model focus on application of cattle manure, use of draught oxen and improved fodder management. But our findings show many farmers are following strategies in the short term – and pathways of change over the longer term – that diverge from this idealised model. There is no single ideal pathway of agricultural intensification that all households will, or should, follow. Farmers' access to land, livestock and external sources of income govern the options open to them. And the trade-offs farmers make are mediated by institutional arrangements and are influenced by conjunctures of certain events.

Those who are able to follow these recommendations are thus only a minority elite – the 'progressive' Master Farmers. Becoming part of the mixed farming vision and therefore beneficiaries of the considerable research and extension investment over many years in Zimbabwe is only available to a few. The farmer with a few goats and chickens who gets by through making compost from grass and leaf litter, hand-hoeing, or applying goat manure to garden vegetables, by contrast, remains excluded. She or he cannot comply with the mixed farming ideal.

As the world's attention is focused on land and poverty in Zimbabwe, research and development policy needs to take account of the diversity and complexity, as well as the 'invisible' informal institutional arrangements we have outlined, if it is to contribute to the goal of achieving sustainable livelihoods.

5

Crop–Livestock Policy in Africa: What Is To Be Done?

JOSHUA RAMISCH, JAMES KEELEY, IAN SCOONES
& WILLIAM WOLMER

Introduction

This book has explored the dynamics of crop–livestock interactions in three countries of East, West and Southern Africa. These case studies have each identified a diversity of crop–livestock integration pathways in different resource endowment areas and traced changes over the last 50–100 years. This diversity stands in direct contrast to the linear, evolutionary accounts of agricultural change that dominate research and development policy, which see standard types of crop–livestock relations emerging in response to inevitable changes in population pressure and factor proportions.

The diversity of crop–livestock integration pathways has emerged in this study because it explicitly adopted an anthropological and historical approach while examining the three main technical elements of crop–livestock integration (use of manure for soil fertility, draught power for cultivation and transport, and crop residue for fodder). Such an holistic approach has encouraged us to recognise that people make their own history, but not necessarily under conditions of their own choosing. Livelihoods emerge out of past actions and decisions are made within specific historical and agroecological conditions, and are constantly shaped by institutions and social arrangements. This approach has entailed an analytical focus on four elements:

- *Livelihoods* – Cropping and livestock husbandry practices are embedded in broader livelihood contexts.
- *History* – Particular key events and combinations of events affect crop–livestock interactions and influence pathways of change.
- *Social actors* – The dynamics of crop–livestock interactions differ significantly not only by place but also by people. This research has mapped the contrasting experiences of different actors.

- *Institutions* – Uncovering the often invisible social arrangements underpinning farmers' and herders' activities and mediating access to resources is essential to understanding the dynamics of crop and livestock management.

Pathways of change are therefore not linear or deterministic, and no simple typology is sufficient to explain the large diversity of processes and outcomes observed. This is not just the stereotypical, academic conclusion that 'reality is more complicated than we like to think': it has important, real consequences for policy and decision-making. Each of the case study countries has seen changes in agroecological and social conditions, factor prices and crop–livestock strategies; but these have not been inevitable or monolithic evolutions followed by all actors. To make sense of them, the pathways of change need to be understood in context, since a wide range of factors, both exogenous and endogenous, affect how crops and livestock interact within small-scale farming systems. Taken out of context, pathways that diverge from the conventional model of evolution towards 'mixed farming' risk being marginalised as ephemeral 'transitions', while the factors that shaped (and continue to shape) such pathways risk being ignored or misunderstood.

One of the most important factors, and one relatively accessible to both researchers and policy-makers, is the role of institutions – understood as 'regularised patterns of behaviour that persist in society' (see Chapter 1). An institutional analysis pushed us to look at the way informal and formal arrangements interact, allowing different people to gain access to land, labour, draught, manure, fodder, credit, capital, equipment and information. Detailed analysis at the site level also showed how institutions interact, the power relations embedded in such arrangements and the gaps, conflicts and complementarities between different institutions across scales. Despite similar agroecologies or comparable demographic patterns, in different sites the institutional arrangements governing access to resources can widely differ, resulting in divergent pathways of crop–livestock change.

Finally, just as multiple pathways of change were identified across sites, within sites a whole range of other patterns of difference were found. A differentiated analysis across socioeconomic groups highlighted how mainstream policy efforts are often focused on a relatively small proportion of the whole population. The detailed analysis highlighted how wealth, ethnic, age, gender and other differences are key to understanding how different people integrate crops and livestock.

The conventional assumption that farming systems evolve through a suite of crop–livestock relationships in accordance with a Boserupian model of intensification is, therefore, at best an incomplete presentation of the actual pathways of change followed by African smallholders. The standard belief that 'mixed farming' is the most 'sustainable' model of crop–livestock integration (cf. Beets 1990) presents an unrealistic and often unattainable model of integration that is ill-suited to the diversity of agricultural and livestock-keeping practices in Africa.

For all the technical elegance of the fully integrated 'mixed farming' model, crop–livestock integration (in all its various forms) is not something pursued for its own sake by smallholders. Rather, it is an example of one of many possible means of making a livelihood. In many of the case study examples, crop–livestock integration strategies were pursued alongside other diversification efforts off-farm. By increasing its livestock interest, a farming household is simultaneously diversifying its economic base, exploiting a broader resource base and increasing its potential contact with social institutions and networks – not just integrating its farming system. Moreover, no matter how integrated the crop and livestock aspects of soil fertility maintenance, traction or animal nutrition may be, the capitalisation, production objectives and market interactions of livestock production remain distinctly different from those of crop production (cf. Mortimore and Adams 1999).

The worst consequence of the continued dominance of the 'mixed farming' model in research and extension policy is that many farming systems that are important components of viable livelihoods are dismissed as merely 'incomplete' versions of 'mixed farming'. Since the model assumes a linear, evolutionary pathway from less to more integration, based on an individualised farm, exceptions or deviations from this pathway are of little interest, except as systems waiting to be reshaped into more 'sustainable' configurations. Treating such farming systems, and the social arrangements they typically involve, as 'transition' periods has prevented such arrangements from being evaluated in their own right.[1] The coping or adaptive strategies of households that do not (or cannot) follow the 'mixed farming' model are therefore constantly under-researched, since these arrangements are more complex, harder to extrapolate from, and may offer less dramatic production benefits than attention to specialised producers or successful, fully integrated farms.

Current policy has an incomplete focus

Research and extension on crop–livestock integration takes place in specific institutional contexts, which account for a range of embedded theoretical assumptions, and the adoption of certain methodological commitments is a consequence. Mainstream policy prescriptions across all three countries, reinforced by international research and donor funding, have been shaped by the prevailing discourse favouring 'mixed farming'. The lion's share of attention from national and international organisations has addressed the technical aspects of potential crop–livestock integration, with much less regard for the institutional structures and social arrangements that enable them. Research and extension in all the countries studied tends to focus on mixed cattle–cereal farming within privately owned units. As the individual chapters have shown, such a focus on relatively privileged households neglects pathways of crop–livestock integration and agricultural intensification being followed by the majority of households.

The heavy technical orientation of current research and extension policy is demonstrated by a look at African crop–livestock development projects for a major

---

[1] Commentators have dismissed livestock loaning and manuring contracts as 'transitional' relationships of little lasting importance for at least the last three decades (e.g. Jabbar 1993; Winrock International 1992; McIntire *et al.* 1992; Rabot 1990; Lhoste 1987; Delgado 1979; Tourte *et al.* 1971).

international donor (the UK's Department for International Development: 'DfID') and for the CGIAR centre, the International Livestock Research Institute (ILRI),[2] as well as crop and livestock programmes in each of the three case study countries conducted by national and/or international collaborators. Mono-disciplinary fields (such as veterinary research and animal production) figure prominently in all their research portfolios, and only a quarter of these research projects had any socioeconomic-policy focus.[3]

Livestock and crop-production ministries and agencies still bear the legacy of disciplinary territoriality, such that specialist research in animal health, breeding and agronomy is highly valued. Where attention is paid to crop–livestock interactions, such disciplinary foci tend to dominate, leading, as has been argued elsewhere, to a particular interpretation of crop–livestock interaction in a mixed farm model. Under pressure to become more 'multi-disciplinary' it has proven much easier for agronomists and animal scientists to find common ground using the technical model of 'mixed farming' than it has been to add in social science. Mixed farming may be an 'improvement' over mono-disciplinary approaches but it still neglects important contextual elements.

The heavy concentration of project resources in the field of veterinary medicine has in the past been attributed to the controlling position that veterinary specialists established for themselves during the colonial period (Scheper 1978; Landais and Lhoste 1990). This dominance by animal health research has been criticised by livestock policy analysts for at least the last three decades (cf. de Haan 1994; DSA/CIRAD 1985; Toulmin 1984; Sandford 1983; Scheper 1978; IEMVT 1971). Such critics have argued that more funds need to be dedicated to animal nutrition and range management, which are arguably of greater importance in raising productivity.

Much less attention has been devoted to understanding the role of livestock and crop–livestock integration in local livelihoods. This is not for lack of critical pressure, with numerous commentators emphasising the need to situate livestock development within a socioeconomic or livelihood context (Morton and Matthewman 1996; de Haan 1994; Mortimore 1991). ILCA itself was founded with an explicit, farming

---

[2]All DfID livestock-related projects funded in Africa since 1995 are recorded on the NARSIS database. The database was originally set up in 1990 to track projects within the Rural Livelihoods and Environment Division's Renewable Natural Resources Research Strategy. More recently it has been expanded to include information on the range of DfID's natural resources and environmental projects, irrespective of funding source, including bilateral country programmes, Rural Livelihoods Department and Engineering research, ESCOR, Joint Funding Scheme and Challenge Funds. Full records are available for ILRI projects covering all activities (both in-house projects and the activities of research fellows) from the Institute's creation in 1995, out of the twin agencies of ILCA (the International Livestock Centre for Africa) and ILRAD (International Laboratory for Research on Animal Diseases), until 1998. A qualitative assessment was made of the orientation of a given project. This was determined from the end-of-project report or the anticipated output statements. The interpretations may therefore reflect more the rhetoric of the projects' draughting context than their actual successful accomplishments or implementation. The heavy use of participatory rhetoric in project documents therefore may overestimate the actual social component of these projects. However, in the DfID case, social science research may be underestimated as ESCOR research was only added to the NARSIS database more recently.

[3]'Veterinary' projects include animal health, genetics and veterinary staff training. 'Production' projects included all those that emphasised end products rather than processes, such as maximising dairy production and meat processing.

systems approach in mind, but has remained largely wedded to the 'mixed farming' model and an evolutionary approach to farming and livelihood system change.[4] Situating crop–livestock integration or livestock development more generally within a broad, livelihood context is potentially ultimately threatening to professional, disciplinary norms and presents a production-oriented research agenda with priorities and questions that current staffing and expertise are ill-prepared to address. By contrast, broadening livestock development from veterinary to nutrition or range management goals may have been easier steps to have made, since the overall goal of improved animal productivity remained intact and basic assumptions of farming system evolution unchallenged. Within such a framework, social science's understanding of institutions serves only an instrumental role of identifying what existing structures must be changed or exploited to facilitate technology adoption. A pipeline approach to technological development is adopted, whereby research (with all the embedded assumptions unchallenged) takes the dominant role, and results are delivered to the extension system, often as part of a 'Training and Visit' approach to passing on technological messages. The opportunities for reflection, learning and the challenging of assumptions remain limited, and the emphasis is on the transfer of technology, with little appreciation of broader livelihood contexts, social differentiation or institutional processes.

National research and extension priorities

Given the overwhelming technical orientation of research at the international level, it should not be surprising that crop–livestock development projects bear much the same emphasis at the national level. However, each of the case study countries has had a significantly different history of crop–livestock development, and to an extent this is discernible from the assessment of project priorities. Infrastructure development projects addressing water management, resettlement and restocking issues are prominent in national priorities, since agricultural and livestock development agencies are charged with promoting aspects of development beyond research alone. This is especially true of Ethiopia and Mali, where dramatic ecological and political crises have been the impetus for such interventions. Zimbabwe has had a much lower emphasis on such infrastructure projects, but a greater attention to animal production research, a consequence in part of the colonial research priorities, which were influenced by a vocal, wealthy beef-ranching community (Cousins *et al.* 1992). As at the international level, research in all three countries is largely oriented to meat production or animal nutrition rather than to crop–livestock integration *per se*. It is also true that, in an era of structural adjustment and restricted national budgets, delivery of veterinary services has been privatised and veterinary research has increasingly been centralised in international research bodies like ILRI, often at the insistence of national livestock development departments (ILCA 1994).

Although the 1980s and 1990s saw all three case study countries attempting to situate some of their crop–livestock research and extension in broader livelihood

---

[4]Research on draught power, for example, has tended to emphasise ploughing with oxen or other cattle (such as ILRI's work with milk cows). Donkey power has received considerably less attention, as have non-ploughing aspects of draught power, such as carts [Source: NARSIS 2000; ILRI annual reports, 1995,1996,1997,1998].

contexts (through the creation of integrated or farming systems-centred research units), this approach still figures in only a few projects. Approximately twice as many projects address macro-economic and large-scale structural issues of marketing policy or systems of price incentives, with little attention being paid to disaggregated patterns and processes at the local level.

Some of the differences in national priorities can be understood with reference to the history of national research and extension institutions. The following sections briefly outline the emergence of crop–livestock development priorities in each of the case study countries, identifying the target audience and principal beneficiaries of research and extension. This then leads into a discussion of the domains most over-looked by the present approaches.

Ethiopia

Agriculture accounts for about 40 per cent of Ethiopia's GDP, 80 per cent of export earnings, and 85 per cent of employment in diverse traditional subsistence systems for production mainly of cereals, oilseeds and livestock (Herz 1993). Governments have accorded relatively low priority to research for improving smallholder agriculture, but efforts in the last few years have begun to create a more favourable environment.[5] Applied research activity is coordinated by the Ethiopian Agricultural Research Organisation, EARO (formerly the Institute of Agricultural Research, IAR). Before recent restructuring efforts, this had specialised centres dedicated to crop breeding, plant protection, forestry and livestock. Additional adaptive and developmental research was also carried out under the auspices of the ministries. For example, extensive work on soil conservation was carried out by the Ministry of Agriculture's Soil Conservation Research Project. Other research is also conducted at Alemaya and Addis Ababa universities and a number of regional agricultural colleges. The influence of international organisations and donors has been great in Ethiopia, espe-cially given the presence of ILCA (and later ILRI) since 1973 (ILCA 1994). Improved crop varieties, machinery and implements, and methods of livestock husbandry have all been useful outputs of past agricultural research, some of which (such as the crop breeding programme) have had a demonstrable impact on production (Herz 1993). However, much of this research has focused on particular technical elements and not looked at broader systems within which these are set.

Despite the disciplinary separation of much agricultural research, the 'mixed farming' model has had strong advocates in Ethiopia. Mixed farming is often considered the 'traditional' form of crop–livestock integration, from which modern farming systems are perceived to have strayed (Assefa 1990). Improved draught tech-nologies have received relatively little financing relative to production-oriented objectives. Those technologies that have been promoted (such as the broad bed maker or ploughing with milk cows) have had minimal uptake.

Boosting agricultural productivity has long been a major policy priority in Ethiopia. This has become particularly significant following the famine periods since the 1970s. As a result, the objectives of extension and development programmes have focused on securing production increases. This is reflected in the foci of the

---

[5]Cf. National Agricultural Research Policy, October 1994, Addis Ababa.

integrated development programmes of the 1960s and 1970s, the Minimum Package programmes of the 1970s and 1980s, and the 'Global' Package since 1993. These efforts have not been focused on crop–livestock integration *per se*, but more the improvement of agricultural productivity, with a particular emphasis on crop production improvements through external inputs and improved seeds. Production research and infrastructure development (relief, restocking and water development) dominate most projects, well ahead of even veterinary concerns.

However, all of these extension and development programmes have made implicit assumptions about the potential farming systems that would benefit and result. For example, the households most likely to benefit from the improved maize–fertiliser extension package currently being promoted are cereal farmers with access to oxen and sufficient labour, since the crops are supposed to be weeded twice, by hand-hoe (see Chapter 3). In general, crop–livestock research and extension can be faulted for failing to adequately recognise the different constraints of the different study sites. As Chapter 3 shows, land is the most limiting factor in Admencho, while the availability of oxen and sufficient labour constrains activity in Mundena. The vast majority of smallholders in all the study areas were unable to benefit from technologies or packages on offer.

Mali

Agriculture accounts for around half of Mali's GDP and employs more than 80 per cent of the workforce. The livestock sector accounted for 47.5 per cent of the agricultural GDP in 1987 and 35 per cent in 1989 (Témé *et al.* 1996). Cotton, gold and livestock exports are the most important sources of foreign exchange. Agricultural research is the responsibility of the Institut d'Economie Rurale (IER) within the Ministry of Rural Development and Water (MDRE), although significant research on cotton is supported by CMDT, the parastatal cotton company. Research programmes are oriented to agricultural production of industrial crops, cereals and food legumes, horticulture (vegetables and fruit), forestry and inland fisheries, and livestock. Two programmes devoted to natural resources management, and farming systems and rural economics support these production-oriented programmes. The country's diverse eco-regions are served by six regional agricultural research centres, eight experimental stations, and experimental sites. Regional Technical Committees serve to guide planning and build liaison to administrators, extension and the users of research results (Herz 1993).

Present-day policy towards crop–livestock integration has evolved from a specific colonial legacy (see Chapter 2). Most of the early proponents of mixed farming in French West Africa were veterinarians who wanted to see the abundant livestock resources of the semi-arid regions properly exploited – a disciplinary bias that is still observed. In particular, officials and scientists rued the fact that ethnically based livelihoods of 'herder' and 'farmer' in the Sahel appeared to drive a wedge between the presumed rational integration of crop and livestock production systems (Tourte *et al.* 1971). Particularly influential writing from that era, whose resonance is still felt today, identified 'desertification' as the inexorable consequence of the failure to integrate livestock with cropping systems (Aubreville 1949). As a result, the colonial administration sought ways to contain and control the potential of livestock to degrade the environment by finding more socially and economically useful roles for the country's herds. This led to policies of sedentarising pastoralists and their herds, converting former grazing ranges (such as the Niger's Inland Delta) to agricultural production, and promoting export crops like cotton and groundnuts (Feunteun 1955; Becker 1994). Owners of oxen were initially forced to accept ploughs on credit and attend mandatory training at local 'farm schools' run by the national extension service.

Although French West Africa was never home to European settler farmers, the model of *'agriculture mixte'* that was promoted in the colonial 'farm schools' was based explicitly on the experiences of settler farmers in anglophone East and Southern Africa (Curasson 1947). An undue emphasis on the planting of forage crops to improve rangelands, on the adoption of ox ploughing in regions of already sparse labour, and on destocking supposedly overstocked ranges, can be credited with most of the inevitable failures that resulted (Landais and Lhoste 1990). Although the fodder crops or regulated grazing components of the 'farm school' model did not spread, ox ploughing was one component of the model that did become popular in Mali Sud, especially once lighter ploughs pulled by only two oxen were available. Indeed, the interest in ploughs was so great that the colonial government soon found itself trying to *limit* their spread in Mali Sud. Ploughs had to be licensed and 'farm schools' intensified their courses on the 'proper' use of ploughs, to discourage 'environmentally degrading' practices.

Although using a model of *'integration agriculture–élevage'*, the post-Independence CMDT continued to acknowledge that the most important role of livestock (essentially only cattle) in Mali Sud was subordinate to cotton production, as suppliers of manure and draught power (CMDT 1995). The increasing numbers of semi-sedentary, pastoral Fulani herds present in the region since the 1970s are therefore often perceived as a threat to the orderly production of cotton, both by the local populations and by officials (Ramisch 1999). A major part of the national-level discussion of decentralisation, which will promote local management of village resources (*gestion des terroirs villageois*), has been finding ways to ensure that livestock production can be made 'less environmentally degrading' and instead render productive services to agriculture (Bosma *et al.* 1996).

While some of the more recent work by the IER has looked at crop–livestock integration as part of broader livelihood activities, the CMDT and MDRE remain committed to the mixed farming model. Such an approach ignores the many households for whom livestock are the primary livelihood, and accounts for the minimal presence of MDRE extension in Dalonguébougou. It also downplays the fact that farmers are investing in livestock (and herders taking up farming) as much to diversify their livelihood base as to advance the 'integration' of crop and livestock systems. Even in the cotton zone itself, farmers in Zaradougou were intent on diversifying their systems beyond merely integrating livestock, either through external investments in cash crop plantations in Côte d'Ivoire or local development of orchards or *bas fonds* production systems.

Zimbabwe
Agriculture accounts for about 15 per cent of Zimbabwe's GDP, 40 to 50 per cent of export earnings and 26 per cent of the total formal employment. It is characterised by a large- and small-scale commercial farming and a ranching sector, and a communal

land and resettlement sector, with diversified crop–livestock farming systems. Public sector agricultural research is the responsibility of the Department of Research and Specialist Services (DRSS) of the Ministry of Agriculture, with the overall planning and coordinating function carried out by the Agricultural Research Council. DRSS carries out most of the research on crop and livestock commodities other than tobacco, sugarcane, poultry and pigs. Private local and transnational companies undertake research on the latter commodities and in crop plant breeding and testing, seed production and distribution, horticulture, fertilisers and pesticides, machinery and equipment (Herz 1993).

In Zimbabwe, the 'mixed farming' model remains strongly informed by the European experience of owner-occupied homestead farms and is not always relevant to many African smallholder farmers (see Chapter 4, and Agritex's Master Farmer trainee record book). In the colonial era, the attention of crop–livestock development was on the large-scale, commercial sector. This did provide some beneficial spin-offs to small farmers, such as the spread of hybrid maize in the 1950s, but these were relatively isolated and unintentional. Since Independence, the government has been joined by an increasing number of NGOs working in agriculture and resource management (i.e. tree planting, water development, small-scale gardening, soil and water conservation). Research has expanded to include more of the needs of the small-scale sector, turning to such things as drought-resistant millet and sorghum crops, water harvesting technologies and draught power issues. However, despite the activities of groups like the Farming Systems Research Unit (FSRU) of DRSS, there have been no major breakthroughs appropriate to resource-poor farmers in dry areas, nor have NGOs had much impact on the type of recommendations offered by the national extension service (Agritex).

In many respects, Agritex maintains the pre-Independence focus on high-input, technical solutions to farming problems, relying on cattle manure, draught oxen and improved fodder management. This approach obviously favours the 'Master Farmers' already following the recommended practices. At the same time, it underestimates the problems of the risk-prone, resource-poor farmer. Indeed, a variety of land use planning and legal restrictions have reduced the opportunities of such farmers to practise flexible land management (Scoones *et al.* 1996).

The successes of serving the large-scale, commercial sector have been regarded as a suitable model for the post-Independence administration, with adjustments in scale and target group rather than in basic content. As a result, the dominant model continues to emphasise a top-down approach to technology development. For example, the 'Training and Visit' extension approach, which was encouraged by the World Bank in the 1980s, is often in practice limited to a process of calendar-timed and message-based contacts between groups of agriculturalists and extension agents, preventing meaningful exchanges of knowledge or farmer-led influence of the research process.

Continuity and change: understanding policy processes

To summarise these quick sketches of the national settings in Ethiopia, Mali and Zimbabwe: colonial and international donor influences have fundamentally shaped interventions in cropping and livestock in all three countries. Activity has been dominated by technical, science-driven projects focused on the large-scale economic or technical constraints facing the 'average' or 'above average' farmers. Marginal or alternative pathways of change have been consistently under-researched and under-valued, if they have been recognised at all. Chapter 1 explored some of the historical reasons for the adherence to the dominant, evolutionary model of crop–livestock integration and agricultural intensification, but why today do policies remain persistently geared in one direction? Looking at 'policy processes', rather than solely policies, helps explain why such orthodoxies are reinforced and alternative realities systematically sidelined.

It tends to be assumed that once the limitations of a particular set of policy interventions are seen, a new set of technical policies can be neatly arranged, fed into the pipeline and then sequentially implemented. This view misses a whole range of issues around bureaucratic and scientific practices and contexts, including funding structures, disciplinary traditions and institutional conventions and cultures, which go some way towards explaining why policies are as they are and why it is often difficult to change them.

The links between policy and the 'mixed farm' orthodoxy are important. Assuming a particular model and concentrating on developing different aspects of it, or ordering the world in accordance with it, reinforces the dominant model in a circular fashion. As we have seen, much policy has been informed by a story or 'narrative' of change that sees the emergence of an ideal mixed farm as the desirable end. Such narratives may be either explicitly articulated, or implicit in the behaviour and practices of policy-makers. A narrative serves the function of simplifying reality and making complex policy domains manageable. In practice this means that a scenario or a problem is identified, a set of causes is offered, possible future scenarios are set out and negative scenarios averted and favourable ones encouraged by particular interventions. Hence, in this case, the problem of increasing population in the context of land scarcity and a fragile resource base is to be dealt with by agricultural intensification through integrating crops and livestock. This will maximise agricultural output and mitigate possible food gaps while combating environmental degradation. This narrative is so deeply entrenched in the policy process that it may be extremely difficult to move towards another way of operating.

In part the entrenchment of such a narrative can be explained by the nature of the agricultural bureaucracies implementing policies. Bureaucracies tend to favour manageability, regularity, the imposition of order and delivery of standard products. For predictable and regular environments this may work reasonably well, but for situations that are characterised by diversity and complexity, and by the irregular and the informal, this can be problematic. What emerges from the case study chapters is that it is precisely the irregularity – in the sense of dynamic, changing and context-specific settings – and the diversity of informal institutions that are key to the strategies people pursue. However, existing bureaucratic systems in all three countries are organised on sectoral bases, with agricultural ministries geared to improving agricultural production and environment ministries protecting natural resources. Very often this is linked to a production emphasis on modernisation and transformation of agriculture. Research is geared towards producing the new technologies upon which a transformed agriculture would be based, and extension systems are organised in a command-and-control fashion to deliver technologies for adoption, and to guide the transformation of management practices. Incentive systems for staff are frequently geared towards ensuring that field staff follow the prescribed model, with minimum amounts of divergence from what is set out as regular further up the hierarchy. Key to all this, but not always easy to pinpoint, are the political processes that underlie these ostensibly technical objectives. Bureaucratic activity is not simply neutral administration, but rather part of political processes of asserting control over and shaping society.

The ways science is applied, in turn, depend strongly on such bureaucratic contexts. At the same time, science also shapes bureaucratic practice through the knowledge it produces, what it defines as good and valuable knowledge, and through messages that it may be able to convince 'formal' policy-makers with. Thus the specific micro-practices of research contribute to the persistence in policy of particular models, even when these are ill-fitting. Several aspects are important. First, applied research is frequently weak at interdisciplinarity. As we have seen for the cases of national agricultural research systems across the three case study countries, not only do particular technical scientific disciplines often work in isolation, there is also an under-emphasis on the incorporation of social science. This neglect results in a lack of awareness of the differences in society, differences that may be fundamental to the types of development model it would be sensible to promote. But this does not mean that research operates without implicit models of socioeconomic worlds. As Chapter 1 demonstrated, the 'mixed farming' model carries with it a range of assumptions about desirable social and economic norms. Second, the dominance of particular models is further reinforced by the lack of mechanisms for client involvement in priority setting. This lack of inclusivity is a major reason why these implicit models are not held open to scrutiny. Finally, where research is defined as primarily a technical enterprise, research activities tend to concentrate on components of pre-set problems.[6] The 'whole' is then reduced to a series of elements to be worked upon without looking at the relevance of the wider model of which these are components. In the case of crops and livestock integration this means detailed investigation of different aspects of fodder, manure and soil fertility management.

Equally importantly, despite decades of research and development expenditure, the lack of a spectacular, 'Green Revolution'-style research breakthrough in African crop or livestock production has meant that international funding has been easily lured towards other, greener research pastures (de Haan 1994). Chronic under-funding and staffing constraints, particularly since the imposition of structural adjustment programmes, have severely limited the ability of the key government departments to innovate upon, or seek out alternatives to, the existing models on offer and hence reinforced the orthodoxy (Muturi 1981).

Finally, the networks of policy-makers that thread their way between donor head-quarters, government ministries in capitals, provincial capitals and district towns, and NGO field sites, are particularly key to the institutionalising of ideas and practices in scientific and administrative bureaucracies. These 'actor-networks', reinforced by international funding patterns and institutional inertia, support continued adherence

---

[6]This is not atypical, nor a recent phenomenon. Tackling only the economic or technical constraints of African agriculture with 'magic bullet' solutions such as irrigation, 'Green revolution' packages or mechanisation has had a dismal track record (Raynaut *et al.* 1997; Adams 1992; Richards 1985; Williams 1981).

to the dominant, evolutionary models of crop–livestock integration and agricultural intensification leading to 'mixed farming'.

What priorities are missing from current research and extension?

The preceding sections have shown that priorities have been, and continue to be, biased towards addressing crop–livestock problems with technical solutions and evolutionary assumptions, based on the disciplinary strengths already present in national and international development organisations. However, decades of project review and critical evaluation have constantly reminded policy-makers that the list of priorities needs to be broader and more inclusive of marginalised perspectives.

The historical approach taken in this book has demonstrated the numerous attempts at inducing technological change, and the frequency with which such interventions have not met their stated goals. In general, technically oriented packages have assumed that increasing the output of agricultural systems is the only path to economic growth, and (implicitly) that farming can command up to 100 per cent of available labour. When households have failed to commit labour on the scale expected, the factors implicated are inevitably labelled 'social' – and beyond the remit of the technical planners (Mortimore and Adams 1999).

However, the case studies themselves have presented numerous examples of how these 'social' phenomena are integral to understanding the nature and course of crop–livestock integration pathways. The interdisciplinary analysis of farming system change reached several conclusions that prove useful to guiding and reshaping future studies. Each will be treated in detail below:

- Technological change occurs in a broader livelihood context.
- Multiple possible pathways of change co-exist and interact simultaneously.
- Changes to pathways can be incremental or abrupt, depending on conjunctures of particular key events.
- Broader livelihood changes and technology changes are affected by a complex matrix of formal and informal institutions across scales.
- Different policies interact or conflict to shape livelihood and technical changes, sometimes with unintended consequences.

Technological change occurs in a broader livelihood context

Technological change does not occur for its own sake, nor in isolation from other social and economic changes. The development and adoption of new agricultural technologies is part of a broader strategy of maintaining or advancing the viability of individual, household or indeed community livelihoods. As the case study chapters showed, these livelihoods are always dynamic and changing in response to changing circumstances. Farming systems are not self-contained sectors of economies, and the households studied engage in a number of different kinds of economic activities. Agricultural production articulates with a range of agricultural economic activities (wage labour, non-agricultural production, small businesses) and with generational cycles and gender relations.

Analysis needs to take into account the powerful networks of kinship and reciprocal obligation that link households, so that 'clusters' of households that interact closely with each other in agricultural production may often be a more useful unit of analysis than the individual household, however defined. The case study work identified a range of 'actor groups' united by common social institutions and arrangements that are pursuing similar strategies of crop–livestock integration.

The case studies highlighted how gender, age, wealth, ethnic and other differences are key to understanding how different people integrate crops and livestock. For example, in Mali ethnic differences in the Sahelian study site between Bambara farmers and Fulani and Maure pastoralists result in highly differentiated strategies. In Ethiopia, wealth differences reflected in access to land and draught power allow very different options to be pursued by different households. In Zimbabwe, gender differences are important, with women's strategies for managing smallstock as part of both an individual and household farming enterprise often underestimated.

The omnipresence of the 'mixed farming' model in the explicit policies of national and international development agencies has usually implied that it is a model that is somehow 'livelihood-neutral', that it is a shopping list of technologies that all farmers should be able to find appropriate. However, as has been noted above, and throughout this book, this is not the case. 'Mixed farming' is often associated with wealthier groups. This correlation between more complete integrations of crop and livestock systems and greater wealth is often wrongly assumed to be evidence of causation. For example, in the hierarchical model of Mali's CMDT extension approach, it is implicit that 'under-equipped' households can better themselves by adopting more of the crop–livestock integration technologies like ploughs, manure use and carts (Chapter 2).

The 'wealth' and 'livelihood sustainability' ranking exercises carried out in each country served to identify the shorthand that local communities used to identify their relevant social strata. In all cases, livestock ownership figured prominently. Those without livestock (especially cattle, and particularly draught animals) of their own had to employ numerous social arrangements if they were to pursue any forms of crop–livestock integration. Yet the 'mixed farming' model, with the assumption of exclusive, private ownership of the crucial land and livestock elements, begins from a configuration only possible in a privileged minority of households.

Multiple possible pathways of change co-exist and interact simultaneously

The case study chapters have highlighted the range of crop–livestock integration practices present in the three countries. They have also identified how some of these practices are better suited to, and more often adopted by, different groups of actors. The 'pathways of change' that have led to these present practices have been non-linear, and appear non-deterministic inasmuch as various actors, starting from different positions of power and resource endowments, may have arrived at outwardly similar present configurations of crop and livestock systems by very different intermediate steps.

An example of this from Dalonguébougou in Mali (Chapter 2) is the convergence of the practices of the formerly pastoral, stock-wealthy Fulani, and the village Bambara agriculturalists on a farming system based on ox-ploughing, intensive manuring of home fields and a tightly interwoven set of social obligations regulating access to water and land. In Ethiopia's Chokare site (Chapter 3) households that decades ago practised more purely pastoral and agricultural livelihoods find their resource management and production strategies converging.

More interesting, however, are the divergences – the present practices that do not resemble each other any longer despite similar starting points, and which today overlap with each other spatially and temporally on the same landscapes. After all, many of the antecedents of the various intensification or extensification strategies found in these cases studies originally practised some form of hand-hoed, extensive, bush fallow cultivation, with minimal interaction with livestock systems. In many of the systems studied, such as many of the cases in Zimbabwe or Ethiopia, animal traction was adopted first. However, pastoralists like the Sidama or Fulani, already well endowed with livestock, might have begun their agricultural intensification process through manuring and only later adopting ploughs or weeding. In other farming systems, as in southern Mali's cotton zone, hoe-cultivating households, with no easy access to manure, adopted inorganic fertilisers first, and only later acquired ploughs and cattle.

In different agroecological and political contexts, similar stimuli can also lead to vastly different outcomes. In Zimbabwe, the high mortality rate of cattle during recent droughts has resulted in an increasing interest in using donkeys rather than oxen as draught animals. In contrast, the loss of cattle to disease outbreaks in southern Mali stimulated an increasing interest in plantation agriculture in Côte d'Ivoire, rather than a search for alternative sources of traction or manure within the village context. Disease losses of oxen in Dalonguébougou were instrumental in promoting an increase in water-for-draught contracts between the village Bambara and cattle owners. This has corresponded with a diminished prevalence of water-for-manure exchanges, reducing access to an important means of sustaining the fertility of village fields' soil.

From the combined examples of the case study work, it is possible to dismantle the pathways of change into the different components of technological change and identify the enabling social institutions. Table 5.1 presents an assemblage of all the observed technological transformations in one column, and all the various social and institutional arrangements that mediated crop–livestock integration strategies in another. This is not to assume that a particular pathway of change in a given domain (say the maintenance of soil fertility) must be accompanied by a corresponding transformation in another domain (for example, means of cultivation, weeding or animal nutrition).

Smallholders' adoption of technologies has been much more disaggregated and diverse than simple progress or regression along a pathway towards fully integrated 'mixed farming'. At any given time, in a given locale, a household may experience certain relative, local availabilities of land, labour, capital, information and access to social networks or institutions. Different components of a land holding can therefore simultaneously receive different inputs or benefit from different technologies. Extensification and intensification of labour or capital are often rational land use choices simultaneously within the same household's farming system. For example, the *darkua* fields in southern Ethiopia, the gardens and 'niches' in Zimbabwe, and the village fields of Dalonguébougou in Mali are intensively manured, while the *shoqa*, 'away' or 'bush' fields are not.

Table 5.1 Multiple strategies, multiple pathways.

Domain	Observed pathways of change	Possible facilitating institutions
Cultivation method	Hoe (no change) Ox-plough (no change) Hoe → ox-plough (and hoeing) Hoe → donkey-plough Hoe → (ox-plough) → tractor Hoe → ox-plough → hoe Hoe → ox-plough → donkey-plough Hoe → plough → tractor → ox-plough	Household/personal labour only Kinship/collective labour exchanges Kinship/collective equipment exchanges Pairing/teaming animals Shared ownership (i.e. *kotta*) Share-rearing (i.e. *hara*) Tenant–landlord labour obligations Manure–draught labour exchanges Market-based labour hiring/ contracts Market-based equipment hiring/contracts Cooperatives Begging/religious obligations
Weeding method	Hoe (household labour) Hoe (household labour) → women's labour Hoe → ox-drawn weeding (i.e. *shilshallo*) Hoe → donkey-drawn weeding	Household/personal labour only Kinship/collective labour arrangements Market-based equipment hiring
Soil fertility	Extensive fallow (no change) Corralled cattle herds Bush fallow → transported cattle manure Bush fallow → tpt'd smallstock manure Manured → bush fallow Bush fallow → inorganic fertiliser Bush fallow → manure + fertiliser	Share-rearing/Shared ownership Profit sharing arrangements (*tirf yegera*) Watering rights–manure exchanges *Jatigi* (ad hoc or long term) Contract farming NPK purchased on credit versus cash crop yield (i.e. cotton)
Transport	Head-load Donkeys and/or donkey-carts Head-load → donkey-cart Head-load → ox-cart Head-load → ox-cart → head-load Head-load → ox-cart → donkey-cart	Private ownership Cart sharing/hiring Cooperatives
Animal nutrition	Extensive communal grazing Extensive grazing → individualised Grazing crop residues *in situ* only *In situ* grazing → crop residue stocking	Watering rights–manure arrangements Watering rights–draught arrangements *Jatigi* (ad hoc or long term) Cash market for cut-and-carry

The diversity of social institutions listed in Table 5.1 also attests to the importance of institutions in supporting technology adoption. Highly flexible and adaptive sharing arrangements appear particularly common, and serve to familiarise households with new technologies by both spreading the risks of investment and introducing new management options and opportunities. Young oxen can be trained in teaming or labour sharing. The benefits of manuring can be greatly augmented and the costs of fencing and moving reduced by share-rearing animals. Establishing host–visitor relations (as in the *jatigi* system of Mali) also links pastoral and agricultural livelihoods' knowledge and experiences, as well as sharing benefits of crop residue grazing and manuring. Ignorance of such institutions misses a key feature of the dynamics of crop–livestock integration, especially for those actors with the least secure access to livestock, or the latest experimenters with new technologies.

Changes to pathways can be incremental or abrupt, depending on key events

A virtue of the Boserupian model of intensification is that it acknowledges that farming systems are dynamic, and that farmers and herders are constantly interacting with and shaping their environments. However, the classic evolutionary model conceives of change as a single, continuous process of improvement and refining in response to changing factor scarcities. Along this evolutionary path, it is assumed that systems steadily advance to more intensive practices as a resource becomes scarcer, or regress to more extensive ones if the resource's abundance increases (see Chapter 1). As the case studies have shown, the pathways of change included shifts in practice that were incremental or sudden, depending on the conjunctures of particular key events, not just changes in factor scarcities.

Such key events can often be located in the changing policy environment, and the methods used to promote technologies on offer. For example, the promotion of ox ploughs in Mali met with considerable resistance so long as it was associated with forced labour, taxes paid in cotton and reliant on unwieldy ploughshares that required four oxen in the team. When the interests of France turned from its colonies to rebuilding the war-ravaged metropole, and when lighter ploughs were made available, ploughs were readily adopted. A research-led modification of the technology, and a combination of geopolitical forces with an inadvertent impact on colonial policy, had direct implications on introducing animal traction to Malian smallholders (see Chapter 2).

Similarly abrupt events, this time at a much smaller scale, conspired to introduce the households of Zaradougou to cash crop plantations in Côte d'Ivoire – a resource not commonly available to other villages in Mali Sud. The personal history of one man, sold into slavery and earning his freedom in Ivoirian coffee and cocoa fields, created a particularly resonant narrative of success and entrepreneurship for Zaradougou. Today, the village's plantations are important sources of revenue and destinations of investment: a means of diversification that now ranks along with cotton and livestock (Chapter 2).

Less abrupt, but equally significant, changes have also been triggered by key, exogenous events. The steady eradication of tsetse flies, and the changing politics of migration to neighbouring countries have been of greater consequence than increasing population pressure in setting the pace of integration and disintegration for Zimbabwe and Mali. Other key events can be traced to changing agroecological conditions. A perceived increasing variability in the onset, frequency and duration of rains has served to alter the value of land to favour extensification and diversification in each of the countries studied. For example, in Zimbabwe the combination of structural adjustment and drought in the early 1990s resulted in major shifts in the crop–livestock system, with the growth of hoe-based gardening systems that responded to emerging market opportunities and the lack of draught power (Chapter 4).

Finally, the retrospective view allows us to see that a given technology may have been adopted, rejected, and readopted repeatedly in a process leading up to the present practice. The use of manure as a means of maintaining soil fertility has undergone numerous such fluctuations in all of the systems considered. This iterative process of learning (from initial awareness, experimentation, evaluation, through to adoption, refashioning or rejection) is dependent on multiple sources of knowledge, especially social and institutional networks. It is also contingent on the environmental factors influencing agricultural conditions over at least several years. It is therefore likely to be a much longer and more thorough process than commonly allowed by extensionists for a majority of farmers to adopt and use a technology (Tyndall 1996). It also demonstrates that the practices described as existing in the 'present' (even in these case studies) are themselves far from static, being situated in the midst of constant reassessment and a search for alternatives.

Livelihood and technical changes are strongly influenced by institutional dynamics

In the light of historical legacies, power relations and the social and cultural setting, some actors are better able to negotiate access to resources via institutional arrangements. It follows that different actors are better able to follow certain paths of agricultural change than others, as following a particular pathway of change depends on access to crucial resources and thus particular forms of institutional involvement.

In the case study sites there are many institutions that may be used for on-farm and off-farm activities, as well as for non-productive activities. Typically household-based institutions are the 'first step' for accessing these resources, and those without sufficient resources within their own household will then look to institutions outside the domain of the household to enable them to access resources. These include cash and non-cash inter-household practices as well as larger and more formal institutions. As Table 5.1 showed, there are many such institutions – particularly at the inter-household level, but operating at all scales – available to households, but they are not necessarily all available in each of the sites.

The role and importance of small-scale, informal institutions have changed significantly over the historical periods studied. In some cases, these have been radically altered by dramatic political changes brought about by revolution in Ethiopia or Mali, or the Liberation War in Zimbabwe. For example, Ethiopia's 1974 Revolution abolished slavery and landlordism, formally ending long-established landlord–slave relationships, and forcing a search for new institutions to regulate access to crucial resources. Arrangements similar to those of today's *hara* share-rearing used to exist in Admencho between landlords and their tenants and slaves, but since the Revolution *hara* arrangements between non-relatives have been stigmatised and are generally avoided. However, in the other sites, migrants to urban areas often use *hara* arrangements to invest in livestock in their home area. Animals belonging to migrants are kept by relatives who use the products of the animal, giving gifts (often butter) to the owner (see Chapter 3).

Another trend has been the perceived increase in the importance of market-based transactions over social networks, with social arrangements becoming less stable and more opportunistic than they were. In Zimbabwe, there was some evidence that mutual aid institutions may be fading in importance for some people, in some situations. However, in the face of marketisation and individualisation of labour relations, others are relying more on social networks. In Chikombedzi, for example, *kufiyisa* livestock loaning arrangements have become important in the wake of drought in the 1990s. Prior to the Liberation War only large herd owners engaged in *kufiyisa*. However, with many households now owning draught animals, loaning out animals is considered a way to protect them from the greater perceived threat of drought and disease (see Chapter 4). New social networks are also emerging as older, 'traditional' institutions are supplanted by market transactions. Church-based congregational work groups have proven important for mobilising labour and spreading information in Zimbabwe, while in Mali Village Associations have provided a new institution for organising collective labour, credit and technical innovation.

However, the dynamics of institutional change are not simply the replacement of older forms of reciprocity with less personal, market-based transactions. In Dalonguébougou, Mali, the power of the once-dominant village Bambara house-holds has slowly been undermined by increasing immigrant and transhumant popula-tions. This has translated into a shift away from a regime where the village Bambara could control the location and nature of others' settlement. It has, more importantly, seen a changing role for the arrangements made for watering rights. Where once the village Bambara could demand that visiting herds be camped on the lands of the well-owner as payment, today herd owners are more likely to manure their own fields, and offer instead the services of plough teams in exchange for water (see Chapter 3).

Finally, national-level, formal institutions have also seen their power and influence altered. Structural adjustment has ended subsidised credit programmes and made inorganic fertiliser inputs more expensive and harder to provide. In Mali's cotton zone, this has seen smallholders turn towards a greater reliance on manure, but a simultaneous privatisation of veterinary care, and an outbreak of CBPP, has meant that strategies based on manure are perceived to be increasingly risky.

A close analysis of the institutional matrix (see Chapter 1 and the case study-specific examples in Chapters 2–4) – differentiated by site and by social group – therefore provides an opportunity for identifying ways in which external interventions focused on institutional issues might result in greater access to key resources, and so positive shifts in strategies, which reduce poverty and improve sustainable livelihoods.

Policy interactions and conflicts shape livelihood and technical changes

A key aspect of assessing priorities for institutional interventions is the interaction between local, informal and more meso or macro formal institutional arrangements. The case study research highlights how, in a range of cases, such interactions were too often ignored, with external interventions either contradicting or undermining local institutions with detrimental consequences for poor and marginalised groups. The policies that matter are not just ones focused on technical, research and extension issues, but include all intersecting policy impacts, especially those addressing tenure and market reforms.

Tenure issues have been particularly contentious in all three countries. Uncertainty over tenure rights in Ethiopia has been a major feature over the last decades. With land reform and villagisation in the Derg period, the pattern of settlement and agriculture in the study area changed significantly, with major impli-cations for who controlled land and resources. In the Transitional Government period of the 1990s, State Farms went through yet another convulsion as tenure became more individualised. In Mali, tenure insecurity mounted in anticipation of eventual decentralisation and Forest Code reforms, and was expressed as using ploughs to expand cultivated areas of farmland to assert ownership through use. Tensions over land in Zimbabwe have been a recurrent feature of the post-Independence period, rising to a head in the run-up to the elections in 2000 and afterwards. Difficult relations between communal and commercial farm areas have simultaneously made informal, even illicit, arrangements more important as a means of accessing traction, manure and fodder and, at the same time, made these arrangements more risky and opportunistic. The recent invasions of commercial farms, for example, have enabled extensification of arable and grazing lands with varying degrees of tenure security.

Market and fiscal reforms (especially in the wake of structural adjustment programmes) have also intersected in unanticipated ways with both official policies and informal institutions. In Mali, the devaluation of the CFA franc in 1994 had a major impact on the relative profitability of different cropping options. In the cotton zone, this resulted in increasing investment in cotton, but, with the costs of imported fertilisers also rising after devaluation, the soil fertility strategy to support this had to increasingly rely on integrated options, including a rise in demand for manure. The devaluation was enacted without significant consultation with national ministries, but had an especially profound impact on livestock policy by increasing the incentives for livestock sales to Côte d'Ivoire's markets, including strategies popular with many households and individuals that fatten smallstock for export.

At the same time, structural adjustment reforms in each country have also slashed national research and extension budgets. As mentioned above, this seriously constrains the options available to national systems trying to find local solutions to crop–livestock integration problems. Yet another impact has been the widespread privatisation of veterinary health services. During the 1990s, services have tended to become concentrated only in those markets where they would be most profitable. Drought and disease outbreaks have therefore had important impacts in undermining crop–livestock integration strategies in the more marginal areas in each country, especially for those households without other opportunities to diversify their livelihoods.

Finally, even interventions targeted especially to help marginalised communities, such as the promotion of subsidised inputs or credit schemes, have often failed to consider local institutional contexts. Subsidised resources have a long record of being co-opted by wealthier, better-equipped households in all three countries. With better access to information and social networks, wealthy households have managed to monopolise the benefits of well-digging, traction/mechanisation programmes, and subsidised inorganic fertilisers. This has often forced poorer households to either negotiate with potential patrons to gain access to these resources, or seek alternatives using their own resources. Credit programmes in drier areas of Ethiopia and Zimbabwe have also had the consequence of increasing the debt burden of the poorest households when crop failures or disease have made repayment impossible.

All five of these conclusions make it clear that technology choice has social, economic and institutional determinants and that these have to be seen in historical context. Assuming that the practices of the 'mixed farming' model will all gradually be acquired by households as they intensify their production systems takes an inappropriate, ahistorical view of crop–livestock integration. To remedy the limitations of an excessive focus on the 'mixed farming' model, research and development policy needs to take these conclusions into account when prioritising technological options, defining scientific questions or allocating resources. By identifying the linkages between technologies, pathways of change, institutions and existing policies, the range of entry points for interventions should become clearer.

New approaches to technology design and choice

Assuming that smallholdings differ from large commercial enterprises only in terms of scale, and that input–output analyses of crop–livestock integration strategies provide the best lens for investigation, has led to the advocacy of labour-saving and yield-enhancing technologies in order to increase household or individual incomes from agriculture. However, smallholdings are not just 'micro large-holdings' situated on a trajectory towards more integration and commercialisation: they are qualitatively different in terms of their diversity, variability and multi-dimensionality (cf. Mortimore and Adams 1999: 189). In the same way, the inappropriate targeting of interventions at some putative 'average' household will inevitably fail to meet the needs or understand the true constraints facing the actual majority of households (Ramisch 1998). The most impressive stories of development are those where a need for multiple choices, to suit a range of smallholder families, has been met, implicitly or explicitly, in the type of interventions and opportunities affecting rural households (Tiffen et al. 1994).

In each of the three case study countries, considerable effort was spent in discussions with potential users of the research. These included researchers in government departments, extensionists, NGO workers, donors and others. Workshops were also held with key people to gain feedback on the results. However, the research outputs are not easily amenable to such direct forms of dissemination and uptake. The research has not produced a 'technology' for adoption, and its ideas cannot be easily slotted into existing practices and procedures. Instead, as this book has shown, the research presents some fairly major conceptual challenges to the way intensification processes (and crop–livestock integration in particular) are seen in small-scale farming systems in Africa, with significant implications for how research and development priority setting is carried out. Indeed, the research results can be seen as a fairly fundamental critique of much current practice, both in terms of government research and extension strategy and in international research and donor support.

In this sense, the 'uptake' pathways for the research are not immediately obvious. The impact of this type of strategic research is likely to be long-term, and the consequence of basic shifts in perspectives and priorities. This does not happen overnight, nor as a result of a single research programme. Yet what is clear is that a response to the limitations of the current situation will not come from 'more of the same'. The conclusion that processes of crop–livestock integration are more complicated than the evolutionary, 'mixed farming' model would suggest is not a prescription for throwing that model out, or having it somehow enlarged to engulf every possible crop–livestock configuration. As this book has illustrated for a variety of settings, the pathways of change are, almost by definition, locally situated, differentiated by actor group and highly dynamic. A simple response of demanding that more data be collected will not necessarily produce better, more accurate prescriptions. Similarly, attempts to quantify and classify farming systems may indeed ultimately obscure our understanding of smallholders' livelihoods, if this type of dynamic variability is obscured by simple typologies and descriptions.

What is needed is to encourage those involved in technology development, design and dissemination to think about options in a broader context, taking on board the key themes highlighted by this research. This requires asking a series of questions often not posed by those working within a technical domain, and setting such reflections within a wider understanding of livelihoods contexts and dynamics. Fig. 5.1 presents a framework developed for research on sustainable livelihoods (Scoones 1998; see also Carney 1998). The key questions posed by the framework are:

> Given a particular *context*, what combination of *livelihood resources* result in the ability to follow what combination of *livelihood strategies* with what *outcomes*? What *institutional processes* mediate the ability to carry out different livelihood strategies and achieve (or not) such outcomes? (Scoones 1998:3)

For crop–livestock integration we are interested in one particular livelihood strategy, but need to set this within a broader understanding of the potentials and limitations of other options. As the case studies have demonstrated, even within the livelihood strategy of 'crop–livestock' farming there are huge variations. These are affected by contexts in various ways. As we have seen, policy conditions, agroecology, social differentiation and power relations all affect the type of strategy adopted. Such contexts influence the availability of different livelihood resources. Access to land, labour, capital, social networks, information, technology and physical infrastructure have all been seen to be important in different settings. Different people have access to different combinations of such livelihood resources, resulting in quite different strategies being followed and, ultimately, livelihood outcomes resulting.

As we have discussed, much existing work focuses on technology-generated production increases as the key objective of intervention. But a livelihoods approach requires us to sit back from this, and ask in what ways this has an impact on poverty and livelihoods. The range of outcome indicators listed in Fig. 5.1 is simply illustrative, but highlights the variety of ways that livelihood sustainability can be looked at, ranging from simple income or consumption measures of poverty through labour/employment measures to broader notions of well-being. Such livelihood indicators must be complemented by indicators dealing with sustainability, both of the resource base and livelihoods. Thus productivity increases may be important, but the link between these and broader poverty, livelihood and sustainability measures must be assessed.

A key feature of Fig. 5.1 is the role of institutions and organisations that mediate access to livelihood resources and affect the type of strategies followed. As we have emphasised throughout this book, it is the range of institutional processes, operating across a range of scales and in a variety of domains, that is key to understanding pathways of change. In Chapter 1 we introduced a simple matrix for analysing the range of institutions. As the case study chapters have shown, this must be a key step in any analysis, as the identification of institutional gaps, complementarities, overlaps and conflicts may be essential in identifying entry points for external intervention.

A livelihoods analysis of this sort, then, opens up a range of questions that might not otherwise be asked. For work focused on crop–livestock issues an indicative checklist

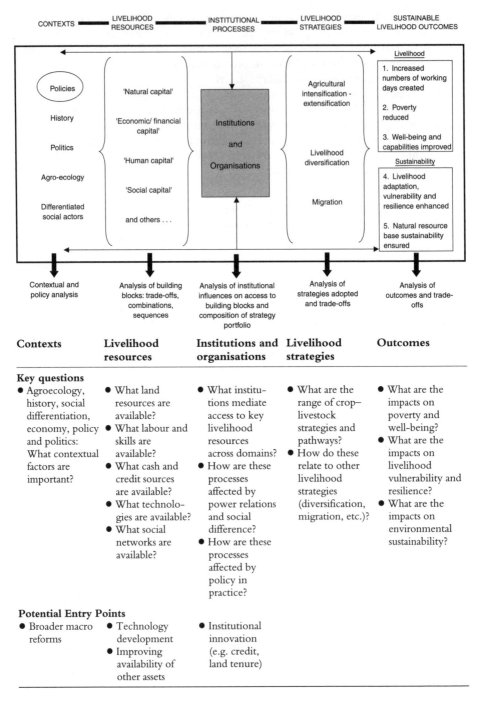

Figure 5.1 A framework for the analysis of sustainable livelihoods: key questions and potential entry points for crop–livestock work

of key questions is linked to various parts of the framework in Fig. 5.1 (see also Morton and Meadows 2000). The analysis of such questions, in turn, suggests a range of potential entry points for intervention. This expands the potential opportunities beyond the highly technical focus of most efforts to date. Of course, technology development remains important (as a route to improving livelihood resources), but this may be complemented by interventions aimed at the long-term task of shifting broader contextual factors or, potentially more immediately, influencing institutional processes or organisational structures. A recognition of social differentiation and the influence of institutions on the non-deterministic pathways of technological change, we argue, must be central to any policy decisions or else 'livelihood-blind' packages like 'mixed farming' will endure.

So what would be the consequences of pursuing such an approach? Table 5.2 summarises crop–livestock integration strategies presently pursued in each of the three countries, listing the relative prevalence (rare or common), the actors most likely to be following the strategy, and the asset or institutional requirements. Clearly, diversity is already present, but more strategies favour richer groups. Poorer households are more likely to be following labour intensification, extensification or livelihood diversification strategies than following the 'mixed farming' or capital intensification strategies of the ideal models promoted. Such households would be better served by adaptive technologies that enabled indigenous crop–livestock integration, such as credit schemes for non-cash crop agropastoralists in Mali or improved donkey ploughs for Zimbabwean farmers.

Table 5.2 Current crop–livestock integration strategies in the case study communities: their prevalence and their requirements.

Strategy	Ethiopia	Mali	Zimbabwe
Extensification	Rare (unless social network allows access to land)	Common on bush fields (group needs access to land, i.e. all of Zaradougou, only village and visiting Bambara)	Only richer groups in Neshangwe, Chikombedzi (need access to land and labour)
Capital intensification and 'mixed farming'	**Global model:** Common for richer groups (requires infrastructure, extension support) **Irrigation:** Rare (irrigable land is nearly all taken) **'Mixed farming' model:** Common for richer groups	**Inorganic fertiliser and herd manure:** Common on village fields (needs wells, water–manure contracts, capital for NPK) **Cotton–maize (CMDT model, Mali Sud):** Only richer households can increase input use > rate of extensification (requires extension support) **Cotton–maize, supported by Ivorian plantations:*** Common in Zaradougou (requires large labour commitment)	**'Mixed farming' model:** Common for richer groups ('Master Farmers') in Chipuriro, Ngundu, Neshangwe **Inorganic fertiliser and/or irrigation:** Richer groups in all sites (requires contract farming, markets, subsidies, credit) **'Mixed farming' with donkeys and cows, not oxen:** Common in Chipuriro, Ngundu, Neshangwe (result of migration, tsetse, or drought)

★Other off-farm capital sources may be valuable in other villages

Separation of agriculture and livestock	Common for richer groups	Common for groups without secure access to land (i.e. visiting Bambara)	Common in Neshangwe, Chikombedzi (non-livestock owners)
Labour intensification	Common for poorer groups Common for all on at least *part* of farm	Common for poorer groups Common for all on at least *part* of farm	Common for poorer groups
Livestock extensification & agricultural intensification	Common for all	Common for Dalonguébougou's Maures and Fulani (requires water–draught contracts)	Rare (limited by lack of grazing land)
Agricultural specialisation	Common for all (requires markets) **Vegetable garden focus:** Common for poorer groups	**Vegetable garden focus:** (requires markets, lineage access to *bas fonds*) **Fruit production focus:** (requires capital, markets)	**Intensive gardening and 'niche farming':** Common in Ngundu, Chipuriro (requires markets, favours contract farmers and co-ops)
Livestock specialisation	**Cattle:** Rare except for richer Sidama (ethnically based livelihood, limited by disease, grazing/fodder) **Replacing cattle with smallstock:** Common for poorer groups (needs markets)	**Cattle:** Rare except for richer Fulani, Maures (ethnically based livelihood, limited by disease, grazing/fodder) **Smallstock fattening:** Common for individuals (requires access to markets)	**Cattle:** Rare except for richer groups, Chipuriro (pen-fattening) **Smallstock fattening:** Common in Chikombedzi, Chivi, Chipuriro, esp. men (requires local and external markets)
Abandon agriculture (as coping or accumulating strategy)	**Livelihood diversification:** Common for all **Migration:** Common, esp. for young	**Livelihood diversification:** Common for all **Migration:** Common, esp. for young	**Livelihood diversification:** Common for all **Wage labour:** Common for poor individuals **Migration:** Common for all

Challenges for the policy process

Can such a broad-based, poverty reduction/sustainable livelihoods approach be pursued in the case study countries? This section explores some of the challenges of shifting policy processes to be more attuned to the evident diversity and complexity of farmers' and herders' livelihoods, and so allowing a recognition of the technical and institutional implications of multiple pathways of change.

Across the case study countries it is possible to identify the beginnings of new policy approaches, and the emergence of new types of policy process (Box 5.1). Potentially this might lead to more sophisticated understandings of different types of pattern of crop and livestock management. However, positive experiences so far can be seen only as relatively isolated and sporadic. Stronger and longer-lasting effects would entail more systematic reflection on and a more thorough engagement with the policy process.

Box 5.1   Opportunities for change

In Tigray, *Ethiopia* connections with senior figures in the bureaucracy mean there is a critical 'green light', as it is put locally, allowing experimentation with new approaches, such as building farmer capacity and confidence to innovate and develop new types of relationship with those promoting technical development. Work on soil management and land husbandry in the region has been employing travelling seminars and networkshops, where farmers learn from each other and where Development Agents are exposed to new ways of thinking and acting. Research too may be changing. A high percentage of proposed research projects at the key Mekelle University College in Tigray specifically emphasise farmer participation.[7]

In *Mali* two factors stand out. First, formal processes of decentralisation are under way, with election of councillors for newly formed rural communes in July 1999. At the time of writing it is still too early to judge effectiveness, but it is possible that a move away from previously highly centralised planning models may create opportunities for programmes and local policies with greater sensitivity to diverse conditions and circumstances. Second, there has been a mushrooming of civil society organisations in Mali. Recently many NGOs have shifted towards a more livelihoods focus in their activities. Building on this start, and in response to some of the discontent expressed about the dominant approach being pushed in the cotton zone,[8] if links are made to state structures, there may be possibilities of much broader change

In *Zimbabwe*, the Contill project, which was based in Masvingo Province, has helped to challenge the fundamental premise of research and extension institutional practice, namely that something cannot be extended unless it has been 'proven and tested' by research. Essentially, extensionists made use of their connections to a nearby research station to get away with a very liberal definition of 'testing' technologies together with farmers. Through links across projects and with government officials in the research and extension bureaucracy, a foundation was built, which has gradually resulted in a shift in bureaucratic practice through the initiation of a 'change process' within Agritex, and official endorsement of Participatory Extension Approaches.

---

[7]Pers. comm. from the Dean of the college.

[8]Within the CMDT zone there has been an increasing number of protests by farmers, such as burning of company lorries. These to some extent represent a straight conflict over surplus appropriation, and a push for a better deal for farmers. The emergence of the cotton farmers' union (SYCOV) in the early 1990s has offered some potential remedies, but having won some early victories for farmers, SYCOV's leadership must now balance grassroots solidarity with the risks of co-option by the CMDT and other actors (Bingen 1996). However, the protests can also be seen to represent a deeper frustration with the dominant cotton production model, the systems of credit provision associated with it, and the lack of flexibility in relation to other livelihood opportunities. These currents could potentially open possibilities for the creation of new networks linking NGO activity, critical voices within the CMDT and new forms of farming systems research.

The basic problem with existing policy processes is that they deal poorly with complex and diverse practices and strategies. A major reason for this is that policy formulation is not sufficiently open to allow for the articulation of different interests and knowledges. The idea of participation is, of course, fast becoming the conventional development solution to these kinds of dilemmas. Because participation is high-fashion in the development industry, there is a real danger that there will be much show with relatively little substance. Participatory appraisals with no link to action, or consultations that extract information but change little are all examples of what might be called 'instrumental participation'. Hence, if the aim is to build policy processes that capture the non-linearity of people's livelihood and farming practices more effectively than the 'mixed farming' model does, then there is a real need to make sure that participation is more than isolated good practice. There must be real and effective links changing the way choices are made and resources are allocated.

As we have seen, narratives and paradigms die hard. The 'mixed farming' model is one such survivor. They can appear to have disappeared but then they re-emerge. Counter-narratives too can risk becoming quickly absorbed as the new orthodoxy, with all the resulting simplifications and short cuts that characterised their predecessors. There is always a powerful urge to simplify complexity. This makes sense on one level, but there is always a need to ensure flexibility and openness to new insights. One answer to this is to try to incorporate forms of reflexivity in policy processes, where there is a continuously critical reflection on process, norms and emerging outcomes (Rein and Schön 1993). Other implications would include examination of the sectoral lines on which development planning is managed.

Livelihoods-friendly governance would entail more 'joined-up' bureaucracy and decision-making than exists at present. Critically, this may not sit easily with the dominant governance agenda pushed by donors. This tends to look at making bureaucracies more efficient, limiting corruption, promoting democratic accountability and expanding the role of civil society. While all these things may be desirable in themselves, they do not add up to more inclusive and reflexive policy processes. More efficient and less corrupt governments may simply pursue old, top-down models more effectively than ever before. Indeed, good governance is often seen in terms of promoting standard-fit bureaucracy more effectively, bureaucracy that delivers regular products reliably. This may not be at all what is needed for the promotion of awareness of very diverse realities and support for very diverse livelihood pathways. Equally, support for civil society may not quite do the trick either, as there is no guarantee that civil society organisations will not articulate dominant narratives in essentially the same vein as others.

There are, however, some basic things that can be done by those who want to influence the policy process (cf. Keeley 2000). A key starting point is to document diversity, whether it be diversity of social context, diversity in terms of values or in terms of experiences and practices. From this, it may be possible to develop new models that take adequate account of this complexity, variability and diversity. This means developing counter-narratives that bring more complexity within a storyline than the existing crop–livestock integration model. In some respects, this book has begun to do this. Further to this, it may be possible to develop 'success stories' that help communicate – preferably visually – the core ideas of a new approach to policy-makers. The experience of Chivi in Zimbabwe, or the work on farmer innovation in Ethiopia are examples (see Box 5.1). With something to show that illustrates a message it may be possible to construct new actor-networks and to begin to change policy.

For crop–livestock issues this would mean actor-networks that reach into the extension departments of Ministries of Agriculture and into research stations and research administrations, as well as reaching higher political levels to build support. This type of activity cannot be undertaken on a haphazard basis, it entails systematic analysis of whom and where to target. As well as targeting the obviously influential, it is important to build capacity and voice at lower levels, specifically the capacity of farmers – or rural people more broadly – to articulate their demands and to learn from each other. Redefining the extension and research cadres to build on complementarities with private and non-governmental sectors could improve the expression of demand-led agricultural research and extension, by giving effective mechanisms for stakeholders' lobbying and influence. Such a redefinition would be institutionally difficult, but the payoffs should ultimately outweigh the considerable challenges.

Conclusions

The aim of externally generated development interventions is not to reinforce a particular status quo, but to encourage changes that reduce poverty and improve the sustainability of livelihoods. Continuing critical interest in the role of crop–livestock integration in supporting sustainable livelihoods for Africa's poor demands, we suggest, that present policy shed its emphasis on simple evolutionary models. Overall, the case study material suggests the ultimate goals of technological change should include the following:

- Promoting diversity in adaptive technologies and enabling indigenous crop–livestock integration, rather than promoting particular, idealised packages like 'mixed farming'.
- Situating crop–livestock integration within a broader livelihood context of farm and non-farm commitments.
- Engaging variability directly, to formally integrate concepts of risk and vulnerability into development planning.
- Directly addressing poverty among vulnerable groups, such as poor households and women.

The results from Ethiopia, Mali and Zimbabwe suggest new priorities for technology choice if a wider range of beneficiaries is to be reached, particularly poorer and marginal groups. In addition, a technology-focused approach may be insufficient, and greater attention needs to be paid to institutional contexts. While particular technologies and management techniques remain important, by identifying institutional blockages and opportunities for change, a range of other entry points for development intervention can be identified.

By emphasising non-deterministic pathways, social differentiation and processes of institutional mediation, this book has provided the beginnings of an alternative framework for thinking about pathways of agricultural and livelihood change, and the role of technologies for crop–livestock production within this. Research and development priority setting, we argue, must take these issues seriously if a poverty reduction and sustainable livelihoods approach is to be truly central.

References

Abiye Astake and Mohammed-Saleem, M.A. (1996). 'Draught animal power for land-use intensification in the Ethiopian highlands', *World Animal Review (FAO)*,86(1): 3–11

Abiye Astake, Jutzi, S. and Abate Tedla (1989). 'Sequential cropping of vertisols in the Ethiopian Highlands using a broadbed-and-furrow system', *ILCA Bulletin*, 34, July

Adams, W.M. (1992). *Wasting the Rain: Rivers, People and Planning in Africa.* London: Earthscan Publications and Minneapolis: Minnesota University Press

Alvord, E.D. (1943). *Agricultural Position in Reserves, Selukwe Reserve – Report of the Agriculturalist for Natives.* National Archives of Zimbabwe, S2386

Alvord, E.D. (1948). 'The progress of Native Agriculture in Southern Rhodesia', *The New Rhodesia*, 15: 18–19

Anderson, D.M. (1984). 'Depression, dust bowl, demography, and drought: the colonial state and soil conservation in East Africa during the 1930s', *African Affairs* 83(332): 321–43

Anderson, D.M. (1988). 'Cultivating pastoralists: Ecology and economy among the Il Chamus of Baringo, 1840–1980'. In Johnson, D. and Anderson, D. (eds.) *Ecology and Survival. Case Studies from Northeast African History.* London: Lester Crook Academic Publishing: 241–260

Anon. (1947). *Rapports Economiques.* Bamako: Archive National du Mali, Document IQ–360

Assefa, T. (1990). 'Livestock development in the peasant sector of Highland Ethiopia: Some policy issues and implications', *ALPAN Network Paper*, No. 24. Addis Ababa: ILCA, African Livestock Policy Analysis Network (ALPAN)

Astor, Lord and Seebohm Rowntree, B. (1946). *Mixed Farming and Muddled Thinking.* London: Macdonald

Aubreville, A. (1949). *Climats, forêts et desertification de l'Afrique tropical.* Paris: Société d'Editions Géographique Maritime et Coloniale

Bannerman, J. H. (1980). 'A short political and economic history of the Tsovani, Chisa and Mahenye: Dynasties of the Ndanga, Chiredzi and Chipanga Districts to ca. 1950'. Manuscript, National Archives of Zimbabwe

Bassett, T.J. and Crummey, D.E. (1993). *Land in African Agrarian Systems.* Madison: University of Wisconsin Press

Bayer, W. and Waters-Bayer, A. (1995). 'Forage alternatives from range and field: Pastoral forage management and improvement in the African drylands'. In

Scoones, I. (ed.) *Living with Uncertainty: New Directions in Pastoral Development in Africa*. London: Intermediate Technology Publications: 58–78

Becker, L.C. (1994). 'An early experiment in the reorganisation of agricultural production in the French Soudan (Mali), 1920–1940', *Africa*, 64(3): 373–390

Beets, R.C. (1990). *Raising and Sustaining Productivity Small-holder Farming Systems in the Tropics*. Alkmaar: AgBe Publishing

Behnke, R.H. (1994). 'Natural resource management in pastoral Africa', *Development Policy Review:* 12(1): 5–27

Behnke, R.H. and Scoones, I. (1993). 'Rethinking range ecology: Implications for rangeland management in Africa.' In Behnke *et al.* (1993) *Range Ecology at Disequilibrium*

Behnke, R.H., Scoones, I. and Kerven, C. (1993). *Range Ecology at Disequilibrium: New Models of Natural Variability and Pastoral Adaptation in African Savannas*. London: Overseas Development Institute

Beinart, W. (1984). 'Soil erosion, conservationism and ideas about development: A Southern African exploration, 1900–1960', *Journal of Southern African Studies*, 11(1): 52–83

Berry, S. (1984). 'The food crisis and agrarian change in Africa: A review essay', *African Studies Review,* 27(2): 59–112

Berry, S. (1989). 'Social institutions and access to resources in African agriculture', *Africa,* 19: 41–55

Berry, S. (1993). *No Condition is Permanent: The Social Dynamics of Agrarian Change in Sub-Saharan Africa*. Madison: University of Wisconsin Press

Bingen, R.J. (1996). 'Leaders, leadership, and democratisation in West Africa: Observations from the cotton farmers' movement in Mali', *Agriculture and Human Values*, 13(2): 24–32

Binswanger, H.P. and Ruttan, V. (1978). *Induced Innovation: Technology, Institutions and Development*. Baltimore: Johns Hopkins University Press

Boserup, E. (1965). *The Conditions of Agricultural Growth: The Economics of Agrarian Change Under Population Pressure*. London: Allen & Unwin

Boserup, E. (1981). *Population and Technological Change: A Study of Long-term Change*. Chicago: University of Chicago Press

Bosma, R., Bengaly, K., Traoré, M. and Roeleveld, A. (1996). *L'élevage en Voie d'Intensification: Synthèse de la Recherche sur les Ruminants dans les Exploitations Agricoles Mixtes au Mali-Sud*. Amsterdam: Royal Institute of the Tropics (KIT) and Bamako: Institut d'Economie Rurale

Bourn, W. and Wint, W. (1994). 'Livestock, land use and agricultural intensification in Sub-Saharan Africa'. *Pastoral Development Network* Paper 39a. London: Overseas Development Institute

Bowler, P.J. (1989). *The Invention of Progress: The Victorians and the Past*. Oxford: Basil Blackwell

Bratton, M. (1984). 'Draft power, draft exchange and farmer organisations', *Working Paper No. 9/84*, University of Zimbabwe: Department of Land Management

Brock, K. (1999). 'Implementing a sustainable livelihoods framework for policy-directed research: Reflections from practice in Mali'. *IDS Working Paper*, 90. Brighton: Institute of Development Studies, Sussex

Brock, K. and Coulibaly, N. (1999). 'Sustainable rural livelihoods in Mali'. *IDS Research Report,* 35. Brighton: Institute of Development Studies, Sussex

Bromley, D.W. and Cernea, M.M. (1989). *The Management of Common Property Natural Resources: Some Conceptual and Operational Fallacies.* Washington, DC: World Bank

Bruce, J. (1993). 'Do indigenous tenure systems constrain agricultural development?' In Bassett, T. and Crummey, D. (eds.). *Land in African Agrarian Systems.*

Bruce, J. and Migot-Adholla, S. (eds.) (1994). *Searching for Land Tenure Security in Africa.* Washington, DC: World Bank

Bryceson, D.F., Kay, C. and Mooij, J. (2000). *Disappearing Peasantries? Rural Labour in Africa, Asia and Latin America.* London: Intermediate Technology Publications

Butterfield, H. (1963). *The Whig Interpretation of History.* London: Bell

Campbell, B.M.S. and Overton, M. (1993). 'A new perspective on medieval and early modern agriculture: Six centuries of Norfolk farming c.1250 – c.1850', *Past and Present,* 141: 38–105

Campbell, B., Frost, P., Kirchman, H. and Swift, M. (1998). 'A survey of soil fertility management in small-scale farming systems in north-eastern Zimbabwe', *Journal of Sustainable Agriculture,* 11(2/3): 19–39

Carney, D. (1998). 'Implementing the sustainable rural livelihoods approach'. In Carney, D. (ed.). *Sustainable Rural Livelihoods. What Contribution Can we Make?* London: Department for International Development

Carswell, G., Data Dea, De Haan, A., Konde, Alemayehu, Seba, Haileyesus and Sinclair, A. (2000). 'Ethiopia Country Report'. *IDS Research Report,* 44. Brighton: Institute of Development Studies, Sussex

Clay, D. (1998). 'Sustainable intensification in the highland tropics: Rwandan farmers' investments in land conservation and soil fertility', *Economic Development and Cultural Change,* 48(2): 351–377

Cliffe, L. (1986). *Policy Options for Agrarian Reform in Zimbabwe.* Harare: FAO

CMDT (1995). 'L'intégration agriculture-élevage en 3e région'. Sikasso: Compagnie Malienne de Développement des Textiles (mimeo)

Cohen, J. (1987). *Integrated Rural Development. The Ethiopian Experience and the Debates.* Uppsala: Scandinavian Institute for African Studies

Comaroff, J. and Comaroff, J. (1992). 'Home-made hegemony: Modernity, domesticity and colonialism in South Africa'. In Hensen, K.T. (ed.), *African Encounters with Domesticity.* New Brunswick: Rutgers University Press

Comte, A. (1875). *System of Positive Policy.* London: Longmans Green

Connelly, W.T. (1994). 'Population pressure, labor availability and agricultural disintensification: The decline of farming on Rusinga Island, Kenya', *Human Ecology,* 22(2): 145–170

Coulibaly, B. (1979). 'Monographie d'un village en milieu Sénoufo: Zangasso'. Unpublished Mémoire de fin d'étude. Bamako: Ecole Normale Supérieure

Cousins, B., Weiner, D. and Amin, N. (1992). 'Social differentiation in the Communal Lands of Zimbabwe', *Review of African Political Economy,* 53: 5–25

Crole-Rees, A. (1997). 'Diversification des revenus en milieu rural: Le cas de Mali-Sud', *Research Report.* Zurich: Centre Suisse pour l'Agriculture Internationale

Croppenstedt, A. and Mulat Demeke (1996). *Determinants of Adoption and Levels of Demand for Fertiliser for Cereal-growing Farmers in Ethiopia.* Oxford: Centre for the Study of African Economies.

CSA (1996). *The 1994 Population and Housing Census of Ethiopia: Results for Southern Nations' Nationalities' and Peoples' Region,* Vol. 1, Part IV. Addis Ababa

Curasson, M.-G. (1947). 'Le rôle et importance du pâturage dans l'économie des pays chauds', *Elevage et Médecine Vétérinaire des Pays Tropicaux,* 1(4): 279–289

Dagnew Eshete (1995). 'Food shortages and household coping strategies by income groups: A case study of Wolaita District in Southern Ethiopia'. In Dejene Aredo and Mulat Demeke (eds.), *Ethiopian Agriculture: Problems of Transformation.* Proceedings of Fourth Annual Conference on the Ethiopian Economy, Addis Ababa

Data Dea (1998). 'Soil fertility management in its social context. A study of local perceptions and practices in Wolaita, southern Ethiopia', *Managing African Soils,* 1. London: International Institute for Environment and Development

David, R. and Ruthven, O. (1993). 'The effects of male out-migration on women's management of the natural resource base in the Sahel: Summary report of the first phase of the research in Diourbel (Senegal)'. UK: SOS-Sahel International

Davies, S (1997). 'Livelihood adaptation'. Paper for workshop 'Making Livelihoods Work – Women, Men and Children in Rajasthan'. Mimeo. Brighton: Institute of Development Studios, Sussex

de Haan, C. (1994). 'An overview of the World Bank's involvement in pastoral development', *Pastoral Development Network Paper,* 36b. London: Overseas Development Institute

de Leeuw, P.N. (1997). 'Crop residues in tropical Africa: Trends in supply, demand and use'. In Renard, C. (ed.), *Crop Residues in Mixed Farming Systems.* Wallingford: CAB International

de Leeuw, P.N., Reynolds, L. and Rey, B. (1995). 'Nutrient transfers from livestock in West African agricultural systems'. In Powell, J.M., Fernandez-Rivera, S., Williams, T.O. and Renard, C. (eds.), *Livestock and Sustainable Nutrient Cycling in Mixed Farming Systems of Sub-Saharan Africa. Volume II: Technical Papers.* Addis Ababa: ILCA

Dejene Aredo and Mulat Demeke (eds.) (1995). 'Ethiopian agriculture: Problems of transformation', *Proceedings of Fourth Annual Conference on the Ethiopian Economy.* Addis Ababa

Delgado, C. (1979). 'The southern Fulani farming system in Upper Volta. A model for the integration of crop and livestock production in the West African savanna', *African Rural Economy* Paper No. 20. East Lansing: Michigan State University, Department of Agricultural Economics

Demsetz, H. (1967). 'Towards a theory of property rights', *American Economic Review,* 57: 357–359

Derman, B. (1995). *Changing Land-use in the Eastern Zambezi Valley: Socio-economic Considerations.* Centre for Applied Social Sciences/World Wide Fund for Nature Joint Paper. Harare

Dessalegn Rahmato (1990). *A Resource Flow Systems Analysis of Rural Bolosso (Wollaita).* Addis Ababa, Addis Ababa University: Redd Barna and Institute of Development Research

Dessalegn Rahmato (1992). *The Dynamics of Rural Poverty: Case Studies from a District in Southern Ethiopia,* Monograph Series 2/92. Addis Ababa: Institute of Development Research

Dessalegn Rahmato (1994). 'Land tenure and land policy in Ethiopia after the Derg: Proceedings of the second workshop of the Land Tenure Project'. In Dessalegn Rahmato (ed.), *Land Tenure and Land Policy in Ethiopia after the Derg*. Addis Ababa: Institute of Development Research

Diabaté, D. (1986). 'Analyse des mécanismes de mutations socio-économiques au sein des sociétés rurales Sénoufo du Sud du Mali'. Ph.D. thesis, Paris, Ecole des Hautes Etudes en Sciences Sociales

Drinkwater, M. (1991). *The State and Agrarian Change in Zimbabwe's Communal Areas*. London: Macmillan

DSA/CIRAD (1985). 'Relations agriculture-élevage. Actes du IIe séminaire du Département Systèmes Agraires du CIRAD'. Conference held at Montpellier, France, 10–13 September. Montpellier: DSA/CIRAD

Dyke, G.V. (1993). *John Lawes of Rothamsted: Pioneer of Science, Farming and Industry*. Harpenden: Hoos Press

El Wakeel, A. and Astake, A. (1996). 'Intensification of agriculture on vertisols to minimize land degradation in parts of the Ethiopian Highlands', *Land Degradation and Development*, V(7): 57–67

Ellis, F. (1998). 'Household strategies and rural livelihood diversification', *Journal of Development Studies,* 35(1)

Eyasu, Elias (1997). 'Soil fertility decline and coping strategies: The case of Kindo Koisha, southern Ethiopia'. PhD thesis, Norwich, University of East Anglia

Eyasu, Elias and Scoones, I. (1999). 'Perspectives on soil fertility change: A case study from southern Ethiopia', *Land Degradation and Development*, 10: 195–206

Eyasu, E., Morse, S. and Belshaw, D.G.R. (1998). 'Nitrogen and phosphorous balances of Kindo Koisha farms in southern Ethiopia', *Land Degradation and Development*, 10: 195–206

Fairhead, J. and Leach, M. (1996). *Misreading the African Landscape. Society and Ecology in a Forest–Savanna Mosaic*. Cambridge: Cambridge University Press

FAO (1979). 'The impact of food assistance: WADU 1971–1976, Ethiopia. A case study for A Study of the Impact of WFP Assistance on Local Food Production in Food Priority and Least Developed Countries', Addis Ababa: FAO

Feder, G. and Noronha, R. (1987). 'Land rights systems and agricultural development', *World Bank Research Observer*, 2: 143–169

Feunteun, L.M., (1955). 'L'élevage en AOF. Son importance économique et sociale; les conditions de son développement et de son amélioration', *Revue d'Elevage et Médicine Vétérinaire en Pays Tropiques*, 8(2–3): 137–162

Fok, M. (1994). 'Evolution du système coton au Mali', *Cahiers Agricultures*, 3: 329–336

Gass, G.M. and Sumberg, J.E. (1993). *Intensification of Livestock Production in Africa: A Review of Experience and Issues with Special Reference to Poverty and the Environment*. University of East Anglia: Overseas Development Group, School of Development Studies

Gavian, S. (1993). *Land Tenure and Soil Fertility Management in Niger*. Stanford University: Food Research Institute

Getachew Asamenew *et al.* (1993). 'A survey of the farming systems of vertisol areas of the Ethiopian highlands'. In Tekalign Mamo *et al.* (eds.), *Improved Management of Vertisols for Sustainable Crop-Livestock Production in the Ethiopian Highlands*.

Synthesis report 1986–92. Addis Ababa: Technical Committee of the Joint Vertisol Project

Giddens, A. (1984). *The Constitution of Society: Outline of the Theory of Structuration.* Cambridge: Polity Press

Giraudy, F. and Niang, M. (1996). *Impacte de la Dévaluation sur les Systèmes de Production et les Revenus Paysans dans la Zone Mali-sud.* Sikasso: CMDT Suivi-Evaluation

Gould, S.J. (1996). *Life's Grandeur. The Spread of Excellence from Plato to Darwin.* London: Jonathan Cape

Gryseels, G., Abiye Astake, Anderson, F.M. and Getachew Assemenew (1984). 'The use of the single oxen for crop cultivation in Ethiopia', *ILCA Bulletin* (18), April

Gryseels, G., *et al.* (1987). 'Draught power and smallholder grain production in the Ethiopian Highlands'. In *Proceedings of the First National Livestock Improvement Conference.* Addis Ababa: Institute of Agricultural Research

Guillard, D. (1993). *L'Ombre du Mil: Un système Agro-Pastoral Sahelien en Aribinda (Burkina Faso).* Paris: Editions ORSTOM

Hall, A.D. (1905). *The Book of Rothamsted Experiments.* London: John Murray

Hall, A.D. (1936). *The Improvement of Native Agriculture in Relation to Population and Public Health.* London: Oxford University Press

Hampshire, K. (1998). 'Seasonal labour migration and livelihood security in the Sahel', *Research Report.* London: University College

Hardin, G. (1968). 'The tragedy of the commons', *Science* 162: 1234–1248

Harris, F. (1996). *Intensification of Agriculture in Semi-Arid Areas: Lessons from the Kano Close-Settled Zone, Nigeria.* IIED Gatekeeper Series No. SA59. London: International Institute for Environment and Development

Hayami, Y. and Ruttan, V. (1985). *Agricultural Development: An International Perspective.* Baltimore: Johns Hopkins University Press

Herskovitz, M.J. (1926). 'The cattle complex in East Africa', *American Anthropologist,* 23: 230–272, 362–388, 494–528, 633–644

Herz, K.O. (1993). 'Report of the Expert Consultation on Funding of Agricultural Research in Sub-Saharan Africa'. Kenya Agricultural Research Institute (KARI), 6–8 July. http: //www.fao.org/WAICENT/FAOINFO/SUSTDEV/RTdirect/RTre0002.htm 'RT: Resources Africa' [accessed 5/10/2000]

Hesseling, G. and Coulibaly, C. (1991). *La Législation et la Politique Foncières au Mali: Rapport dans le Cadre de la Schéma Directeur de Développement Rural.* Bamako: Institut Malien des Recherches appliquées au Développement and Leiden: Centre d'Etudes Africaines

Hulme, M. (1996). 'Recent climate change in the world's drylands', *Geophysical Research Letters,* 23(1): 61–64

Humphreys, L.R. (1994). *Tropical Forages: Their Role in Sustainable Agriculture.* Harlow: Longman Scientific and Technical

IAR (1991). 'Areka area mixed farming zone, North Omo Region. Diagnostic Survey', *IAR Research Report* No. 15. Areka: Institute of Agricultural Research

IEMVT (1971). 'Etude de la structure des activités des institutions à la recherche en matière d'élevage et de santé animale'. Paper presented to the Conference on Agricultural Research in Africa, AAASA, University of Ibadan

ILCA (1994). *Improving Livestock Production in Africa: Evolution of ILCA's Programme 1974–94.* Addis Ababa: International Livestock Centre for Africa

Illius, A. and Ncube, S. (unpublished). 'Environmental variability and productivity of semi-arid grazing systems. Project summary'. Livestock Production Programme, DFID. Chatham: Natural Resources Institute

INRA/IRAM/UNB (1991). *Cereals, Trade and Agricultural Policies in the Western Sub-Market: What Prospects?* Paris: CILSS document SAH/D/91/376

Jabbar, M.A. (1993). 'Evolving crop–livestock farming systems in the humid zone of West Africa: Potential and research needs', *Outlook on Agriculture,* 22(1): 13–21

Jabbar, M. (1996). 'Energy and the evolution of farming systems: The potential of mixed farming in the moist savannah of Sub-Saharan Africa', *Outlook on Agriculture,* 25(1): 27–37

Jahnke, H. (1982). *Livestock Production Systems and Livestock Development in Tropical Africa.* Kiel: Kieler Wissenschafterverlag Vauk

Jenden, P. (1995). *Cash for Work and Food Insecurity in Koisha, Southern Ethiopia.* London: Overseas Development Institute

Jutzi, S., Anderson, F.M. and Abiye Astake (1987). 'Low cost modifications of the traditional Ethiopian tine plough for land shaping and surface drainage of heavy clay soils: Preliminary results from on-farm verification trials', *ILCA Bulletin* (27), April

Keeley, J. (2000). 'Understanding and influencing policy processes for soil and water conservation'. In Reij, C. *et al.* (eds.), *Farmer Innovation in Africa: Sources of Inspiration.* London: Earthscan Publications

Keeley, J. and Scoones, I. (1999). 'Understanding environmental policy processes: A review', *IDS Working Paper,* 89. Brighton: Institute of Development Studies, Sussex

Keeley, J. and Scoones, I. (2000a). 'Global science, global policy: Local to global connections in the policy process surrounding soils management in Africa', *IDS Working Paper,* 115. Brighton: Institute of Development Studies, Sussex

Keeley, J. and Scoones, I. (2000b). 'Knowledge, power and politics: The environmental policy-making process in Ethiopia', *Journal of Modern African Studies,* 38: 98–120

Keeley, J. and Scoones, I. (2000c). 'Environmental policy-making in Zimbabwe: Discourses, science and politics', *IDS Working Paper,* 116. Brighton: Institute of Development Studies, Sussex

Keeley, J. and Scoones, I. (2000d). 'Environmental policy-making in Mali: Science, bureaucracy and soil fertility narratives', unpublished paper.

King, J.G.M. (1939). 'Mixed farming in northern Nigeria. Part 1: origin and present conditions', *Empire Journal of Experimental Agriculture,* 7: 271–284

Kleene, P., Sanogo, B. and Vierstra, G. (1989). *A partir de Fonsébougou: Présentation, objectifs et méthodologie du Volet Fonsébougou (1977–1987).* Amsterdam: Royal Institute of the Tropics (KIT)

Landais, M. and Lhoste, P. (1990). 'Crop–livestock association in intertropical Africa: A technological myth confronted with field realities', *Cahiers des Sciences Humaines,* 26 (1–2): 217–235

Landais, E. and Lhoste, P. (1993). 'Systèmes d'élevage et transfert de fertilité dans la zone des savanes africaines. 2. Les systèmes de gestion de la fumure animale et leur insertion dans les relations entre l'élevage et l'agriculture (Livestock systems and fertility transfer in the African savanna zone. 2. Farmyard manure management methods in crop–livestock interactions)', *Cahiers Agricultures,* 2(1): 9–25

Leach, M. and Mearns, R. (eds.) (1996). *The Lie of the Land: Challenging Received Wisdom on the African Environment.* London: James Currey

Leach, M., Mearns, R. and Scoones, I. (1997). 'Environmental entitlements: A framework for understanding the institutional dyanamics of environmental change', *IDS Discussion Paper*, 359. Brighton: Institute of Development Studies, Sussex

Lele, U. and Stone, S.W. (1989). *Population Pressure, the Environment and Agricultural Intensification: Variations on the Boserup Hypothesis*. Washington, DC: World Bank

Lhoste, P. (1987). *Elevage et relations agriculture–élevage en zone cotonnière: Situation et perspectives*. Montpellier: CIRAD-IEMVT

Lugard, F. (1922). *The Dual Mandate in British Tropical Africa*. London: Frank Cass

Maïga, A.S., Témé, B., Coulibaly, B.S., Diarra, L., Kergna, A.O., Tigana, K. with Winpenny, J. (1995). 'Structural adjustment and sustainable development in Mali: A World Wildlife Fund for Nature Study', *ODI Working Paper*, 82. London: Overseas Development Institute

Manyuchi, B. and Smith, T. (1992). 'Improving the feeding value of low quality roughages using urea treatment', *The Farmer*, 13

McCann, J. (1995). *People of the Plow: An Agricultural History of Ethiopia, 1800–1990*. Madison: University of Wisconsin Press

McCown, R.L., Haaland, G. and de Haan, C. (1979). 'The interaction between cultivation and livestock production in semi-arid Africa'. In Hall, A.E., Cannell G.H. and Lawton, H.W. (eds.), *Agriculture in Semi-Arid Environments*. Berlin: Springer-Verlag

McGregor, J. (1995). 'Conservation, control and ecological change: The politics and ecology of colonial conservation in Shurugwi, Zimbabwe', *Environment and History*, 1(3): 257–279

McIntire, J. and Gryseels, G. (1987). 'Crop–livestock interactions in sub-Saharan Africa and their implications for farming systems research', *Experimental Agriculture*, 23: 235–243

McIntire, J. and Powell, J.M. (1995). 'African semi-arid tropical agriculture cannot grow without external inputs'. In Powell, J.M., Fernandez-Rivera, S., Williams, T.O. and Renard, C. (eds.), *Livestock and Sustainable Nutrient Cycling in Mixed Farming Systems of Sub-Saharan Africa. Volume II: Technical Papers*. Addis Ababa: ILCA

McIntire, J., Bourzat, D. and Pingali, P. (1992). *Crop–Livestock Interaction in Sub-Saharan Africa*. Washington, DC: World Bank

Mehta, L. *et al.* (1999). 'Exploring understandings of institutions and uncertainty: New directions in natural resource management', *Discussion Paper*, 372, Brighton: Institute of Development Studies, Sussex

Mengistu Buta and Shapiro B. (1997). 'Use of crossbred cows for milk and traction in the highlands ecoregion : A whole-farm evaluation', Agricultural Economic Society of Ethiopia, Third Conference, 2–3 October. Addis Ababa

Mohammed-Saleem, M.A. and Astake, A. (1996). 'Options to intensify cropland use for alleviating smallholder energy and protein deficiencies in the East African Highlands', *Field Crops Research*, V(48 (2,3)): 177–184

Mohammed-Saleem, M.A. and Fitzhugh, H.A. (1995). 'An overview of demographic and environmental issues in sustainable agriculture in sub-Saharan Africa'. In Powell, J.M., Fernández-Rivera, S., Williams, T.O. and Renard, C. (eds.), *Livestock and Sustainable Nutrient Cycling in Mixed Farming Systems of Sub-Saharan Africa. Volume II: Technical Papers*. Addis Ababa: ILCA

Mohammed-Saleem, M.A. and Mendera, E.J. (1997). 'Balancing livestock, environment and needs – Ethiopia'. Paper presented to Electronic Conference on Balancing Livestock, Environment and Human Needs. International Development Research Centre (IDRC), Ottawa; the International Livestock Research Institute (ILRI), Addis Ababa; and the Food and Agricultural Organization of the United Nations (FAO) Rome. 10 March–24 May.

Morrison, K.D. (1996). 'Typological schemes and agricultural change: Beyond Boserup in precolonial South India', *Current Anthropology*, 37(4): 583–597

Mortimore, M. (1991). 'A review of mixed farming systems in the semi-arid zone of sub-Saharan Africa', *ILCA Working Document*, No. 17. Addis Ababa: ILCA, Livestock Economics Division

Mortimore, M. (1993). 'The intensification of peri-urban agriculture: The Kano Close Settled Zone, 1964–86'. In Turner, B.L, Kates, R. and Hyden, G. (eds.), *Population Growth and Agricultural Change in Africa*. Gainesville: University of Florida Press: 358–400

Mortimore, M. and Adams, W.M. (1999). *Working the Sahel: Environment and Society in Northern Nigeria*. London: Routledge

Mortimore, M. and Turner, B. (1993). 'Crop–livestock farming systems in the semi-arid zone of sub-Saharan Africa: Ordering diversity and understanding change', *Agricultural Administration Network Paper*, 46. London: Overseas Development Institute

Morton, J. and Mathewman, R. (1996). 'Improving livestock production through extension: Information needs, institutions and opportunities', *Natural Resources Perspectives*, 12. London: Overseas Development Institute

Morton, J. and Meadows, N. (2000). 'Pastoralism and sustainable livelihoods: An emerging agenda', *Policy Series*, 11. Greenwich: Natural Resources Institute

Mtetwa, R.M.G. (1976). 'The "political" and economic history of the Duma people of south-eastern Rhodesia from the early eighteenth century to 1945'. Ph.D. Thesis, Salisbury, University of Rhodesia, Department of History

Muchena, M. (1989). 'The effect of ox-sharing arrangements on the supply and use of draft animals in the Communal Areas of Zimbabwe – preliminary findings'. In Cousins, B. (ed.), *People, Land and Livestock. Proceedings of a Workshop on the Socio-Economic Dimensions of Livestock Production in the Communal Lands of Zimbabwe*. University of Zimbabwe: Centre for Applied Social Sciences

Mugwira, L.M. and Murwira, H.K. (1997). *Use of Cattle Manure to Improve Soil Fertility in Zimbabwe: Past and Current Research and Future Research Needs*. Harare: International Maize and Wheat Improvement Centre (CIMMYT)

Mukhebi, A.W., Knipscheer, H.C. and Sullivan, G. (1991). 'The impact of foodcrop production on sustained livestock production in semi-arid regions of Kenya', *Agricultural Systems*, 35(3): 339–351

Mulat, Demeke (1995). 'Constraints to efficient and sustainable use of fertilizers in Ethiopia'. In Dejene Aredo and Mulat Demeke (eds.), *Ethiopian Agriculture: Problems of Transformation*, Proceedings of Fourth Annual Conference on the Ethiopian Economy. Addis Ababa

Mulat, Demeke et al. (1997). *Promoting Fertilizer Use in Ethiopia: The Implications of Improving Grain Market Performance, Input Market Efficiency, and Farm Management*. Addis Ababa: Ministry of Economic Development and Cooperation (MEDAC)

Munguri, M.W., Mariga, I.K. and Chivinge, O.A. (1996). 'The potential of optimizing cattle manure use with maize in Chinyika Resettlement Area, Zimbabwe'. In *Research Results and Network Outputs in 1994 and 1995*, Proceedings of the Second Meeting of the Soil Fertility Network Working Group, Harare: CIMMYT: 46–53

Murton, J. (1997). 'Sustainable livelihoods in marginal African environments? The social and economic impacts of agricultural intensification in Makueni District, Kenya'. Draft paper presented to the ESRC Conference on Sustainable Livelihoods in Marginal African Environments, Sheffield University, 10–11 April

Murwira, K.H.,Swift, M.J. *et al.* (1995). 'Manure as a key resource in sustainable agriculture'. In Powell, J.M., Fernández-Rivera, S., Williams, T.O. and Renard, C. (eds.), *Livestock and Sustainable Nutrient Cycling in Mixed Farming Systems of Sub-Saharan Africa. Volume II: Technical Papers*. Addis Ababa: ILCA

Muturi, S.N. (1981). 'The system of resource allocation to agricultural research in Kenya'. In Daniels, D. and Nestel, B. (eds.) *Resource Allocation in Agricultural Research*. Ottawa: International Development Research Centre (IDRC)

NARSIS (2000). Natural Resources Information Systems, Department for International Development, United Kingdom http://nt1.ids.ac.uk/narsis/narsis.htm

Ndlovu, L. and Francis, J. (1997). *Performance and Nutritional Management of Draft Cattle in Smallholder Farming in Zimbabwe*. Harare: University of Zimbabwe Publications

Nengomasha, E. and Jele, N. (1995). 'The potential of the donkey as draft power resource and implications for communal area farming in the semi-arid regions of Zimbabwe'. In Ellis-Jones, J., Ndlovu, L.R., Pearson, R.A. and O'Neill, D. (eds.), *Improving the Productivity of Draft Animals in Sub-Saharan Africa*. Proceedings of a Planning Workshop Meeting, Matopos Research Station, Bulawayo, 23–26 September

Netting, R. McC. (1974). 'Agrarian ecology', *Annual Review of Anthropology*, 3: 21–56

Netting, R.M. (1993). *Smallholders, Householders, Farm Families and the Ecology of Intensive, Sustainable Agriculture*. Stanford: Stanford University Press

Nnadi, L.A. and Haque, I. (1988). 'Forage legumes in African crop–livestock production systems', *ILCA Bulletin* (30), April

Noronha, R. (1985). *A Review of the Literature on Land Tenure Systems in Sub-Saharan Africa*, Research Unit of the Agricultural and Rural Development Department, Washington, DC: World Bank.

OMBEVI (1984 through 1995). *Statistique du bétail et de la viande, Rapports Annuels*. Bamako: Office Malienne du Bétail et de la Viande (OMBEVI)

Painter T., Sumberg, J. and Price, T. (1994). 'Your "terroir" and my "action space": Implications of differentiation, mobility and diversity for the *approche terroir* in Sahelian West Africa', *Africa*, 64: 447–464

Palmer, R. (1977). *Land and Racial Discrimination in Rhodesia*. London: Heinemann

Phimister, I. (1986). 'Discourse and the discipline of historical context: Conservationism and ideas about development in Southern Rhodesia 1930–1950', *Journal of Southern African Studies*, 12(2): 263–275

Pieri, J.M.G. (1992). *Fertility of Soils: A Future for Farming in the West African Savannah*. (Translated from French by P. Gething.) Berlin: Springer-Verlag

Pingali, P.L., Bigot, Y. and Binswanger, H.P. (1987). *Agricultural Mechanisation and the Evolution of Farming Systems in Sub-Saharan Africa*. Baltimore and London: Johns Hopkins University Press

Pinstrup-Andersen, P., Pandya-Lorch, R. and Rosegrant, M. (1999). 'World food prospects: Critical issues for the early twenty-first century'. *2020 Vision Food Policy Report*. Washington, DC: International Food Policy Research Institute

Place, F. and Hazell, P. (1993). 'Productivity effects of indigenous land tenure systems in sub-Saharan Africa', *American Journal of Agricultural Economics*, 75: 10–19

Platteau, J.-P. (1996). 'The evolutionary theory of land rights as applied to Sub-Saharan Africa: A critical assessment', *Development and Change*, 27: 29–86

Popper, K.R. (1972). *Objective Knowledge: An Evolutionary Approach*. Oxford: Clarendon Press

Powell, J.M. and Williams, T.O. (1993). 'Livestock, nutrient cycling and sustainable agriculture in the West African Sahel'. *Sustainable Agriculture Gatekeeper Series*, SA37. London: International Institute of Environment and Development

Powell, J.M. and Williams, T.O. (1995). 'An overview of mixed farming systems in sub-Saharan Africa'. In Powell, J.M., Fernández-Rivera, S., Williams, T.O. and Renard, C. (eds.), *Livestock and Sustainable Nutrient Cycling in Mixed Farming Systems of Sub-Saharan Africa. Volume II: Technical Papers*. Addis Ababa: ILCA

Rabot, R. (1990). 'Transferts de fertilité et gestion des terroirs… Quelques points de vue', *Les Cahiers de la Recherche Développement*, 25: 19–32

Ramisch, J.J. (1999). 'The long dry season: Crop–livestock linkages in Southern Mali'. *Drylands Programme Issue Paper*, 88. London: International Institute of Environment and Development

Ramisch, J.J. (1998). 'Cattle, carts, and cotton: Livestock and agricultural intensification in Southern Mali'. Ph.D. Thesis, Norwich: University of East Anglia

Ranger, T. (1985). *Peasant Consciousness and Guerrilla War in Zimbabwe. A Comparative Study*. London: James Currey and Harare: Zimbabwe Publishing House

Raynaut, C. (1984). 'Outils agricoles de la région de Maradi (Niger)', *Cahiers ORSTOM, Série Sciences Humaines*, 20(3–4): 505–536

Raynaut, C., Grégoire, E., Janin, P., Koechlin, J. and Lavigne Delville, P. (eds.) (1997). *Societies and Nature in the Sahel*. London: Routledge

Reardon, T. (1997). 'Using evidence of household income diversification to inform study of the rural nonfarm labor market in Africa', *World Development*, 25(5): 735–747

Reed, J.D. and Goe, M.R. (1989). 'Estimating the nutritive value of cereal crop residues: Implications for developing feeding standards for draught animals', *ILCA Bulletin*, 34, July

Rein, M. and Schön, D. (1993). 'Reframing policy discourse'. In Fischer F. and Forester, J. (eds.), *The Argumentative Turn in Policy Analysis and Planning*. London: University College London Press

Richards, P. (1985). *Indigenous Agricultural Revolution: Ecology and Food Production in West Africa*. London: Unwin Hyman

Roberts, R.L. (1996). *Two Worlds of Cotton: Colonialism and the Regional Economy in the French Soudan, 1800–1946*. Stanford: Stanford University Press

Robins, S. (1994). 'Contesting the geometry of state power: A case study of land-use planning in Matebeleland, Zimbabwe', *Social Dynamics*, 20(2): 91–118

Rocheleau, D. (1995). 'More on Machakos', *Environment* 37(7): 3–5

Roe, E. (1991). 'Development narratives or making the best of blueprint development', *World Development*, 19(4): 287–298

Rondeau, C. (1980). 'La société Sénoufo du Sud Mali (1870–1950) de la "tradition" à la dépendance'. Ph.D. Thesis, Paris: Département de géographie et sciences de la société

Rostow, W.W. (1960). *The Stages of Economic Growth: A Non-Communist Manifesto.* Cambridge: Cambridge University Press

Ruthenberg, H. (1980). *Farming Systems in the Tropics.* Oxford: Oxford University Press

Sampson, H. and Crowther, E. (1943). Report on Crop Production and Soil Fertility Problems. London: West Africa Commission and Leverhulme Trust

Sandford, S. (1982). *Livestock in the Communal Areas of Zimbabwe.* Government of Zimbabwe, Ministry of Lands, Resettlement and Rural Development

Sandford, S. (1983). *Management of Pastoral Development in the Third World.* Chichester: John Wiley

Sandford, S.G. (1989). 'Crop residue/livestock relationships'. In *Soil, Crop and Water Management Systems for Rainfed Agriculture in the Sudano-Sahelian.* Proceedings of an International Workshop, 7–11 Jan. 1987. Niamey, Niger: ICRISAT

Sandford, J. (1992). *Land Tenure in Wellaita, South West Ethiopia: An Anthropological Perspective*, MA thesis, University of Edinburgh: Department of Social Anthropology

Sanogo, B. (1989). *Le rôle des cultures commerciales dans l'évolution de la société Sénoufo (sud du Mali).* Collection 'Pays Enclavés', no. 2. Bordeaux: CRET, Université de Bordeaux III

Sanogo, I. (1984). 'Etude sur la jeunesse rurale: Espoirs et frustrations – le cas de quatre villages Sénoufo'. Unpublished Mémoire de fin d'étude, Bamako: Ecole Normale Supérieure

Scheper, W. (1978). 'Economic aspects related to projects of veterinary medicine and animal production in developing countries'. In *Second International Conference on Institutions of Tropical Veterinary Medicine.* Eschborn, Germany: GTZ

Schumpeter, J.A. (1934). *The Theory of Economic Development: An Inquiry into Profits, Capital, Credit and the Business Cycle.* Cambridge, MA: Harvard University Press

Scoones, I. (1991). 'Wetlands in drylands: key resources for agricultural and pastoral production in Africa', *Ambio*, 20: 366–71

Scoones, I. (1995). 'New directions in pastoral development in Africa'. In Scoones, I. (ed.), *Living with Uncertainty: New Directions in Pastoral Development in Africa.* London: Intermediate Technology Publications

Scoones, I. (1997). 'Landscapes, fields and soils: Understanding the history of soil fertility management in Southern Zimbabwe', *Journal of Southern African Studies,* 23(4): 617–636

Scoones, I. (1998). 'Sustainable rural livelihoods. A framework for analysis', *IDS Working Paper*, 72. Brighton: Institute of Development Studies, Sussex

Scoones, I., Chibudu, C., Chikura, S., Jeranyama, P., Machaka, D., Machanja, W., Mavedzenge, B., Mombeshora, B., Mudhara, M., Mudziwo, C., Murimbarimba, F. and Zirereza, B. (1996). *Hazards and Opportunities. Farming Livelihoods in Dryland Africa: Lessons from Zimbabwe.* London: Zed Books

Seur, H. (1992). *Sowing the Seed. The Interweaving of Agricultural Change, Gender Relations and Religion in Serenje District, Zambia.* Wageningen: Proefschrift

Shackley, S. and Wynne, B. (1995). 'Global climate change: The mutual construction of an emergent science-policy domain', *Science and Public Policy,* 22

Simmons, E. (1987). 'Policy and structural reform of grain markets in Mali'. Paper at Conference on The Design and Impact of Adjustment Programmes on Agriculture and Agricultural Institutions. London: Overseas Development Institute

Smaling, E., Fresco, L. and de Jager, A. (1996). 'Classifying, monitoring and improving soil nutrient stocks and flows in African agriculture', *Ambio*, 25: 492–496

Smith, J.W., Naazie, A., Larbi, A., Agyemang, K. and Tarawali, S. (1997). 'Integrated crop–livestock systems in Sub-Saharan Africa: An option or an imperative?' *Outlook on Agriculture*, 26(4): 237–246

Spencer, H. (1972). *On Social Evolution: Selected Writings*, edited by J.D.Y. Peel. Chicago: University of Chicago Press

Spierenburg, M. (1995). *The Role of the Mhondoro Cult in the Struggle for Control over Land in Dande (Northern Zimbabwe): Social Commentaries and the Influence of Adherents*. Harare: University of Zimbabwe, Centre for Applied Social Sciences

Staatz, J.,Dione, J. and Dembele, N.N. (1989). 'Cereals liberalisation in Mali', *World Development*, 17(5): 701–718

Stangel, P.J. (1995). 'Nutrient cycling and its importance in sustaining crop–livestock systems in sub-Saharan Africa: An overview', In Powell, J.M., Fernández-Rivera, S., Williams, T.O. and Renard, C. (eds.), *Livestock and Sustainable Nutrient Cycling in Mixed Farming Systems of Sub-Saharan Africa. Vol. 2 Technical Papers*. Addis Ababa: International Livestock Centre for Africa: 37–59

Stanning, J. (1985). 'Sengwe Cattle Development Project, Chiredzi District, Masvingo Province'. Unpublished Report for Republic of Zimbabwe and Federal Republic of Germany

Starkey, P. (1990). 'Animal traction for agricultural development in West Africa: Production, impact, profitability and constraints'. In Starkey, P. and Faye, A. (eds.), *Animal Traction for Agricultural Development, Proceedings of the Third Workshop of the West Africa Animal Traction Network, 7–12 July 1988, Saly, Senegal*. Ede-Wageningen: Technical Centre for Agricultural and Rural Cooperation (CTA).

Starkey, P. and Kaumbutho, P. (eds.) (2000). *Meeting the Challenges of Animal Traction*. Harare: ATNESA and London: Intermediate Technology Publications

Steinfeld, H., De Haan, C. and Blackburn, H. (1997). *Livestock–environment Interactions. Issues and Options*. Brussels: EC DG for Development Policy, Sustainable Development and Natural Resources

Steward, J.H., Steward, J.C. and Murphy, R.F. (eds.) (1977). *Evolution and Ecology: Essays on Social Transformations*. Urbana: University of Illinois Press

Stocking, G.W. (1987). *Victorian Anthropology*. New York: Free Press

Sumberg, J. (1998). 'Mixed farming in Africa: The search for order, the search for sustainability', *Land Use Policy*, 15(4): 293–317

Sumberg, J. and Gilbert, E. (1992). 'Agricultural mechanisation in the Gambia: Drought, donkeys and minimum tillage', *African Livestock Research*, 1: 1–10

Sutter, J.W. (1987). 'Cattle and inequality: Herd size differences and pastoral production among the Fulani of northeastern Senegal', *Africa*, 57: 196–218

Swift, M.J., *et al.* (1989). 'Nitrogen cycling in farming systems derived from savanna: Perspectives and challenges'. In Charholm, M. and Bergström, L. (eds.), *Ecology of Arid Lands*. Amsterdam: Kluwer Academic Publishers

Takele Gebre (1996). 'SG2000 Project in Sustainable Intensification of Agriculture in Ethiopia'. In *Sustainable Intensification of Agriculture in Ethiopia*, Second Conference of Agricultural Economics Society of Ethiopia, Addis Ababa

Témé, B., Breman, H. and Sissoko, K. (1996). *Intensification Agricole au Sahel: Mythe ou Réalité?* Proceedings of a Conference held in Bamako, 28 November–2 December 1995. Wageningen: Production Soudano-Sahelienne (PSS)

Tempany, H. (1949). 'The practice of soil conservation in the British colonial Empire', *Technical Communication*, 45. Harpenden: Commonwealth Bureau of Soil Science

Tempany, H., Rodden, G. and Lord, L. (1944). 'Soil erosion and soil conservation in the colonial empire', *Empire Journal of Experimental Agriculture*, 12: 121–153

Tiffen, M. (1995). 'Population density, economic growth and societies in transition: Boserup reconsidered in a Kenyan case study', *Development and Change*, 26(1): 31–66

Tiffen, M., Mortimore, M. and Gichuki, F. (1994). *More People, Less Erosion: Environmental Recovery in Kenya*. Chichester: John Wiley & Sons

Toulmin, C. (1983). 'Herders and farmers, or farmer-herders and herder-farmers?' *Pastoral Development Network Paper*, 15d. London: Overseas Development Institute

Toulmin, C. (1984). 'The allocation of resources to livestock research in Africa'. *ALPAN Network Paper*, No. 4. Addis Ababa: ILCA, African Livestock Policy Analysis Network (ALPAN)

Toulmin, C. (1992). *Cattle, Women and Wells: Managing Household Survival in the Sahel*. Oxford: Clarendon Press

Tourte, R., Poothier, G., Ramond, C., Monnier, J., Nicou, R., Pailain, J.F., Hamon, R. and Charreau, C. (1971). 'Thèmes Légers – Thèmes Lourds, Systèmes Intensifs, Voies différentes ouvertes au développement agricole au Sénégal', *Agronomie Tropicale*, 5 (May): 636–658

Turner, B.L., Hyden, G. and Kates, R.W. (eds.) (1993). *Population Growth and Agricultural Change in Africa*. Gainsville: University Press of Florida

Turner, M.D. (1994). In 'Comments on "Livestock, land use and agricultural intensification in sub-Saharan Africa (paper 37a)" by D. Bourn and W. Wint', *Pastoral Network Paper 37b*. London: Overseas Development Institute

Turner, M. (1995). 'The sustainability of rangeland to cropland nutrient transfer in semi-arid West Africa; ecological and social dimensions neglected in the debate'. In Powell, J.M., Fernández-Rivera, S., Williams, T.O. and Renard, C. (eds.) *Livestock and Sustainable Nutrient Cycling in Mixed Farming Systems of Sub-Saharan Africa. Volume II: Technical Papers*. Addis Ababa: ILCA

Tylor, E.B. (1873). *Primitive Culture*. London: Murray

Tyndall, B.P. (1996). 'The anatomy of innovation adoption: The case of successful agroforestry in East Africa'. Ph.D. Thesis, Boulder: Colorado State University

van der Pol, F. (1992). 'Soil mining: An unseen contributor to farm income in Southern Mali', *KIT Bulletin*, 325. Amsterdam: Royal Institute of the Tropics (KIT)

van Keulen, H. and Breman, H. (1990). 'Agricultural development in the West African Sahelian region: A cure against land hunger?' *Agriculture, Ecosystems and Environment*, 32 (3–4)

Veblen, T. (1919). *The Place of Science in Modern Civilisation and Other Essays*. New York: Viking Press

Vincent, V. and Thomas, R.G. (1960). *An Agricultural Survey of Southern Rhodesia. Part 1: Agroecological Survey*. Salisbury: Government Printer

WADU (1976a). *Agricultural Survey of Bolloso (1971)*. Soddo, Ethiopia: Wollaita Agricultural Development Unit

WADU (1976b). *Agricultural Survey of Bele (1971)*. Soddo, Ethiopia: Wollaita Agricultural Development Unit

Weber, G.N. (1996). 'Heterogeneity and complexity in farming systems: Towards an evolutionary perspective', *Journal for Farming Systems Research-Extension*, 6(2): 15–32

Williams, G. (1981). 'The World Bank and the peasant problem'. In Heyer, J., Roberts, P. and Williams, G. (eds.), *Rural Development in Tropical Africa*. London: Macmillan: 16–51

Williams, T.O., Hiernaux, P. and Fernández-Rivera, S. (2000). 'Crop–livestock systems in sub-Saharan Africa: Determinants and intensification pathways'. In McCarthy, N., Swallow, B., Kirk, M. and Hazell, P. (eds.), *Property Rights, Risk, and Livestock Development in Africa*. Nairobi: ILRI, IFPRI: chapter 5

Wilson, K. (1986). 'History, ecology and conservation in southern Zimbabwe'. Paper delivered at a seminar, Department of Sociology, University of Manchester, 12 February

Wilson, N.H. (1923). 'The development of Native Reserves', *NADA*, 1: 83–94

Winrock International (1992). *Assessment of Animal Agriculture in Sub-Saharan Africa*. Arlington, VA. Winrock International Institute for Agricultural Development

Wolmer, W. (1997). 'Crop–livestock integration: The dynamics of intensification in contrasting agroecological zones: A review', *IDS Working Paper*, 63. Brighton: Institute of Development Studies, Sussex

Wolmer, W. and Scoones, I. (2000). 'The science of "civilised" agriculture: The mixed farming discourse in Zimbabwe'. *African Affairs*, 99(397): 575–600

Wood, C. (unpublished). 'Effects of harvest and post harvest practices on the production and nutritive value of maize and sorghum residues in Zimbabwe'. Project Summary. Livestock Production Programme, DFID. Chatham: Natural Resources Institute

Worby, E. (1995). 'What does agrarian wage-labour signify? Cotton, commoditisation and social form in Gokwe, Zimbabwe', *Journal of Peasant Studies*, 23(1): 1–29

Wright, A. (1972). *Valley of the Ironwoods: A Personal Record of Ten Years served as District Commissioner in Rhodesia's Largest Administrative Area, Nuanetsi, in the South-Eastern Lowveld*. Cape Town: T.V. Bulpin

Index